And the wine is bottled poetry...

— **Robert Louis Stevenson**

Other Books in the Show Me Missouri Series

Exploring Missouri WINE Country

Updated & Revised Third Edition

Wine is light, held together by water.
— Galileo

Brett Dufur

Pebble Publishing, Inc.
Rocheport, Missouri

ISBN 1-891708-30-9 $18.95

Editor: Kimberly Small

Cover photograph, small back photograph and Table of Contents verso page watercolor painting by Miriam Krone. Aerial photograph on back cover by Sandy Watts.

Maps by Cartographic Works: Lawrence "Ted" Twenter, Robert Cline and Elizabeth Touchette.

First Edition Printing, July 1997. Second Edition Printing, February 1999. Third Edition Printing, October 2006.

Pebble Publishing, P.O. Box 2, Rocheport, MO 65279
(573) 698-3903 ❖ www.pebblepublishing.com

To Tawnee with love.

Acknowledgments

Many thanks go to all of the vintners who made exploring Missouri wine country such an enriching experience. Murli Dharmadhikari, enology advisor, and Sanliang Gu, the viticulture advisor, at the Department of Fruit Science Research Campus at Missouri State University contributed vital information, as did Sue Berendzen and Jim Anderson of the Missouri Grape and Wine Program.

I am also gratefully indebted to the following people for generously sharing their time and expertise: Mary Mueller of Röbller Winery; Lucinda Huskey of Stone Hill Winery; Greg Stricker, past president of the Missouri Winemaking Society; Dr. Bourgeois of Les Bourgeois Winery & Vineyards; Department of Natural Resources' State Historian Jim Denny and Site Administrator for Deutschheim Historical Site Dr. Erin Renn; Lucy Valbuena, Amy Scheidegger and Jessica Faerber; editors Sandy Watts and Nancy Fagerness of the *Missouri Wine Country Journal;* Julaine Cabot. Thomas Sallee, Agricultural Statistician, USDA; and Marlowe Schlegel, Deputy Director of Missouri Agricultural Statistics, USDA. Thanks also go to Ken Luebbering, co-author of *German Settlement in Missouri,* and Robert Scheef, author of *Vintage Missouri.*

Special thanks also go to friends, family and everyone at Pebble Publishing who went the extra mile on this project: Kimberly Small, Julie D'Auteuil, Martin Bellman, Miriam Krone, R.C. Adams, Brian Beatte, Tawnee Dufur, Neal Dufur, Kathy Dufur, Mark Flakne, Heather Starek, Scott Angus, Jeff Lehman and Pippa Letsky.

CONTENTS

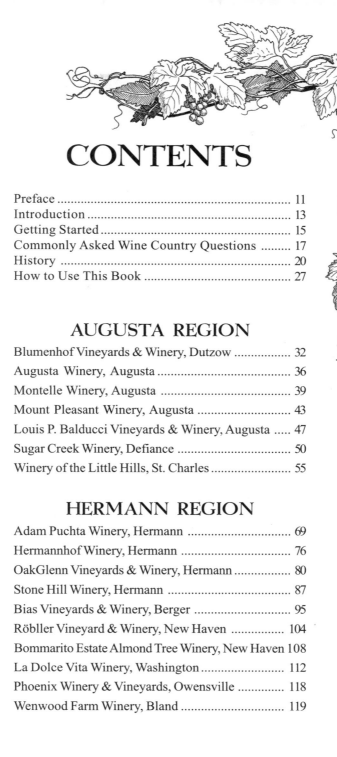

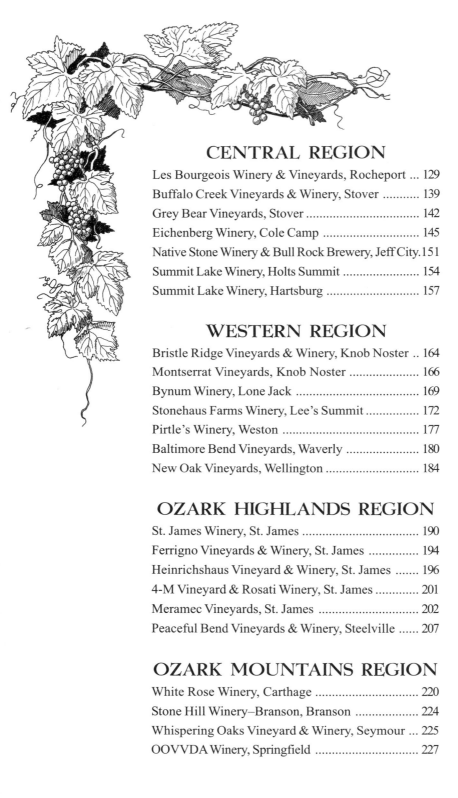

CENTRAL REGION

WESTERN REGION

OZARK HIGHLANDS REGION

OZARK MOUNTAINS REGION

EASTERN REGION

SOUTHEAST REGION

SPECIAL SECTIONS

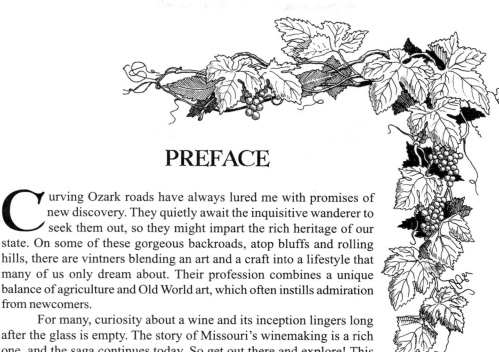

PREFACE

C urving Ozark roads have always lured me with promises of new discovery. They quietly await the inquisitive wanderer to seek them out, so they might impart the rich heritage of our state. On some of these gorgeous backroads, atop bluffs and rolling hills, there are vintners blending an art and a craft into a lifestyle that many of us only dream about. Their profession combines a unique balance of agriculture and Old World art, which often instills admiration from newcomers.

For many, curiosity about a wine and its inception lingers long after the glass is empty. The story of Missouri's winemaking is a rich one, and the saga continues today. So get out there and explore! This guidebook answers many wine questions for both beginners and pros. In addition to highlighting Missouri's wine regions and every winery found within them, this book includes nearby services and history, introduces newcomers to tasting and appreciating wine, explains the grape varieties grown and serves as an introduction to the families and faces of Missouri's burgeoning wine industry.

There are nearly 60 wineries around the state. In 2005, sales of Missouri wine reached a post-Prohibition high of more than 700,000 gallons. So about seven bottles in 100 sold within the state are Missouri-made. This definitely marks a peak in today's wine revolution. But underlying today's success stories is a prolific past. Before Prohibition in 1920, Missouri was home to no less than 65 wineries and was producing ten times as much wine. In 1904 alone, Missouri wineries produced a record 3 million gallons of wine. In fact, 100 years ago, Missouri was the second largest wine-producing state in the nation—behind only New York.

But as much as this book is about today's wine revolution, it's also a book about the immigrants and the rich countryside that supported the initial evolution of such a fruitful wine country. As you drive these hills and walk into today's wineries, remember that by 1860, more than half of Missouri's foreign-born residents were German.

The rich German heritage of our wine regions has left a legacy in winemaking as well as an imprint on our architecture and day-to-day life. It would be hard to imagine a modern-day Missouri without German influence. German immigrants gave us foods such as the jelly doughnut, apple butter, potato salad, hamburgers and sauerkraut. Even kindergarten is a German concept. A family-oriented Christmas, complete with gifts, sweets and a decorated evergreen tree, was introduced to a great extent by these early German settlers. Even "Silent Night," the most popular Christmas carol in America, comes from a German-speaking country. These early immigrants also brought with them an architectural style that is still well preserved today in towns throughout Missouri, such as Hermann and Westphalia. Many of their festivals, like Maifest and Oktoberfest, continue today.

Before that first drop of wine touches your tongue, there are other senses waiting to be tantalized. A stroll through a vineyard hanging heavy with fruit, a bluff-top view of a mist-filled valley below, a gentle breeze enjoyed under a pergola of vines, a taste of a new wine and a walk through the damp coolness of a seasoned wine cellar, all await your exploration.

I hope this book will increase your appreciation of Missouri wine and the progressive winemaking taking place here. The laborious behind-the-scenes work that goes into each bottle is remarkable. Twelve-hour days in sweltering heat. Back-breaking labor. Patience. Ah, the glorious life of winemaking. Yet life among the vines and the art of winemaking have long held a romantic mystique. From the early Greek's homage to a god of wine, alternately called Dionysus and Bacchus, to more modern studies by George Washington and Thomas Jefferson, the process evokes an image of Old World art and celebrates virtues such as patience, hard work and family togetherness.

Nowhere else do these virtues and Old World influence match up so perfectly with back roads and quiet bluff-top settings than in Missouri wine country. The wineries and vineyards throughout the state have become havens for day-trippers, explorers and a growing class of wine drinkers. For me, the beautiful part of exploring Missouri wine country is that there is no strip mall of wineries. To really enjoy these wineries, adventure is in order. As Mark Twain once said, "There's more to traveling than arriving."

Read on to discover the tumultuous evolution of Missouri's wine industry, which has grown immensely in the past 45 years. The vintners themselves have even been surprised by the explosive growth of the last decade. This growth is due to several factors, including the increasing quality of Missouri wines, state assistance, better marketing, a maturing industry, a new generation of well-educated winemakers, healthier lifestyles, the increasing consumer demand for locally brewed spirits and the publication of fine guidebooks (if I do say so myself).

So read on... a journey of discovery awaits!

Brett Dufur
Rocheport, Missouri

INTRODUCTION

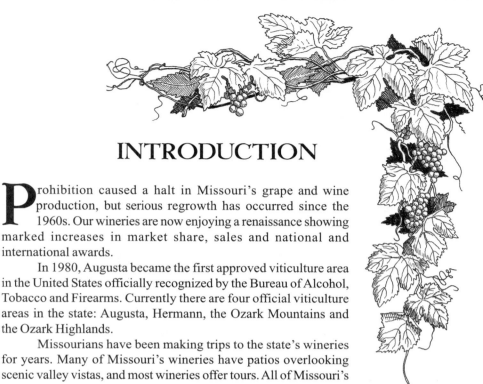

Prohibition caused a halt in Missouri's grape and wine production, but serious regrowth has occurred since the 1960s. Our wineries are now enjoying a renaissance showing marked increases in market share, sales and national and international awards.

In 1980, Augusta became the first approved viticulture area in the United States officially recognized by the Bureau of Alcohol, Tobacco and Firearms. Currently there are four official viticulture areas in the state: Augusta, Hermann, the Ozark Mountains and the Ozark Highlands.

Missourians have been making trips to the state's wineries for years. Many of Missouri's wineries have patios overlooking scenic valley vistas, and most wineries offer tours. All of Missouri's wineries provide tasting rooms and many provide live entertainment and host many fun activities such as grape stomps and festivals.

Over 1 million people visit Missouri wineries each year. Our wineries have shown a continual rise in production, quality, recognition and status in the local, national and international wine industry.

Missouri's vintners are getting fabulous results with the native Norton/ Cynthiana grape, which was designated Missouri's official state grape in 2003. Currently, Missouri has over 1,100 acres of grapes producing over $26 million in wine sales. Missouri wines boast of having captured more than a 7 percent share of the state's wine market, with many varieties consistently taking top honors in prestigious domestic and international competitions.

The Missouri wine industry is growing in several dimensions. We are at a post-Prohibition high with close to 60 bonded wineries, and our production of gallons exceeding 700,000. Missouri wineries are an integral part of the Missouri tourism industry as well. Over 1 million people visit Missouri wineries each year. Our wineries have shown a continual rise in production, quality, recognition and status in the local, national and international wine industry.

Missouri wineries continue to improve their product, refining their winemaking and grape-growing skills to offer quality wines at affordable prices. Most of the state's wine is sold directly through the wineries. The annual Weinstrasse, Maifest and Oktoberfest celebrations bring many people to the wineries, nearby restaurants and local bed & breakfasts. In fact, the *Weinstrasse,* German for "wine road," is a two-lane road along Highway 94 that leads many Missourians to wineries where German settlers found the rich soils of the Missouri River Valley to be ideal for grape-growing.

Efforts to improve the quality of Missouri wine varietals are ongoing and are visible in the highly disciplined and scientific approach of our vintners. Missouri State University's State Fruit Experiment Station at Mountain Grove, Missouri, conducts research to further Missouri's quest for better, hardier grapevines. Primary concerns include identifying new grape varieties that will tolerate cold temperatures and disease, cultural practices on existing grape varieties, integrated pest management studies and improved winemaking.

Legislation passed in 1984 created a four-cent-per-gallon tax on all wine sold in Missouri to be used for research, development and promotion of Missouri grapes, wines and juices. In 1988, the tax was increased to six cents per gallon. Since 2002, a total of 12 cents per gallon has been collected for research and advisory programs. This tax revenue funds the Department of Agriculture's Wine and Grape Board and efforts at the MSU Fruit Experiment Station.

The Wine and Grape Board is making an ongoing, concerted effort to increase recognition of the Missouri wine industry and has several projects completed. With the progress of the industry and increase in the number of wineries in Missouri, the program is keeping pace with a revamp of the industry's image.

Jim Anderson
Missouri Wine and Grape Program

GETTING STARTED
Start . . .
. . . whenever you can
. . . wherever you are

There's never a better time than right now to visit a Missouri winery. A winery tour at any time of the year will likely give you the opportunity to catch some aspect of the winemaking process in action.

Like other forms of agriculture, the cycle of "growing wine" follows the seasons. The vintner's work alternates between growing, processing and marketing the wine. Steps include winter pruning of the vines, caring for the spring's new shoots, tending the vines all summer long, managing the autumn crush and finally guiding the wine through maturity. In this way, winemaking is a craft, demanding continuous labor and care by the artist, from conception through execution.

The seasons change, the vines grow and the grapes are transformed into wine. So many variables are part of the process, yet one aspect remains unchanged—constant contact with the public. Every day the winemaker pours samples of recent releases and receives immediate evaluations for his effort. Missouri winemakers enjoy welcoming visitors, whether introducing them to the world of wine or revealing insights about their craft.

TOUR TIPS
Missouri's Wine Country Can Be Enjoyed in Many Ways

Touring Wine Country by Car

If you are looking for a great back-road adventure, visit a Missouri winery. If you live near St. Louis, a tour on Sunday afternoon can take you to many of Missouri's wineries along Highway 94 and Highway 100. No matter if you live in Kansas City, Springfield, Cape Girardeau or points in between, there are numerous wineries within a two-hour drive.

Use the map at the beginning of each region to help you plan your next excursion. No matter where you live in Missouri, there will almost always be a winery near you or one "just far enough away" for that perfect daytrip or bed & breakfast weekend.

Drink Responsibly!

Don't drink and drive. Part of the fun of any journey is getting to and from your destination safely. A designated driver is always the way to go.

Touring Wine Country by Bicycle

Touring France's wine country by bike is a classic wine connoisseur's dream. Before you learn to say "No" to *Parlez-vous français?* ... a similar experience can be had much closer to home. I recently guided a 5-day bicycle trip along the 225-mile Katy Trail, which passes through Missouri's *Weinstrasse* Region. I was leading a group of wine lovers from Chicago, so we toured many of the wineries along the way. The previous year, they had toured France's wine country by bike and said this trip exceeded their experience abroad. They found great wine, cozy bed & breakfasts and fine dining here—and they were more than happy to pay $10–25 for a bottle of wine instead of $100 a bottle in France. *Vive le Misuri!*

For more complete Katy Trail information, refer to my book, *The Complete Katy Trail Guidebook* or check out the Katy Trail online at: www.bikekatytrail.com.

Touring Wine Country by Train

Amtrak runs daily between St. Louis and Kansas City, with stops in Hermann, Washington, Jefferson City, Sedalia, Warrensburg, Lee's Summit and Independence. You can spend the day enjoying Hermann, for example, or design your own wine country weekend. Round-trip tickets are modestly priced. Call Amtrak at (800) USA-RAIL for more information.

Touring Wine Country by Boat

Several Missouri wineries are also accessible by boat. Both the Missouri and the Meramec Rivers provide convenient access to wine country, and Buffalo Creek Vineyards & Winery has completed a tasting room on the Lake of the Ozarks.

From Washington, heading west, a quick jaunt up the Missouri River to New Haven (along with an adventurous spirit and a friendly person willing to give you a lift) will get you to Röbller Vineyard and Winery.

In Mid-Missouri, a boat trip further west on the Missouri River leads to Rocheport's Les Bourgeois Winery & Vineyards. Their bistro overlooks both the river and the Katy Trail. A wonderful switch-back trail leads boaters and Katy Trail cyclists from the river's edge to their blufftop setting.

In the Ozarks, Peaceful Bend Vineyards & Winery has a set-up smack-dab on the Meramec River. They even offer wine in plastic bottles for boaters. A short hike takes you through their forested property and up to the main tasting room.

COMMONLY ASKED WINE COUNTRY QUESTIONS

How do I use this book?
We've divided the book into eight regions. Find a specific winery using the table of contents or index.

How many wineries are there in Missouri?
There are close to 60 wineries in the state, with new ones opening their doors every season. Call the Grape and Wine Program at (800) 392-WINE for more details.

What should I expect when I visit?
Expect a totally new experience. Missouri wines consistently win national and international awards. The wines are unique to Missouri, however, so don't be surprised when you don't find your favorite California-style Zinfandel.

What's the best time of day to visit a winery?
Most wineries close at dusk, so get there early. I've shown up at dusk and found tasting rooms already closed.

What's the price range of Missouri wines?
Most Missouri wines retail from $7 to $30 a bottle. Ice wines and other specialty wines are often bottled in 375 ml "half bottles" to keep the prices below $25. Most wineries give quantity discounts when you purchase four or more bottles. Prices are not listed in this book since offerings and prices change frequently.

Should we bring our kids?
Definitely! All wineries sell juices and pop to quench their thirst. They make a special effort to accommodate the entire family—so bring the kids!

What's the best winery to visit?
My advice is—visit as many as you can and decide for yourself. From one-man operations to multimillion-dollar ventures, every winery offers something worth exploring.

What's the best month to see grapes being harvested?
The picking season begins in August and ends in October. At smaller wineries and vineyards you may even get a chance to help.

How about a wine country weekend. Any suggestions?
I've included bed & breakfast listings, other services and histories for each town to help you plan your perfect wine country weekend.

Questions

How far in advance do I need to make reservations at a B&B?
To insure a successful wine country weekend, book your reservations well in advance. During Oktoberfest in Hermann, most B&Bs are booked a year in advance, but this is certainly not the norm.

How is wine made?
We've included a special section that takes you from the vine to the wine. Refer to the back of this book for answers.

What makes a wine a Missouri wine?
Missouri wine must be produced from at least 85 percent Missouri-grown grapes. When harvests are below average, this can be reduced to 75 percent.

What's ice wine?
Ice wines are super-sweet dessert wines, made from grapes with a high sugar content. These grapes are harvested in late fall, after cold weather has increased the grape's sweetness. Authentic ice wine is made from grapes that have been left to freeze on the vines.

I need help! I just bought your book and I'm desperate to impress my girlfriend this weekend.
No sweat. We've included *The Basics of Tasting Wine* just for you.

GRAPE FACT

Augusta:
America's First Approved Viticultural Area

Four of more than 175 viticultural areas in the United States are in Missouri. They are the Hermann, Augusta, Ozark Mountains and Ozark Highlands viticultural regions. Each federally recognized area has defined borders and specific qualities of climate, soil, elevation and geographic features that distinguish it from other areas. In 1980, Augusta was the first region in the country to be approved by the Bureau of Alcohol, Tobacco and Firearms.

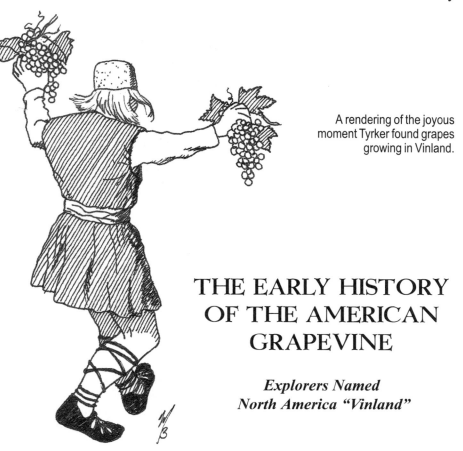

A rendering of the joyous moment Tyrker found grapes growing in Vinland.

THE EARLY HISTORY OF THE AMERICAN GRAPEVINE

Explorers Named North America "Vinland"

The written history of North American vineyards begins with the legend of Leif Ericsson's voyage to an unknown land in 1000 A.D. One version of this much-disputed account tells how Tyrker, a German on Ericsson's ship, discovered a plant with wine berries. Impressed by this discovery, Ericsson named the new land "Vinland" and returned home with samples.

Many historians believe that Tyrker probably found wild cranberries. They cite evidence that Ericsson landed on the northern coast of present-day Newfoundland, where the climate is too cold for grapevines. Nevertheless, future Europeans would come to marvel at the abundance and tenacity of North America's native grapevines. In fact, there are more native grape species in North America than on any other continent.

Fertile soils and an amicable growing climate set the stage for the development of a North American wine industry. Later, even George Washington and Thomas Jefferson grew vines for winemaking and were early supporters of the idea of turning America into a world-class wine producer.

THE HISTORY OF MISSOURI WINE

Immigration Surges with Missouri's Entry into Statehood

When Missouri achieved statehood in 1821, tens of thousands of immigrants came looking for a better life. Many were escaping political, religious and economic oppression in Europe. Missouri's abundant and virtually untapped resources attracted large numbers of immigrants from Germany, France, Switzerland, Austria and eventually Italy. The rich soils, expansive waterway connections, timber and abundant game made Missouri a veritable Eden for the poor and landless.

German Author Favors Settlement in Missouri

In 1824, Gottfried Duden, an optimistic traveler from Germany, arrived on Missouri soil. He believed that many of Germany's woes resulted from overpopulation and poverty. Thinking emigration was the solution to these problems, Duden and his friend Louis Eversmann had set sail for America to study the possibilities of German settlement in the United States.

Arriving in St. Louis, Duden and Eversmann found Nathan Boone, son of Daniel Boone and surveyor of government lands. Boone led them on a tour of the Missouri River Valley. Leaving the area several days later, the German duo lost their way and headed west instead of east. Soon they found the home of Jacob Haun, of Pennsylvania German descent. Haun talked them into purchasing adjoining tracts of land, near present-day Dutzow, and offered to shelter and feed them until they could establish their own farms. Duden agreed. For almost three years he lived in a cabin near Lake Creek, recording the weather, growing conditions and daily doings on his farm. In 1829 he published his findings back in Germany and his report soon became a best-seller. The next excerpt is from his initial observations.

"I do not conceal the fact from you that the entire life of the inhabitants of these regions seemed to me like a dream at first," Duden wrote. "Even now, after I have had three months to examine conditions more closely, it seems to me almost a fantasy when I consider what nature offers man here." He went on to describe "acorns... as big as hen's eggs and wild grapevines... heavy with sweet fruit."

The Editor's Introduction to the English translation of Duden's book called the *Report of a Journey to the Western States of North America:*

> *... a masterpiece of promotional literature. Duden's adroit pen wove reality with poetry, experience with dreams, and contrasted the freedom of the forests and democratic institutions in America with the social narrowness and political confusion*

of Germany. He glorified the routine of pioneer existence, praised Missouri's favorable geographical location, and emphasized its mild and healthy climate... So overwhelmed with what he saw and experienced, Duden feared Germans would not believe him: "It appears," he wrote, "too strange, too fabulous."

To struggling—even starving—Germans back home, these words offered an almost irresistible allure of freedom and plenty. Feeling the oppression back home, the promotional writings of many Germans, including Duden's glowing account, inspired thousands of Germans to emigrate to the "New Rhineland."

Old World Winemaking Reaches Missouri

A s German settlers pushed westward, many carried carefully wrapped clippings from their Old World vineyards. Many of the groups traveled down the Ohio River from Cincinnati, to the Mississippi and up to the mouth of the Missouri River at St. Louis, right in the wake of Gottfried Duden.

Moving to a new land caused a deep yearning to preserve their heritage. In 1836, the German Settlement Society was intent on establishing a new "Fatherland" in America. They selected some land on the south bank of the Missouri River, west of St. Louis, and founded Hermann. The original town was laid out with some plots originally sold as wine plots, beginning in the 1840s. Though their settlement met with many hardships and the soil on the hills nearby wasn't appropriate for many forms of agriculture, by 1846 they had produced their first wine from locally cultivated grapes. In 1848, the town's wineries produced 1,000 gallons. By 1855, 500 acres of vineyard were in production and wine was being shipped to St. Louis and beyond.

But wine in Hermann didn't become a huge money-maker until after the Civil War. It was in 1866 that Missouri surpassed Ohio as the second largest wine producing state in the Union. By 1869, 42 percent of America's wine was produced in Missouri.

The Isabella

GRAPE FACT

The first Native American grape on record to be made into wine in Missouri was the Isabella. This grape is believed to have its "roots" in South Carolina. Hermann farmers planted Isabella, hoping to capitalize on the tenacity of the stock. Unfortunately, Isabella didn't produce the results they desired, so it was abandoned for varieties like Catawba and Norton.

Railroads further boosted the growth of the Missouri wine industry, but the completion of the first transcontinental route in 1869 also made it possible to market California wines in the eastern United States. These California wines became very popular because they were made from grapes more familiar to the Europeans. However, Missouri's wine production continued to flourish. It remained second only to California until Prohibition.

By the turn of the century, Stone Hill Winery, which the German immigrant Michael Poeschel began building in 1847, was the third largest winery in the world (second largest in the United States), producing more than a million gallons of wine a year. Its wines, such as Hermannsberger, Starkenberger and Black Pearl, won eight gold medals at world fairs between 1873 and 1904.

Italian immigrants also played an important role in Missouri's first vineyards. Many Italians had ventured to Arkansas with the intention of working as sharecroppers on the cotton plantations. Some members ended up in the Ozark Highlands of Missouri near St. James. It was here that they began to cultivate vineyards in keeping with the traditions of their homeland.

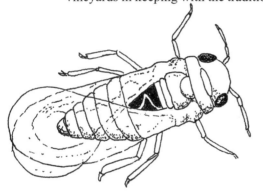

Missouri Vines Save European Vineyards from Parasites

As trellises spread across the landscape, Missouri viticulture soon raised another flag of worldwide acclaim. In 1867, an insidious louse began a relentless assault on vineyards throughout France. The parasite had come from America and found the French roots particularly appealing—pushing the French wine industry to the brink of ruin.

Fortunately, Missouri's first entomologist (bug scientist) Charles V. Riley, together with the work of other pioneeers such as George Husmann, made an important discovery. In 1871, at the invitation of the French government, they inspected France's ailing grape crop. The problem was diagnosed as an infestation of *phylloxera,* an American plant louse. It was found that some Native American rootstocks were immune to the advances of the dreaded louse. By grafting French vines onto them, healthy grapes could be produced. Millions of cuttings of Missouri rootstock were shipped to save the French wine industry from disaster. A statue in Montpelier, France, commemorates this rescue (see drawing next page).

Although this next fact has nothing to do with wine, its worth mentioning and highlights Charles V. Riley's flair for innovative problem solving. During a severe grasshopper plague in western Missouri in 1875, Riley suggested that rather than go hungry, farmers should eat the insects. To introduce people to the delicacy he offered his friends fried grasshoppers. Once he even served a four-course meal consisting of grasshopper soup, baked grasshoppers, grasshopper cakes, grasshoppers with honey and just plain grasshoppers.

Elbert Pirtle, of Pirtle Winery, explains how Missouri grapevines also benefited from the work of these early pioneers:

"Starting in the 1860s, French vineyards were devastated by vine diseases that were probably accidentally imported from America. One of these was phylloxera, a tiny insect which, in one stage of its development, lives in the soil and destroys the vine roots. The Old World vines had no resistance at all. Wine production dropped 75 percent, a catastrophe. George Husmann, then Professor of Agriculture at the University of Missouri, suggested that they graft their vines onto Missouri root stock. The Missouri vines were resistant to phylloxera. It worked. In the late 1880s Missouri exported ten million root stocks and literally saved the French vineyards. Husmann was given the Legion of Honor by the French government. Then, a few amateur viticulturists in France and Germany decided that grafting might not be necessary if they could cross their vines with ours and get what they called 'direct producers.' In the early 1930s, some of the resulting vines were imported. It was discovered that their American blood had given them the winter hardiness needed for Eastern and Midwestern winters. So now, in Missouri, a region that has the summer climate and soils equal to the best wine-growing regions in Europe, we now have the vines for good wines. After nearly 100 years, the French have unwittingly repaid us."

A statue stands in Montpelier, France, of two women, one young and one old, symbolizing the vines of the New World saving those of the Old World.

Prohibition—The Dark Years

Before Prohibition, there were wineries in 48 Missouri counties. Bluffton, Boonville, Cape Girardeau, Hannibal, Owensville, and Stanton were just a few of the many towns that boasted wineries. Long before anyone had ever heard of Harry Truman, Independence was known for its wine production by companies such as Shaffer's Winery and Lohse's Native Wine Garden.

In fact, Missouri's Weinstrasse region grew to include more than 100 wineries before coming to an abrupt halt in 1920 with the addition of the 18th Amendment to the Constitution—Prohibition—which prohibited the manufacture and sale of alcohol in the United States. This amendment dealt a fatal blow to Missouri's wine industry. Vines were burned or abandoned and winemaking equipment was destroyed. Many families lost their livelihoods. At Stone Hill Winery, Ottmar Stark ordered all of his vineyards destroyed, virtually ruining the local economy.

In fact, the survival of many historic buildings in Hermann is largely attributed to the economic downturn caused by Prohibition. Instead of destroying older homes and building new ones, the old buildings were continually lived in and kept up, which allows us to appreciate early German construction today.

The only Missouri winery to survive this dry period was the St. Stanislaus Novitiate, located in St. Louis, where Jesuits continued to produce sacramental wine. Following repeal of the act in 1934, Missouri's wine industry was nothing but a memory. High liquor taxes and license fees discouraged the industry's rebirth. A few dozen wineries did reopen, but much of Missouri remained legally dry, and there was little demand for anything other than sweet, dessert-style wines.

GRAPE FACT

Cass County Carry

One Missouri woman's painful marriage to a heavy drinker fueled the drive to Prohibition. When her marriage was over, Cass County native Carry Nation spent the rest of her life in a crusade against alcohol. She wrote editorials, gave lectures and formed temperance groups—but she really put the cork on her place in history by smashing up saloons with a hatchet. She usually went to the bar mirror first, which left her in hatchet-range of all the bottles and decanters.

Edward Kempf of Hermann is pictured with the
grape that he developed, the Aroma, circa 1906.

Missouri's Wine Industry Revival

In the last 35 years, a handful of visionary vintners have labored to restore many of Missouri's vineyards and wineries to their pre-Prohibition levels of excellence. It's fitting that this rebirth started in Hermann, when Jim and Betty Held switched from raising mushrooms in Stone Hill's cellars to making wine again.

The state government has helped promote the rebirth of Missouri viticulture. In 1980 the Missouri Wine Advisory Board was formed and a state enologist was hired. Since that time a new tax on wine sales has helped generate funds for a state-run Grape and Wine Program. A portion of this money supports a research program at Missouri State University's Fruit Experiment Station. Scientists there are studying varieties of grapes from around the world in hopes of identifying those varieties best suited for Missouri viticulture.

In 1980, Augusta became the first official viticultural region in the country, approved by the Bureau of Alcohol, Tobacco and Firearms. Since then, Hermann, the Ozark Highlands Region, and the Ozark Mountains Region have also made this list.

Today, close to 60 wineries are pressing grapes for wine every fall. Gallonage of wine produced in Missouri has nearly doubled since 1998. A new generation of Missouri vintners, many schooled in California, are working with proven grape varieties and methods, producing increasingly complex and sophisticated wines.

Many wineries, old and new, are winning medals at home and abroad. Much to the pleasure of wine lovers in Missouri and elsewhere, the state's wine industry is thriving once again.

Map of Missouri Wine Regions

Winery Location Symbol

Legend

- ☆1 **Augusta Wine Region**
- ☆2 **Hermann Wine Region**
- ☆3 **Central Wine Region**
- ☆4 **Western Wine Region**
- ☆5 **Ozark Highlands Wine Region**
- ☆6 **Ozark Mountains Wine Region**
- ☆7 **Eastern Wine Region**
- ☆8 **Southeastern Wine Region**

This book is divided into eight geographic regions: Augusta, Hermann, Central, Western, Ozark Highlands, Ozark Mountains, Eastern and Southeastern. To locate a specific town or winery, please refer to the Table of Contents or the Index.

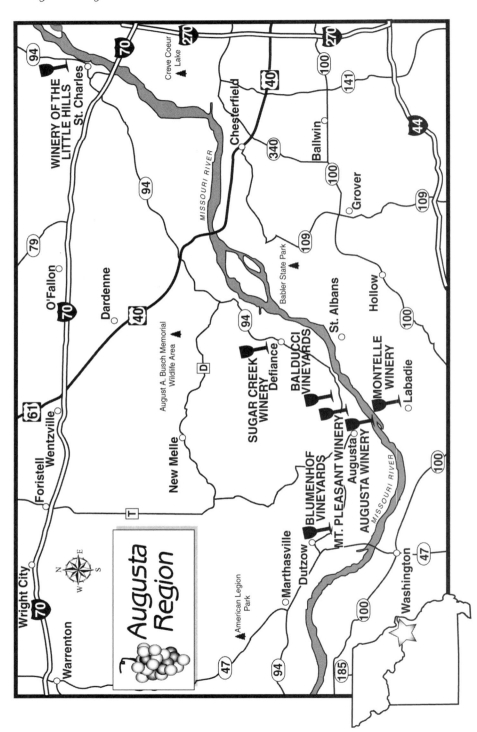

AUGUSTA REGION

Most of the wineries in this region lie along the *Weinstrasse* (German for "wine road"). This corridor runs along the Missouri River, following Highway 94. The wineries here are popular destinations for St. Louisans eager to spend a weekend in the countryside, head out on a short daytrip or simply find a quiet place to watch another day come to a close.

Most of the wineries are located within an hour of each other, making for a fun-filled daytrip.

If you are looking for a day packed with adventure that will take you to a wide range of Missouri wineries, the Augusta Wine Region is a fine place to start.

Daniel Boone was originally buried near present-day Defiance.

EXPLORING DUTZOW

Blumenhof Vineyards & Winery

B&B • Bikes • Eats • Parking • Post Office • Restrooms
Marthasville Chamber of Commerce: (636) 433-5242

Missouri's German heritage first took root in Missouri around present-day Dutzow. In the 1820s, Gottfried Duden established a farm on nearby Lake Creek and sent enthusiastic accounts of his experiences (compiled into a book, *Report on a Journey to the Western States of North America*) back to Germany. In 1832, Baron Wilhelm von Bock founded the town of Dutzow, making it the first German settlement in Missouri.

Many early intellectuals' romantic notions of living on the frontier quickly dissolved, too daunted by their lack of farming skills to stay in the wilderness. Many soon returned to city life in St. Louis or headed back to Germany.

A second wave of German settlers, however—knowing full well the challenges that lay ahead—soon arrived in the area. They were led by Friedrich Muench and Paul Follenius. Muench planted several vineyards around Dutzow and became well known for his expertise in the cultivation of grapes. He also went on to become a Missouri senator. A stone barn with Muench's name in the keystone still stands in Dutzow.

By 1839, Jesuit priests were also coming regularly to Dutzow. A parish was soon established and the first Saint Vincent de Paul Church was built in 1842.

The railroad followed in the 1890s and the town prospered. Like most river-town sagas, however, the railroad era soon gave way to interstate commerce. Dutzow remains a small, vibrant town that is a favorite destination for day-trippers out of St. Louis on a weekend drive, for antique hunters and for bikers who come here to ride the Katy Trail.

Not far from Daniel Boone's burial site outside of Marthasville lies his home near Defiance (shown below). The house is only a few miles from the Katy Trail. It is furnished as it was when Daniel died on September 26, 1820. Boone's home can be visited. Call: (636) 798-2005.

Also located on the grounds is Boonesfield Village, a replica of an early community. Structures reflect the era of the Louisiana Purchase and the early days of Missouri's statehood, offering a living-history experience throughout the year.

Boone came to Missouri in 1799, after spending most of his life in North Carolina, Virginia, Kentucky and West Virginia. Spain still controlled the Missouri country then and Boone was one of the first Americans to respond to the Spanish government's invitation to settle the territory. He was appointed chief officer to the Femme Osage area in 1800. His duties included justice of the peace and militia commandant. He also divided up land for incoming pioneers. It was from his home in Defiance that Boone wrote the following passage: *"I am hire With my hands full of Bisness and No athoraty, and if I am Not indulged in What I Do for the best it Is Not worth my While to put my Self to all this trubel..."*

How to Get to the Daniel Boone Monument: The monument shown on the opposite page is on... you guessed it... Daniel Boone Monument Road, a blacktop road 1.5 miles east of Marthasville. From Dutzow, take 94 west to Hwy 47. Keep an eye out for the signs, and a white house and tan shed off to the north. Take this road north (toward the bluff). The road Ts within sight of the Katy Trail. Go left and follow the road 1.2 miles and the monument is on the right.

Daniel Boone spent his last days at this picturesque home built in the early 1800s.

The Blumenhof's tasting room and deck.

BLUMENHOF VINEYARDS & WINERY

Highway 94, Dutzow, MO 63342
(636) 433-2245 or (800) 419-2245
Hours of Operation:
Monday through Saturday 10:30 a.m. to 5:30 p.m.
Sunday Noon to 5:30 p.m.

HOW TO GET THERE: Less than an hour by car from the St. Louis area, Blumenhof Winery is located in Dutzow on Hwy 94, just 8 miles west of Augusta. Blumenhof is also a convenient stop for bicyclists on the Katy Trail, since the trail passes right in front of the winery.

This winery offers a casual and relaxing atmosphere in German decor. Blumenhof's name, which translates from German as "Court of Flowers," honors the Blumenberg family's ancestral farm located in the foothills of the Harz Mountains in Northwest Germany.

The 2007 growing season will mark the 20th anniversary for this winery, owned by the father and son team of Mark and Jim Blumenberg. Mark planted the first cuttings here in 1979. Since then, the Blumenhof Winery has established itself as an award-winning winery. More than 80 wine bottles now line the tasting room along with dangling medals and acclaims from California to New York.

Blumenhof's wines have won medals at the Missouri State Fair, from the *Dallas Morning News*, the Florida State Fair, the International Eastern and the California National Orange Show wine competitions. Their wines are produced almost exclusively from grapes grown in the Blumenhof vineyards.

Chief vintner Mark Blumenberg currently has about 19 acres in production. The Blumenhof Winery places special emphasis on the production of dry varietals but also has a variety of wines to suit a wide range of preferences. Open 361 days a year, the winery hosts outdoor concerts in the spring and fall. Tours are given by appointment and complimentary tastings are offered in their tasting room.

Many visitors to Blumenhof show up on two wheels, since the Katy Trail State Park, America's longest rails-to-trails project, is located just steps away.

"This is the only winery we go to," says Dawn Matschiner, from St. Louis, enjoying a sunny Monday afternoon with her friends.

BLUMENHOF WINE LIST

Current Offerings:

CHAMBOURCIN: A medium-bodied varietal wine with firm berry fruit tones complemented by toasty oak.

CHARDONEL: A dry white wine fermented and aged in French oak barrels.

DEVIL'S DEN RED: Named for "Devil's Den Hollow," located in the hills near the vineyard. Served chilled, warm or even (apropos the name) hot. Double gold medal winner at the 2005 International Eastern Wine Competition and a silver medal winner at the 2006 Tasters Guild International Wine Judging.

FEMME OSAGE: A floral semi-dry white made from the Traminette grape. Gold medal winner at the 2006 Tasters Guild International Wine Judging.

GOLDBLUMEN: Made from the Vidal Blanc grapes picked in December. A flavorful after-dinner wine.

KATY'S BLUSH: Made in the style of a White Zinfandel.

LA CHARRETTE: Formerly known as "Charrette White," this fruity wine's new name and label commemorated the bicentennial (on May 25, 2004) of Lewis and Clark's departure from the village of La Charrette, the last outpost of Europeans encountered by the Corps of Discovery as they began their epic journey.

MISSOURI WEINLAND: A semi-dry Vidal Blanc. Floral aromas and a bit of spiciness.

RAYON D'OR: A semi-dry white wine with a ripe apple character and a light, slightly sweet finish. Gold medal winner at the 2006 Tasters Guild International Wine Judging

SEYVAL: A crisp, light varietal wine with a bouquet of cut hay and spearmint.

VIGNOLES: Scents of pears, pineapples and spring flowers. A flavor of rich, ripe, succulent fruit. Gold medal at the 2006 Tasters Guild International Wine Judging.

EXPLORING AUGUSTA

Augusta Winery, Louis P. Balducci Vineyards, Montelle Winery,
Mount Pleasant Wine Company

B&Bs • Bikes • Craft shops • Eats • Gas • Lodging
Parking • Post Office • Restrooms
Greater Augusta Chamber of Commerce: (636) 228-4005
www.augusta-missouri.com

L eonard Harold, one of Daniel Boone's followers to St. Charles, founded this
town in 1836. The site was chosen for its excellent river landing. Before
Harold's survey, it was a campsite for French fur traders and a spot along
one of the more popular Native American trails.

By the time of its incorporation in 1855, the town was known as Mount
Pleasant. The town changed its name to Augusta when it applied for a post office
and learned that the name Mount Pleasant was already in use.

Augusta was also a popular riverboat landing known as Augusta Bend. In
1872, flooding of the Missouri River caused the river to fill in its main channel,
changing its course and cutting Augusta off from the river. Fortunately for the
town, the railroad was soon to follow. The new land between the town and the
river also provided great commercial potential.

Located atop a gently rolling landscape, the vineyards surrounding Augusta
have been recognized for their ability to produce superior wine grapes since the
1800s. Augusta actually became America's first recognized viticultural area, or
official wine district, in 1980, because of the distinctive soil type and the length of
growing season within this 15-square-mile region.

As other towns have gone by the wayside, Augusta, with its 300 residents,
is still a thriving small town. Much of the tourist interest, which was spurred by
the revival of the vineyards in the late 1960s, has blossomed into the many home-
based businesses you see today. According to the locals, if a flag is flying near the
door, you can be sure the business is open. Visit the Augusta Brewing Company
for some locally microbrewed beers: (636) 482-BEER.

Bed & Breakfasts

Ashley's Rose Restaurant and B&B
(636) 482-4108

Femme Osage Haus B&B
(636) 482-4005

Anchor Mill Inn
(636) 228-4850

H.S. Clay House
(314) 504-4203 or (888) 309-7334

Augusta Wine Country Inn
(636) 795-5807

Lindenhof B&B
(636) 228-4617

Cottage Guest House
(636) 228-2024

Old Town Augusta Inn
(636) 482-4654

Augusta Winery's owner and vintner Tony Kooyumjian has long
been a leader in Missouri wine country's resurgence.

AUGUSTA WINERY

Corner of Jackson & High Streets, Augusta, MO 63332
(636) 228-4301 or (888) MOR-WINE (667-9463)
www.augustawinery.com
Hours of Operation: Monday through Friday 10 a.m. to 5:30 p.m.
Saturday 10 a.m. to 6 p.m. • Sunday Noon to 6 p.m.

HOW TO GET THERE: From St. Louis, take Hwy 40 west to Hwy 94. Go south for
18 miles to Augusta. From K.C., take I-70 east to Hwy 47. Go south to Hwy 94. Take
94 north to Augusta.

A drive of less than an hour from St. Louis, through the scenic Missouri
River Valley, brings you to Augusta Winery. This winery is located in the
center of town on the corner of High and Jackson Streets. The winery
features wines ranging from dry dinner wines to sweet dessert wines. Owner/
vintner Tony Kooyumjian and his staff craft all of Augusta Winery's wines from
locally grown grapes. Tony's 2002 Norton won the Governor's Cup, Best of Show,
Best Varietal and Gold at the 2004 Missouri Wine Competition. The winery produces
up to 20,000 gallons each year. Sample many varieties in the tasting room. Step
outside and enjoy the terrace with a chilled bottle of wine and a picnic lunch.
Locally produced cheese and sausage are also available.

Augusta Wines Recognized by German Press

For the first time since Prohibition, Missouri wine has been exported to Germany. 615 cases of Missouri wine arrived in Germany—335 cases from the Augusta Winery, 120 cases each from St. James and Stone Hill and 20 cases from Montelle. Three prominent German distributors have been exposing their country to Missouri's fine wines and the exposure has paid off.

On January 16, 2003, Tony Kooyumjian, owner of Augusta and Montelle Wineries, received notice from Germany that the Augusta Winery 2001 Chardonel had received a prestigious award from the German wine magazine *Selection*, which holds a competition once a year. This year over 900 premium white wines from 27 regions from around the world competed. The United States was one region.

The Augusta Winery 2001 Chardonel was voted the Best USA Wine with the Montelle Winery 2001 Dry Vignoles being the runner up. From the winners of these 27 regions, the best six are selected for presentation at a grand six-course tasting dinner and awards ceremony at the Kupferberg Winery in Mainz, Germany. Tony Kooyumjian attended the awards ceremony to do a presentation on his 2001 Chardonel and talk to the German press. He said, "Not only is this shipment of wine an historic moment for Missouri, but we have shown the world that Missouri wines can rival the best wines the world has to offer. This is a feather in our cap for Augusta and for Missouri wines as a whole."

— www.STLtoday.com

The Augusta Winery is located in the middle of town.
Its tasting room and wine garden please the palate.

AUGUSTA WINE LIST

Current Offerings:
BLACKBERRY: A semi-sweet fruit wine made from 100 percent blackberries. Rich, fresh blackberry bouquet and flavor and a long and slightly sweet finish.
CHAMBOURCIN: A dry red. Full-bodied, rich, complex fruit flavor.
CHARDONEL: A dry white, barrel fermented, apple & citrus fruit bouquet, full-bodied, rich, smooth finish.
ICEWINE: A sweet dessert wine. Intense, rich, concentrated fruit flavors and bouquet, long, rich finish. Made after the ice has been removed from frost. Very rare and extremely limited.
NORTON: A full-bodied, dry red. Intense flavors, mouth-filling, oak aged.
RESERVE RED: A semi-dry red, light-bodied with a fruity, soft finish.
RIVER VALLEY BLUSH: Semi-dry with a light salmon color, floral bouquet, luscious fruit, and a pleasant finish.
RIVER VALLEY WHITE: A sweet dessert wine. Rich fruit bouquet and flavor. Long, luscious finish.
RIVER VALLEY RED: A sweet dessert wine with beautiful cherry color, fresh berry flavors and aroma, and a long finish.
RASPBERRY: A semi-sweet fruit wine made from 100 percent raspberries, crisp, fresh raspberry bouquet and flavor, and a slightly sweet finish.
SEYVAL BLANC: A semi-dry white. Crisp acidity. Intense, tropical fruit. Lingering finish.
VIDAL BLANC: Dry, toasty, floral bouquet, crisp acidity, spicy, rich finish.
VIGNOLES: A semi-sweet white. Pineapple, tropical fruit bouquet, fresh crisp fruit body with a hint of sweetness.
VINTAGE PORT: Deep burgundy color, rich ripe fruit flavors and bouquet, full-bodied with a long finish.

AUGUSTA
W I N E R Y

RIVER VALLEY
RED
MISSOURI TABLE WINE

Visitors to Montelle Winery enjoy an astounding view and a steady breeze.

MONTELLE WINERY

201 Montelle Drive, Augusta, MO 63332

(888) 595-WINE or (636) 228-4464

www.montelle.com

Hours of Operation:

Monday through Friday 10 a.m. to 5:30 p.m.

Saturday 10 a.m. to 6 p.m.

Sunday 11 a.m. to 6 p.m.

May to September:

Open until 9 p.m. on Fridays and 10 p.m. on Saturdays.

HOW TO GET THERE: From St. Louis take Hwy 40-64. Take Hwy 94 south 15 miles to the winery. Watch for their signs.

The Montelle Winery sits 400 feet above the Missouri River Valley. Up to 500 visitors at a time can enjoy a great view from the barnlike tasting room or the picnic area. Montelle Winery is a destination that brings you through the heart of the Augusta Region. The winding highway twists and turns, carrying you past picturesque hillsides, meadows and farmland. A daytrip here provides many opportunities to explore.

Owner Tony Kooyumjian, who also owns Augusta Winery, has been a winemaker for over 24 years. Tony proudly describes his wines as an expression of the Augusta area, reflective of the unique microclimate and soil. It is said that the distinctiveness of Augusta's soil came from deposition of soil and debris by glaciers that moved through the area some 10,000 years ago. The minerals deposited in the soil are said to be what gives the area's grapes and subsequent wines their distinctive flavors. The proof is in the pudding, or in this case the wine. Montelle Winery's 2004 Chardonel won a Best of Class and a Gold in the 2005 Indy International Wine Competition.

MONTELLE WINE LIST
Current Offerings:

BLACKBERRY	RIVER COUNTRY RED
CHAMBOURCIN	RIVER COUNTRY WHITE
CHARDONEL	ROSE GOLD
CYNTHIANA	SEYVAL
CYTHIANA PORT	ST. WENCESLAUS
DRY VIGNOLES	STONE HOUSE RED
FRAMBOISE	STONE HOUSE WHITE
HIMMELSWEIN	STRAWBERRY
RED RASPBERRY	VIDAL ICE WINE

The tasting room at Montelle Winery offers a chance to sample a variety of award-winning wines, including the 2004 Chardonel, which won a Best of Class and Gold in the 2005 Indy International Wine Competition.

NOTES

Awaiting harvest at their peak, Mount Pleasant's Dechaunec grapes are a deep purple—almost black—grape.

The road into Augusta is flanked by rows of healthy vines.

MOUNT PLEASANT
WINERY

5634 High Street, Augusta, MO 63332

(636) 482-WINE or (800) 467-WINE (9463)

www.mountpleasant.com

Hours of Operation:

Monday through Friday 11 a.m. to 5:30 p.m.

Saturday and Sunday open until dusk from April to October

HOW TO GET THERE: From St. Louis, take Hwy 40 west to Hwy 94. Travel south on 94 for 18 miles to Augusta. From Kansas City, take I-70 east to Hwy 47. Travel south on 47 to Hwy 94. Take 94 north to Augusta.

George Muench and his brother Fredrick began planting the Mount Pleasant vineyards in the late 1800s. The brothers had emigrated from Germany with the idea of establishing a classic, Old World winery in the heart of Missouri's Rhineland. The buildings were built using Augusta limestone and handmade bricks manufactured on the property. Their wines were receiving international acclaim when Prohibition put an end to their endeavor. During this dark period, all activity at the winery stopped and vineyards were destroyed.

Some 40 years later, the vineyards were replanted and the Mount Pleasant winery was resurrected. Today, the winery is once again producing award-winning wines from grapes grown in the 80-acre vineyard. Mark Baehmann is the resident

Visitors from Germany... ferrets... You never know who or what you're going to run into.

vintner, and Phillip Dressel and his children, Charles and Anne, are the owners. Each year they produce about 50,000 gallons of wine, including ports and champagnes. Many varieties have returned Mount Pleasant to the winner's platform at international wine competitions. Mount Pleasant was recently voted "Best Missouri Winery" by *Sauce Magazine,* and their 2003 Norton won the Governor's Cup in 2005 at the Missouri Grape and Wine Program Competition.

Visits to Mount Pleasant often begin in the tasting room. After a selection is made, their spacious and inviting decks, gazebos and patio offer a front-row view of the sun setting across the Missouri River Valley.

The winery hosts live music, barbecues, private parties and receptions. The terrace rooms hold up to 250 people and are perfect for special gatherings.

MOUNT PLEASANT WINE LIST

Current Offerings:

AUGUSTA VILLAGE: Blended into full body with fruit and berry flavors.

BRUT IMPERIAL: A sparkling blend of Vidal Blanc and St. Vincent. Dry and crisp.

CABERNET SAUVIGNON: A full-bodied, ruby red-violet with a finish of cherry. Can be enjoyed immediately or cellared to further soften and mellow.

CHARDONEL: A soft and creamy hybrid.

CHARDONNAY RESERVE: Fruit, oak and butter flavors give this wine flavorful balance.

CUVEE' BLANC: Known as Missouri Chardonnay. Fermentation in French oak gives this wine rich fruit flavors with oak and butter notes.

HARVEST RED: A sweet red blend.

HARVEST WHITE: A sweet white blend loaded with citrus flavors and aromas.

HIGHLAND: A fruity red with a touch of sweetness.

LATE HARVEST CUVEE: A smooth, fruity dessert wine.

NORTON: Aromas of currant, toast and blueberry mingle with black fruits, light oak and mineral notes.

RHINELAND: A semi-dry and fruity wine.

TAWNY PORT: A silky smooth dessert wine with nuts, caramel and butterscotch flavors.

TEN BUCKS: A sweet, creamy smooth blend.

VILLAGIO: A sweet, deliciously fruity off-dry wine with a floral nose and crisp finish.

VINTAGE PORT: Cellar this wine to soften flavors of chocolate, dark cherry, currant and anise.

WHITE PORT: A sweet port loaded with fresh tree fruits flavors.

WHITE ZEN: A fresh, fruity, semi-dry blush aged in stainless steel.

Nearby: In the summer of 2006, Bethlehem Valley Vineyards opened a tasting room in historic Augusta. Stop in for a visit and taste what the Missouri hills, sun and rain have helped create in every bottle. Bethlehem Valley Vineyards grows Norton and Chardonel grapes on a 200-acre farm in the Missouri River Valley. They focus on the quality of their grapes by planting only the most advantageous slopes with grapes suited to Missouri's climate. The vineyard partners with Mount Pleasant Winery in Augusta. They work together to ensure that the Norton and Chardonel wines they produce reflect the attention given to every grape. Bethlehem Valley wines are found on the tables of several fine restaurants in Missouri and are carried on the shelves of wine shops across the state. Bethlehem Valley wines can also be purchased through Mount Pleasant Winery: (636) 482-4419.

Carol Balducci greets guests in the Balducci Vineyard tasting room, which features a mural by Jane Rohlfing, a local artist.

LOUIS P. BALDUCCI VINEYARDS

6601 Highway 94, South Augusta, MO 63332

(636) 482-VINO

www.balduccivineyards.com

Hours of Operation:

Monday through Thursday 11 a.m. to 5:30 p.m.

Friday and Saturday 11 a.m. to 8 p.m.

Sunday 11 a.m. to 6 p.m.

Kitchen open Friday through Sunday

HOW TO GET THERE: Located 3.5 miles west of Augusta on Hwy 94.

L ouis P. Balducci was active in the wine business in Missouri for 50 years. He began working in the wholesale wine business in 1946. He would eventually introduce many new brands and types of wines to Missourians. He became a highly respected wine specialist in St. Louis, where his reputation as a speaker and wine educator drew him acclaim from all over the Midwest.

Mr. Balducci was associated with Balducci's Restaurant in St. Louis and with Rick and Carol Balducci's vineyards in Augusta. Mr. Balducci passed away in 1995, but his enthusiasm for life and his love for family, friends and fine wines are honored and preserved at this sophisticated winery.

Louis P. Balducci Vineyards has quickly become a hit with visitors and wine fans from all around the state. The winery offers wines and food, along with regularly scheduled live music and beautiful views.

LOUIS P. BALDUCCI WINE LIST

Current Offerings:

ARIA: A dry, light-bodied red blend of Chambourcin and St. Vincent grapes.

BOCCE BLUSH: A semi-dry wine aged in stainless steel.

CHIARETTO: A light-bodied, semi-dry red blend aged in stainless steel.

DOLCE BIANCO: A sweet white with fruity flavors.

DOLCE RUSSO: A sweet red with fruity flavors.

NATALIA: An off-dry white wine with citrus overtones.

NORTON: A dry, medium-bodied red wine aged in oak.

PORT: A sipping wine that is brandy fortified.

SONATA: A semi-dry blend of white varietals aged in stainless steel.

VIDAL BLANC: A dry white with a hint of green apples and a touch of French oak.

Live music and expansive country views await visitors at Louis P. Balducci Vineyards.

A river bottom view along Highway 94, near Dutzow.

EXPLORING DEFIANCE

Sugar Creek Winery

B&Bs • Bikes • Eats • Lodging • Parking • Post Office • Restrooms

Early settlers in the Defiance area were of English descent, from Virginia and Kentucky. In 1798, David Darst settled in the area and Thomas and Phoebe Parsons purchased the claim of Joe Haynes (land grant number 14) in 1839. The Parsons family owned most of the land where the town was built and constructed a brick house on the bluff. James Craig, aware of the significance of the railroad to small towns, led a crusade to build a depot and a farm-to-market road (now Defiance Road). The town was then named Defiance because it had lured the railroad depot away from Matson in 1893. The Schiermeier building here represents the interdependence between farmers and the railroad. It has two opposite-facing fronts. This boomtown phenomenon allowed one front to face the railroad, while the other front faced the farmers. Today, this building houses Katy Bike Rental, a great place to rent a cruiser to enjoy this scenic stretch of trail.

Bed & Breakfasts

Das Gast Haus Nadler B&B
125 Defiance Road
(636) 987-2200

Elysian Fields B&B
2981 S. Highway 94
(636) 798-7426

Bike Rentals

Katy Bike Rental • 2998 S. Hw 94 • (636) 987-2673 • www.katytrailbikerental.com

Sugar Creek offers an abundance of outdoor seating.

SUGAR CREEK WINERY

125 Boone Country Lane, Defiance, MO 63341
(636) 987-2400
www.sugarcreekwines.com
Hours of Operation:
Monday through Saturday 10 a.m. to 5:30 p.m., Sunday Noon to 5:30 p.m.
Closed Thanksgiving, Christmas and New Year's.
Winter hours vary, so please call for information.

HOW TO GET THERE: The winery is located 12 miles southwest of Hwy 40-61 on Hwy 94. Follow 94 west of Defiance to a steep hillside that rises from the Katy Trail and overlooks the broad Missouri River Valley. Watch for the signs.

The Sugar Creek Winery is located along the Katy Trail in a turn-of-the-century Victorian home that embodies the romantic atmosphere of the wine industry.

Ken and Becky Miller make their wines from American and French hybrid grapes, grown in their vineyards surrounding the winery. Inside the house you will find the Sugar Creek tasting room housed in an intimate parlor, wrapped in fantastic stained glass, which also has many wine-related souvenirs for sale.

The Millers' winery was formerly Boone Country Winery, but they renamed it when they purchased the property in August of 1994. They made the move from Kirkwood (a suburb of St. Louis) to Defiance and brought the name of their former neighborhood with them—Sugar Creek. A colorful mural on the side of a shed, an expansive view and abundant outdoor seating just steps from the vineyard make this a great place to sip a new wine and relax with a friend. Next to their winery is an ornate gazebo where live music and specialty foods are offered every Sunday from April through October.

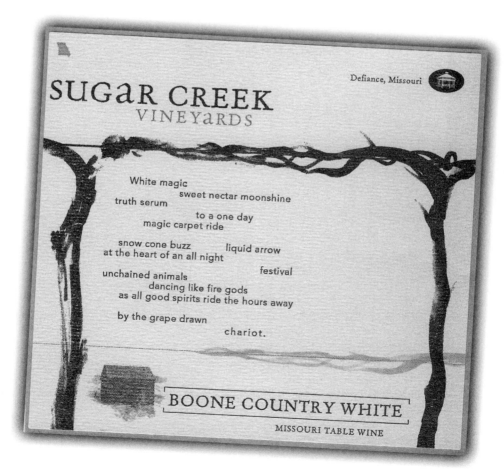

Sugar Creek's turn-of-the-century Victorian home offers a great backdrop for enjoying live music, admiring the views of the river bottoms and drinking a bottle of wine.

SUGAR CREEK WINE LIST

Current Offerings:

BIRDLEGS BLUSH: A Chambourcin and Chenin Blanc blend with fresh citrus tones with a lively finish.

BLACKBERRY THICKET: A classic fruit wine.

BOONE COUNTRY WHITE: A crisp, fragrant Riesling-style wine.

CHARDONEL: A full-bodied dry white aged in French oak. Estate bottled.

CHAMBOURCIN: Bright berry tones with layers of oak flavor. Estate bottled.

CYNTHIANA: A concentrated, full-bodied, thick dry red with tones of black cherry and black licorice. Estate bottled.

LA RUSTICA RED: Four grape varieties blended together offer a sweet wine ripe with cherry and wild berry flavors.

LA RUSTICA WHITE: A balanced blend of Seyval and Vidal grapes. A slightly sweet and fruity start with a dry finish.

MICHAEL'S SIGNATURE RED: A medium-bodied, Merlot-style wine with ripe fruit and berry tones, aged in American oak.

PEACH HOLLOW: A fruit wine with a light and sweet texture.

RASPBERRY PATCH: A fruit wine with strong raspberry tones.

SEYVAL BLANC: A crisp, fruity dry white wine aged in French oak.

SIGNATURE PORT: After-dinner dessert wine.

SUNSET RED: This smooth, semi-dry red has spicy berry flavors.

VIDAL BLANC: A dry, light Chardonnay-style dinner wine aged in French oak.

EXPLORING ST. CHARLES
Winery of the Little Hills

B&Bs • Bikes • Camping • Casino • Crafts • Eats • Gas • Hostel • Lodging
Microbrewery • Parking • Restrooms • RV hookups
Greater St. Charles Visitors Bureau: (636) 946-7776 or (800) 366-2427
www.historicstcharles.com

A visit to downtown St. Charles, which was once the capital of Missouri, feels like walking into an historical photo. The cobblestone of Main Street works its rhythm beneath your feet as you stroll past antique shops and ice-cream parlors along this friendly ten-block corridor into the past.

Pass the afternoon in the shade, walk the Katy Trail or join in a game of frisbee down by the river. The activity in St. Charles doesn't set with the sun. So if you're not in a hurry, you might try your luck on one of the riverboat casinos docked within walking distance of the Katy Trail or dine outside at one of the many tempting restaurants and cafés nearby.

Founded as Les Petites Cotes (The Little Hills) by French Canadian fur trader Louis Blanchette in 1769, this area became the headquarters for the fur-trading industry along the Missouri River. By 1791, the population had grown to 255 and the second Catholic church was dedicated to San Carlos Borromeo (1538–1584), archbishop of Milan and patron saint of Charles IV, King of Spain. On the day the church was dedicated, the town changed its name to San Carlos.

San Carlos was "Americanized" to St. Charles in 1804 during the formalization of the Louisiana Purchase. In subsequent years, St. Charles, like many other Missouri towns, was greatly affected by western expansion, German immigration, the 1849 California Gold Rush and railroad and river trade.

Before Missouri was granted statehood in 1821, various locations had served as the government seat for territorial affairs. As statehood became a certainty, the permanent site of Jefferson City was chosen. But until the new Capitol could be constructed, nine cities vied for the honor of hosting the state's temporary seat of government. The citizens of St. Charles furnished free meeting space for the legislators and won the honor.

The state's first legislators met here from June 1821 through October 1826, when the new Capitol was ready in Jefferson City. Today, the Missouri Department of Natural Resources gives tours of the fully restored first Capitol, where frontiersmen and scholars alike met atop the Peck Brothers General Store. Tours are available Monday through Saturday every hour. The First Missouri State Capitol is located at 200 S. Main. Call (636) 940-3322 for more information.

There are also many interesting buildings throughout town. In the basement of 318 South Main Street there are bars on the windows and pegs in the wall, because this is the site of Missouri's first prison. The house at 724 South Main Street was the local presidential campaign headquarters for Abraham Lincoln.

Augusta Region

The Lewis and Clark Boat House and Nature Center is a real highlight. It is located at 1050 Riverside Drive, or call (636) 947-3199 for tour information. On your way out, the riverfront park's winding path takes you past the restored train depot and numerous benches, offering a great view of the Missouri River and a perfect way to round out the afternoon.

The St. Charles Convention and Visitors Bureau has several free brochures, which include histories on specific parts of town. The bureau also publishes an eco-tourism series of free booklets on hiking, bicycling, bird watching and a fall leaves tour of St. Charles County.

Annual events include the Lewis and Clark Rendezvous the third weekend of May; the Festival of the Little Hills, the third weekend in August; Ragfest, each Labor Day; a bluegrass festival each September; and both the Missouri River Storytelling Festival and Oktoberfest, each October. Contact the St. Charles Visitors Center, 230 South Main Street, or call (800) 366-2427 for more information.

Bed & Breakfasts

Boone's Lick Trail Inn		Victorian Memories B&B
(636) 947-7000		(636) 940-8111
Lady B's B&B	The Mueller House	Old Elm Tree Inn
(636) 947-3421	(636) 947-1228	(636) 947-4843
Lococo House II B&B		The Geery's B&B
(636) 946-0619		(636) 916-5344

Bike Rental
Touring Cyclist • 104 South Main Street • (636) 949-9630

WINERY OF THE LITTLE HILLS

501 South Main Street, St. Charles, MO 63301
(636) 946-9339 or (877) LT-HILLS
www.little-hills.com
Hours of Operation:
Monday through Thursday 11 a.m. to 8 p.m.
Friday and Saturday 11 a.m. to 10 p.m.
Sunday 10 a.m. to 9 p.m.

HOW TO GET THERE: Located in the historic district of St. Charles on South Main Street. Take I-70 to the St. Charles Fifth Street exit. Go north to Boonslick Road and turn right. Take Boonslick to Main Street and turn left. The winery is located in the 500 block.

On the cobblestone Main Street of historic St. Charles, the Winery of the Little Hills has a restaurant and gift shop that are both open all year long for lunch, dinner and Sunday brunch. The restaurant serves European cuisine either indoors or outdoors in their beautiful wine garden. The winery's gift shop specializes in beautifully decorated gift baskets that feature Missouri wine, cheese and sausage.

A winery was founded at this location in 1860 by the Wepprich family. Through the years it's been a pharmacy, meat locker and processing plant and is rumored to have served as a base for whiskey bootleggers during Prohibition.

Over a century later, the winery was reopened and is presently operated by David and Tammy Campbell. The primary focus of the winery is serving exceptional wines in conjunction with fine foods. Although their wines are bottled off-site, the Winery of the Little Hills remains a bonded winery.

Winery of the Little Hills offers their own award-winning wine list as well as other varieties of wines, including the renowned Missouri Valley White, winner of Missouri State Fair Gold Medals two years in a row. All production and bottling is done at Augusta Winery. Traditional sausage, cheese and crackers can be purchased to complement the wines, so stop to enjoy the shaded wine garden.

While you're here, be sure and stop for an old-time portrait across the street at The Tintype Photo Parlour, 510 S. Main Street, (636) 925-2155. The clothes fit over your clothes, so there's no changing. Within minutes you'll be transformed into visions of your great grandparents, the Civil War era, prairie pioneers or Victorian-period style. Their motto is "We don't make you look better, we just make you look old."

WINERY OF THE LITTLE HILLS
WINE LIST
Current Offerings:

BLACKBERRY	MON FILS
BRUT	NORTON
CABERNET BLUSH	RASPBERRY
CABERNET SAUVIGNON	RED PORT
CATAWBA BLUSH	RIESLING
CATAWBA ROSE	RIVERS BEND
COBBLESTONE WHITE	SAUVIGNON BLANC
CONCORD	SEYVAL
GEWURZTRAMINER	VERDI
MAIN STREET RED	WHITE ZINFANDEL
MAIN STREET WHITE	

NOTES

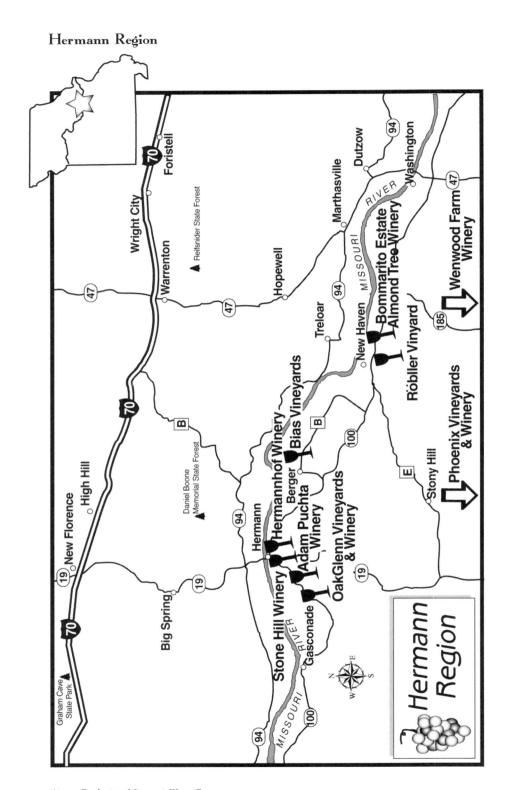

HERMANN REGION

The Hermann wine region is set within the heart of the Missouri Rhineland. It includes Adam Puchta Winery, Hermannhof Winery, Stone Hill Wine Company, Bias Vineyard, OakGlenn Vineyards & Winery, Bommarito Estate Almond Tree Winery, Phoenix Winery & Vineyards, Wenwood Farm Winery and Röbller Vineyard & Winery.

Touring this region will take you through the northern-most rolling hills of the Ozark Plateau. You'll visit Missouri's biggest winery, and some of the smaller ones, as well as one of the most recent additions to the industry. Maifest and Oktoberfest are also celebrated by many of the wineries in this section.

Hermann is home to many annual festivals, including Maifest,
Oktoberfest and the Grape Stomp (shown above).

EXPLORING HERMANN

Adam Puchta Winery, Hermannhof Winery, OakGlenn Winery, Stone Hill Winery

B&Bs • Bikes • Camping • Crafts • Eats • Gas • Lodging • Parking
Post Office • Restrooms • RV Park
Visitors Center, 312 Schiller Street, Hermann, MO 65041, (800) 932-8687
www.hermannmo.com

Hermann was founded by German settlers in 1836 and soon attained world-wide acclaim for its wines. Even today Hermann, located on the southern bank of the Missouri River, remains a hub of Missouri wine production. At one time Hermann was home to 65 wineries, with 40 more dotted along the river valley nearby. Today there are several wineries, including one of Missouri's largest and most awarded wineries, Stone Hill.

Even those not interested in wine will enjoy a visit to Hermann with its rich history and many festivals that celebrate its German heritage. *Midwest Living Magazine* said it best, "Hermann... more German than some cities in Germany."

Hermannites raise their children using "the Hermann formula: the first year wine, the second year wine and sauerkraut."

Hermann was founded in 1836 by the German Settlement Society of Philadelphia, whose members were disheartened at the loss of native customs and language among their countrymen in America. This "Second Fatherland" was intended to be a self-supporting refuge for German heritage and tradition. The proposed community was set up as a joint-stock company and was advertised throughout the United States and Germany. The colony quickly attracted a variety of artisans and laborers drawn by the idea of a "German Athens of the West."

On behalf of the society, one member acquired 11,300 acres of Frene Creek Valley land for $15,612. His choice for the site, bounded by hills and bluffs on three sides and the Missouri River on the north and teeming with wild grapevines, was apparently influenced by its similarity to the Rhine River region in Germany.

Anxious to begin on what they expected to become one of the largest cities in the United States, the German Settlement Society modeled the layout of the colony on that of Philadelphia. The name of Germany's national hero, Hermann (Arminius in Latin), who defeated the Roman legion in 9 A.D., seemed a fitting symbol for the great dream their new settlement embodied.

By 1852, more than 470 acres of vineyards were in production around Hermann. By the turn of the last century, Stone Hill was the third largest winery in the world (second in the United States), producing 1,250,000 gallons a year and winning international gold medals.

Today, Hermann is again home to one of the largest wineries in the state (Stone Hill Winery) and is once again vigorously making wine. More than 200 acres of grapes again grow on the hills around Hermann, and the German heritage of Hermann is as strong as ever. Hermannhof Winery has also been awarded the Brown-Foreman Trophy for Best New World White Wine.

Hermann has remarkably preserved early German architecture, great shops and more than 45 bed & breakfasts. There are many restaurants in town—both German in origin and otherwise. Almost every weekend during the summer months, Hermann plays host to some sort of German festival. The biggest ones are Wurstfest, Maifest and Oktoberfest (a.k.a. October Weekends). The Visitors Center will give you the exact dates. Festivities include traditional German dancing, brats, beer, wine and yodelling. After all, it was the Germans who believed that Sunday's duties included not only church, but revelry after a hard week of work.

Be sure and visit a few of Hermann's countless antique shops. One of my favorites is John and Mae Wilding's Red Barn Craft Shop and Gallery, located at 523 West Ninth Street. Call (573) 486-5544 for more information.

The Kaffee Haus is a great stop if you're looking to cool your heels. It is located across the street from Hermannhof Winery, at 407 E. First Street. They offer great coffee house fare, pastries, sandwiches and baked goods, (573) 486-2010. Directly across the street, Barb's Tin Rabbit is a must stop if you enjoy early Americana and art, or if you are looking to redecorate your home, (573) 486-5307.

The "Hermann Wine Trail" encompasses seven area wineries. These wineries come together to host a series of annual events with unique themes. These events include Wine 101 in January, the Chocolate Wine Trail in February, the Very Berry Wine Trail in July, and the Holiday Fare Wine Trail in November. Visit www.hermannwinetrail.com or call (800) 932-8687 for more information.

In Hermann, there is simply too much to see in one day, so take your cue to stay in one of Hermann's many bed & breakfasts. Hermann's Garden Club has also started garden tours. Call Alice Calhoun for details (573) 486-3060.

Hermann Region

Bed & Breakfasts

There are umpteen B&Bs in Hermann. Call the Visitor Information Center at (573) 486-2744 to book a reservation, or for more information.

Acorn B&B
(573) 486-4003

Alpenhorn Gasthaus B&B
(573) 486-8228

Angels in the Attic
(573) 486-5037 or (888) 264-3553

Ashlee's B&B
(573) 486-2392

Aunt Flora's B&B
(573) 486-5320

Birk's Gasthaus
(573) 486-2911 or (888) 701-2495

Campbell Haus B&B
(573) 486-1093

Captain Wohlt Inn
(573) 486-3357

Captain's Neighbor
(573) 486-3357

Captain's Cottage
(573) 486-2222

Esther's Ausblick
(573) 486-2170

Gatzemeyer Guest House
(573) 252-4380

Hermann Hill Vineyard & Inn
(573) 486-4455

Iron Horse Inn
(573) 486-9152

Klos B&B
(573) 486-5532

Kolbe Guest Haus
(573) 486-3453

Lydia Johnson Inn
(573) 486-0110

Market Street B&B
(573) 486-5597

Montague's B&B
(573) 486-2035

Nestle Inn
(573) 486-5893

Patty Kerr B&B
(573) 486-2510

River Suites
(573) 486-2222

Rose Garden B&B
(573) 486-4736

Schiller Guest Suites
(573) 486-1010

Schmidt Guesthouse
(573) 486-2146

Schneider-Fredrick Guest House
(573) 486-2146

Spirit Hill Guest House
(314) 280-9943

Stone Haus B&B
(573) 486-9169

Mumbrauer Gasthaus
(573) 486-5246

Stuff & Nonsense Guest House & B&B
(573) 486-4444

Weber Schulte Guest House
(314) 808-1493

White Roses
(573) 486-9094

Deutschheim State Historic Site

Deutschheim State Historic Site preserves Missouri's early German heritage. Tour guides share insights into what life was like for German immigrants in the 19th Century. They explain why and how the Germans came, and what they brought with them.

Deutschheim is a museum comprised of the Pommer-Gentner House and the Strehly House and Winery. Tours include the residence, the attached winery and the print shop. The Strehly House was the site of the first print shop in Hermann, and the German newspaper *Lichtfreund* (Friend of Light) was published in the ground floor shop. "But his four plus acres [of grapes] brought him a better income than his newspaper and printing business ever did," said site administrator Dr. Erin Renn.

Within these historic buildings are antique porcelains, furniture, the Midwest's earliest surviving carved wine cask (dated 1875), wooden clogs, early German furniture and a variety of arts and crafts from the past.

Daily tours begin at 109 West Second Street, for a nominal fee. Call (573) 486-2200 for details.

How to get there: Go west on Second Street to 109 West Second Street.

Deutschheim features an early carved wine barrel and these early grapevines, believed to have been planted in the early 1830s. According to site administrator Erin Renn, Ph.D. (pictured), Hermann's original land grants included free land for settlers who promised to grow grapes for at least seven years.

Annual Festivals Honor Hermann's German Heritage

W hen German immigrants settled in Hermann more than 150 years ago, they envisioned a "Second Fatherland" on the Missouri River, where their native customs and traditions could be not only practiced but appreciated. The founders would not be disappointed in the Hermann of today. Each year, area residents, eager to preserve their German heritage, band together in celebration of their town's German roots.

Wurstfest

A two-day celebration of Hermann's sausage making takes place each year in March. During this popular festival, the Hermann Area Chamber of Commerce joins local sausage makers, wineries, breweries, restaurants and shops in reaffirming Hermann as the "Sausage Capital of Missouri." Visitors are invited to sample and purchase Old World delicacies such as Bratwurst, Leberwurst, Schwartenmagen and Sommer Sausage. A statewide sausage-making contest is held, as well as a Brat Knot-Tying Contest. Area shops and museums feature craft demonstrations, and local wineries offer wine tastings and tours. Antique sausage-making and winemaking equipment is displayed around town. The Rhineland "Wurstjaegers" perform each year at the Wurstfest.

The Rhineland "Wurstjaegers" perform throughout the year at German festivals.

At the Maifest picnic in the city park, costumed girls with flowers in their hair danced around a Maypole, one of many Old World customs that survived at the turn of the century. The pole here has a traditional North German leafy tree top. The dance is derived from the ancient ritual of the revival and awakening of life and the ushering out of winter.

Sausage festival? Hmm... this was a new one for me. But after attending the event and sampling dozens of sausages, I was surprised, impressed and found some wonderful new favorites. It quickly became apparent to me that there's more to life than Jimmy Dean sausage. Craftful blends included ingredients as varied as cranberry, maple, blueberry, elk meat, and Stone Hill wine. After sampling the offerings of a dozen different sausage vendors, it became obvious that sausage can have as nuanced a flavor as wine. This was one of those events that left me going "wow." Making sausage really is an art form.

Maifest

Hermann's Maifest dates to the 1870s when, on the last day of school, the children would walk from the German School to the city park, waving flags and singing songs. They played games, ate knockwurst and drank pink lemonade.

Hermann now celebrates Maifest on the third full weekend in May. The community comes alive with German food, music and dancing, just like in the old days. The celebration includes an Entertainment/Food Strasse, where visitors can delight in German fare and enjoy continuous live entertainment. The Volksplatz (open-air market) features the works of quality crafters and artisans. Maypole dancers and Junior Wurstjaegers perform, and there is a heritage tour, a reenactment of the Little Canon Fire, and other activities. The grand finale is the Maifest parade.

Oktoberfest

Be sure to enjoy Hermann's biggest annual festival, Oktoberfest, which takes place every weekend in October. The festival has gained international attention as a celebration of the region's German heritage. Oompah tunes fill the air, and visitors are urged to wear their best German-related dress as they enjoy a cornucopia of sauerkraut, sausages, cheeses and, of course, wine.

During Oktoberfest, Hermann's resemblance to the "Fatherland" is astonishing. This would have pleased Hermann's founders, who envisioned a "Little Germany" in Missouri. Due to the determination of area residents to preserve their heritage, and more than a few annual celebrations, Hermann is undisputedly the most Germann town in Missouri, and perhaps in America.

Say hello to the Pied Piper while munching on some good bratwurst.

Tuba-thumping Polka, brats piled high with sauerkraut, the infamous Duck Dance...
Oktoberfest is one festival you don't want to miss!

One of Kemper's photographs of Hermann's early days shows the first load of leather arriving packed in barrels for Peters Shoe Company in 1902.

For more information on Hermann's colorful past, be sure to look for the book *Little Germany on the Missouri: The Photographs of Edward J. Kemper, 1895-1920*. Edited by Anna Kemper Hesse, the book includes a rare look at early Hermann life including a chapter on the area's fledgling grape and wine industry, captured by Kemper's black-and-white glass-plate negatives. Esteemed photographer Oliver Schuchard teased some amazing prints from these early negatives. The book is available at the Pebble Publishing Bookstore in Rocheport, or contact the University of Missouri Press.

Annual Events in Hermann

March: Wurstfest
April: Artists of Wine Country, Antique Show
May: Maifest—third week in May
June: Annual Quilt Show, Garden Tours
July: Cajun Concert at Stone Hill, Old-Fashioned Fourth of July
August: Great Stone Hill Grape Stomp
September: BBQ & Brats Festival
October: October Weekends
December: Christmas Park of Dreams & Kristkindl Market

Tim Puchta is the owner and winemaker at Adam Puchta Winery. Tim produces award-winning wines from the same fields worked by generations of his family.

The Puchta family began operating a vineyard on their property more than 150 years ago.

ADAM PUCHTA WINERY
Route 1, Box 73, Hermann, MO 65041
(573) 486-5596
Hours of Operation: Monday through Saturday 10 a.m. to 6 p.m.
Sunday 11 a.m. to 6 p.m.

HOW TO GET THERE: Puchta Winery is located 2 miles southwest of Hermann off Hwy 100. Follow the signs to Frene Creek County Road.

Puchta Winery is considered "Hermann's newest old winery." Tim Puchta (pronounced POOK-tah) is the sixth generation in the line of John Henry Puchta, a butcher who immigrated to the 40-acre homestead in 1839. He purchased the land in 1841 and in 1849 purchased 40 more acres. He later sold 40 of those acres to his son, Adam. Adam ran a commercial vineyard here from 1855 to 1919. Prohibition shut him down, and the land was converted to crops.

Future generations of Puchtas preserved the original winemaking equipment and made some fruit wines out of blackberries and elderberries. Tim Puchta was born in 1956 and held on to a lifelong dream of reopening the winery. His dream became a reality in 1990, when Adam Puchta Winery reopened. It established itself as the oldest "family owned" winery operation in the state. The winery celebrated it's 150th anniversary in July of 2005.

The Adam Puchta Winery's tasting room has a great shaded wine garden and indoor seating.

Tim was a respiratory therapist at Columbia Regional Hospital before getting his hands full-time into vines and wines. He continued working at the hospital for several years while he got his winery going and has never looked back.

"This has been a goal of mine for many, many years," Tim said. "I've always loved wine and I'm a farm boy at heart. I love working at home... it leaves time to be with my kids."

Today, Adam Puchta has a production capacity of about 62,000 gallons, up from 8,000 gallons in the year 2000. Wine is sold retail, on the premises, and to other states through mail-order.

As Tim quickly pointed out though, as you're growing, you're constantly updating equipment. Trying to grow a business produces its own problems, what with juggling the books and keeping your livelihood healthy on the vine.

"This isn't like a grain crop. There's a lot of overhead. You spend about $8,000 an acre in the first year for posts, irrigation and vines. Then you wait 4 to 7 years to crop that. Then, for a dry red, you age it in a barrel for 2 years. And remember—that's all before you make dollar one. It's about 10 to 15 years before the break-even point."

And then there's the X factor—the inevitable twist that defies planning. Today, Tim is in the field inspecting his vines, which, without warning, dropped all of their leaves earlier this week. "I don't know what happened. Everything defoliated. Now the secondary leaves are going to get burnt," he said. Tim suspects that herbicide from a neighboring farmer's field has drifted over his vineyard. But he's too busy pruning to dwell on how that will affect his grape production.

"Yeah, I remember being told in 1990 there was no reason to plant [grapes], because there's enough," Tim said, shaking his head. "Since then, though, the industry has grown so rapidly that demand has exceeded supply. No one anticipated such an increase in sales." This means it's harder for smaller wineries to compete, since larger wineries often end up with the lion's share of the harvest.

Another day of hard work lies ahead, as Tim juggles countless variables. As I walk down the hill, into view of the tasting room, I see his sons playing outside, pushing their Tonka trucks around a dirt-mound city. A dozen puppies yip from a pen nearby. Tall oaks are shading the tasting room and the wine cellar, and I see those worn steps trod by his great-great-grandfather Adam Puchta.

As I walk away, I reflect on Tim's hard work, and how he shirked his 9 to 5 job for this demanding lifestyle... and I'm thinking to myself, I wouldn't be looking back either.

ADAM PUCHTA
WINE LIST

Current Offerings:
BERRY BLACK: A sweet red with natural sweet fruit and blackberry characteristics.
BLUSH: A semi-sweet young wine with aromas of watermelon and passion fruit.
CHARDONEL: Light oak complexity with green apple and pear flavors.
HUNTER'S RED: Blended Chianti-style. Red, light and fruity.•
JAZZ BERRY: Fruity and sweet. Intense bouquet and taste of fresh raspberries.
NORTON: A dry oak-aged red wine, similar to a Merlot.
MISTY VALLEY: A sweet white dessert wine with a soft floral nose.
REIFENSTAHLER: A sweet red wine.
ROSE: A dry full-bodied wine with scents of raspberry and pineapple guava.
VIDAL BLANC: A dry Sauvignon Blanc-style white wine.
VIGNOLES: A semi-sweet white wine with strawberry and kiwi tones.
VIVANT: A fruity off-dry white with tropical fruit flavors.

Adam Puchta Winery ~ The First 150 Years

Adam Puchta Winery is the oldest family farm winery in Missouri. The same family has continuously owned it since 1855. Adam Puchta Winery and the Puchta family invited visitors to celebrate those first 150 years in July of 2005.

T he story of the winery actually begins on May 25, 1839, when Adam Puchta, a lad of seven, along with his older brother, Friedrich, his father John Henry Puchta, his stepmother, and three stepsisters ranging in age from five months to five years left the port of Hamburg, Germany, for the United States. The family actually emigrated from Oberkotzau, a village in the northeastern corner of Bavaria near the Czech border, where Adam's father was a butcher.

Upon the family's arrival in Hermann, they settled on a 40-acre tract of land north and adjacent to the land on which the winery is located. Adam's father built a one-room log cabin, approximately 16 feet by 20 feet, for his family of seven, and a small wine cellar with a press house over it. He purchased the land in 1841 and in 1849 purchased 40 more acres, which is now part of the winery farm.

Adam and his brother worked on the family farm until the spring of 1853, when the Puchta brothers and twelve other men left Hermann for California in quest of gold and riches. This group was the first of three to make the trek west. They left on April 15 with three ox teams, six horses and 165 head of cattle.

The trip took four months and twenty days. On reaching the Sierra Nevada Mountains they were met by cattle buyers and sold their stock at a profit. The gold-seekers abandoned their wagons, as they served no further purpose. The party broke up, the Puchta brothers and four others going to the diggings at Downieville on the western slope of the mountains, where they staked off a claim along a good-sized creek. Each man was allowed 100 feet along the creek and the land behind those 100 feet running back to the mountains.

Less than two years after his departure from Hermann, Adam returned to Hermann by way of Nicaragua.

Apparently he had met with some measure of success in California, as on February 28, 1855, Adam purchased 40 acres of land from his father. He built a small log cabin and began clearing land for crops and vineyards. In 1855 he produced his first wine using wild grapes and grapes from his father's vineyard. This first production of wine by Adam Puchta establishes the genesis of Adam Puchta Winery and is the cause for celebration in 2005.

Adam married Clementine Riefenstahl, daughter of George Riefenstahl. George, his wife, Virginia, and five children were among the first seventeen settlers in Hermann. Adam's father-in-law, deceased by the time of his marriage, had been a noted winemaker in Hermann who in April 1847 won a "first-class award in St. Louis" for his wine from the Catawba grape, that he dubbed the "Riefenstahler."

Adam and Clementine first lived in a log cabin but soon built a stone residence. Today, after some restoration and remodeling, it serves as the sales building for Adam Puchta Winery.

In 1858 Clementine died in childbirth. In February 1859 Adam married Bertha Riefenstahl, Clementine's older sister and the first baby girl born in Hermann.

Adam and Bertha had one child, Henry John Puchta, born April 4, 1861.

Adam's early wine production took place in the small cellar under his residence. Within a short time he built a large arched limestone cellar. The stone for both the residence and the wine cellar was quarried on the winery property. A press house and fermentation room were built directly above the cellar and on top of the foundation wall. The cellar and original press house remain today.

Unlike many other vintners in the area, Adam Puchta never abandoned his general farming operation, so that in 1870, in addition to wine, he produced wheat, corn, oats and barley.

In 1882, Adam constructed a brick one-and-a-half story residence just a few feet west of the stone residence. That residence was the third of four early structures on the winery farm, which have been preserved through its long history. The fourth is a brick gable roof smokehouse to the rear of the stone building.

In the 1880s, Adam's son, Henry, joined him in the family farm winery business and operated under the name of Adam Puchta & Son Wine Company. He began to expand the winery's production.

Henry married Amanda Buddemeyer on June 3, 1896, and the couple lived with his parents. Henry and Amanda had two children, Pearl Ethel and Everett Adam, born in 1898 and 1900.

The 18th Amendment to the U.S. Constitution went into effect in 1920. Prohibition destroyed the wine industry nationwide. It dealt a particularly devastating blow to the economy of the Hermann area, because grape growing was the major industry of the area.

The grapevines were pulled out and the vineyards were converted to cropland. Henry and Everett Puchta expanded their production of crops. This father and son, like many other farm families, continued to make wine for family use from a few retained vines, from elderberries and blackberries, and even from dandelions. This practice continued until Everett's death in 1988.

In December of 1933, when Prohibition ended, there were no commercially operating wineries in the Hermann area. It was almost 30 years after Prohibition ended before there was a rebirth of the wine industry in the area.

In 1989, Everett's son, Randolph, born in 1928, and Randolph's son Timothy, born in 1956, began planning the reopening of the Adam Puchta Winery as a commercial enterprise. Randolph had pursued a career in law and Timothy a career in respiratory therapy. Timothy, however, had a dream of one day reopening the winery, and with his father's encouragement and support, that dream was realized when sales and shipment of wine once again began in 1990.

Only old, outdated wooden winemaking equipment remained in 1989 when the rebirth of Adam Puchta Winery occurred. From the time of Prohibition the Puchta family had preserved the dual stone, hand operated grape crusher, the two-man-screw-type press and one large fermenting vat. This original equipment was on display during the 150th anniversary celebration.

Today, all of the winemaking equipment is made of stainless steel—the hoppers and augers, the crusher and destemmer, the pumps, the fermenting tanks and storage tanks, the filters, and the automatic bottling equipment. Most of the tanks are refrigerated.

Pre-Prohibition, family farm wineries marketed most of their wine by shipping five, ten, twenty and thirty-gallon kegs and barrels to taverns in Hermann, New Haven, Washington and St. Louis. Local customers would bring their glass bottles or earthen jugs to the winery for refilling. Most family farm wineries did not bottle or label their products.

Today, Adam Puchta Winery has a production capacity of 62,000 gallons. Adam Puchta wines have won many awards in Missouri, as well as nationally and internationally.

The demand for Puchta wines has increased steadily since 1990 and that trend continues. Adam Puchta & Son Wine Co. proudly continues a family tradition begun 150 years ago in beautiful Frene Creek Valley.

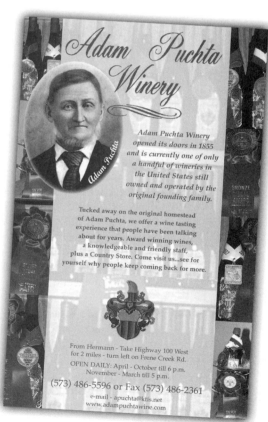

Adam Puchta Winery opened its doors in 1855 and is currently one of only a handful of wineries in the United States still owned and operated by the original founding family.

Tucked away on the original homestead of Adam Puchta, we offer a wine tasting experience that people have been talking about for years. Award winning wines, a knowledgeable and friendly staff, plus a Country Store. Come visit us...see for yourself why people keep coming back for more.

From Hermann - Take Highway 100 West for 2 miles - turn left on Frene Creek Rd.
OPEN DAILY: April - October till 6 p.m.
November - March till 5 p.m.
(573) 486-5596 or Fax (573) 486-2361
e-mail - apuchta@ktis.net
www.adampuchtawine.com

HERMANNHOF WINERY

330 East First Street, Hermann, MO 65041
(573) 486-5959 or (800) 393-0100
Hours of Operation:
Monday through Saturday 10 a.m. to 5 p.m.
Sunday 11 a.m. to 5 p.m.

HOW TO GET THERE: Take Hwy 19 across the bridge into Hermann. Immediately on the south side of the river, head east on Hwy 100 about a mile. Hermannhof is on the south side of the street, on the eastern edge of town. When leaving town watch the posted speed limit—this is a notorious speed trap.

Located on the eastern, "French" edge of town, Hermannhof turned from dream to reality in 1848, when construction began. Hermannhof has been producing wine on and off since 1852, except for the years of Prohibition. The estate was later used as a brewery by Kropp Brewery, then turned into apartments—its intricate series of 10 underground cellars filled with rubbish—until the property was revived under the guidance of owners James and Mary Dierberg. In its most recent evolution, the century-old stone and brick building is once again serving as the foundation for the winemaking art that began long ago.

With over 20 years of experience, Paul LeRoy is the resident vintner. At peak harvest times he oversees a staff of 30 people. They produce about 30,000 gallons of wine annually, 1,500 of which is champagne. LeRoy's expertise guided Hermannhof to an award of "Best New World White Wine" for their Vignoles.

This took place at the New World International Wine Competition in 1997. Judge Jerry Mead summed it up in his newsletter, *Mead on Wine*. (When reading the following excerpt, keep in mind he's addressing people who think there's nothing between the East and West Coasts but desert, cows and hay bales.)

"Knowing the winner of the Brown-Foreman Trophy for Best New World White Wine won't do you much good unless you live in Missouri. I'm not kidding. For the second time in recent years, a Missouri wine produced from a grape called Vignoles (a French-American hybrid) has walked away with this trophy. Hermannhof Winery's 1995 'Missouri' Vignoles is just off-dry, with pleasant fruit and a very long finish. It's not too sweet for food, nor too dry for casual sipping."

Hermannhof Winery is the nation's first two-time winner of the prestigious Brown-Foreman Trophy and has also won top honors at a number of wine competitions around the world.

As with other Hermann wineries, the vineyards are located outside of town. The sights and sounds of exploring this winery do, however, continue below ground. Tour the historic wine cellars, which have been home to winemakers, brew masters and even a wedding. As you tour the cellars 15 feet below ground, you can feel the vibrations as the Amtrak trains rush by only 100 feet away. The tour continues into the modern age and shows you the monolithic stainless steel cooling tanks that may be producing tomorrow's award winners.

Once you're back up top, visit the smokehaus and sample their selection of fine wines, cheeses, breads and sausages. The winery's *weinstube* deli is open for lunch so be sure to picnic under the grape pergola or in the shade of the gazebo.

Hermannhof's vast Festhalle, located across the street just west of the main building, is used for all sorts of activities, including larger-than-life wine tastings, receptions and, of course, bratwurst-swinging, wine-drinking festivals.

Also nearby is the Hermannhof Inn & Gasthaus, offering gracious and casual hospitality. All rooms offer a wide variety of amenities, including fireplaces and jacuzzis. The rooms are all located within formerly working wineries that were carefully relocated to Hermannhof. Each house was restored with special attention to detail, providing simple elegance perfectly suited for family vacations or romantic weekend getaways.

HERMANNHOF WINE LIST

Current Offerings:
BRUT RESERVE: A freshly baked bread nose with fruity and floral notes. Full lemon and grapefruit flavors with a toasty edge. Sparkling wine.
CHAMBOURCIN: A ruby red with a medium body and balanced acidity. Flavors and aromas of cherries, spice and dried fruits. Mildly oaked with an herbal edge.
CHAMBOURCIN VIN-GRIS: Cold pressing dark Chambourcin grapes results in this rosé-style dry red wine with hints of strawberry and rose petal.
CHARDONEL: A cross of Chardonnay and Seyval Blanc. A full-bodied dry white wine with green apple characters and hints of spicy oak.
CHERRY WINE: A medium-bodied ruby-red, naturally sweet and crisp. Produced from Wisconsin cherries and slowly fermented to capture fresh aromas and flavors.

Inside the tasting room. At right, a
Hermannhof all-time favorite—White Lady.

GERMANTOWN: A sweet white wine with luscious fruit flavors.

NORTON: A dark ruby red with concentrated flavors of berries, brown spice and black fruits. Notes of earth and smoky vanilla oak with a long, full finish.

PORT: A vintage blend fortified with brandy and aged two years in mature oak barrels. Rich, complex aromas and flavors. Balance and structure that reward further cellaring.

SEYVAL BLANC: 100 percent estate grown and fermented in stainless steel tanks. A medium body with characters of citrus and lemon peel and mineral notes.

SPRING BLUSH: A semi-sweet, crisp blush that derives its color from a blend of European-hybrid grapes.

STAGSWOOD RED: An old-fashioned red wine made from Concord grapes. European hybrids add crisp, fruity tones to balance the blend.

VIDAL BLANC: Well balanced and bursting with fruit.

VIGNOLES: Semi-sweet and fruity, with citrus flavors and a crisp, lively acidity.

WHITE LADY OF STARKENBURG: A bright semi-dry, Rhine-style white with citrus, green apple and spice characters.

Carolyn Warnebold in front of the view that earned
her winery a feature story in *Southern Living* magazine.

OAKGLENN VINEYARDS & WINERY

1104 OakGlenn Place, Hermann, MO 65041

(573) 486-5057 or (877) 486-5057

www.oakglenn.com

Hours of Operation:

Open daily except Easter, Thanksgiving, Christmas and New Years Day

November through February Noon to 5 p.m.

March through October Noon to 6 p.m.

HOW TO GET THERE: From the intersection of Hwy 19 and Hwy 100 in Hermann, go east 2.7 miles until you see the OakGlenn Place sign.

In 1997, Glenn and Carolyn Warnebold purchased a neglected vineyard in Hermann that once belonged to internationally renowned horticulturist George Husmann. Since then, the Warnebolds have worked diligently to revitalize the vineyard that once belonged to the man who is regarded by most to be the primary influence in establishing the winemaking industry in America from Missouri to California. Five acres of the original vines, planted by Mr. Husmann himself, are now producing amazingly well. In 2000, OakGlenn served its first glass of wine since the pre-Prohibition era.

The residence at OakGlenn has been renovated into a state-of-the-art facility. A massive stone wine cellar built in the 1800s is still intact and is being used today. OakGlenn is perched among the blufftops overlooking the river with rows of gently sloping vineyards. The unmatched view earned the winery the feature story in an issue of *Southern Living* magazine. The author, Clay Nordan, is quoted: "A fabulous drive under a canopy of hardwoods leads to the most scenic of all the wineries."

The Warnebolds named the property OakGlenn for the towering oak tree that stands near the driveway entrance and in honor of the owner's first name, Glenn. Later, they learned through research that in 1890 George Husmann had opened another winery in California and named it "Oak Glen Husmann Winery." Chance or Fate? You decide.

What first struck me were the smoky red blooms of the Mimosa trees along the edge of the old fields as the road crested atop the bluff at the winery's door. Come see for yourself what OakGlenn has to offer. With more than 15 selections of wine, live music at the George Husmann Wine Pavilion, and a photographic exhibit on the lifetime achievements of Mr. Husmann, there's something here for everyone.

The property at OakGlenn Winery was once owned by George Husmann, who is regarded as "The Father of the Missouri Grape Industry." Husmann would later travel to California, where he was instrumental in developing their wine country.

The tasting room at OakGlenn offers more than 15 selections of wine.

OAKGLENN WINE LIST

Current Offerings:
BLUSH: In the tradition of White Zinfandel. A light, semi-sweet blended wine with a fruity aroma and sweet smooth finish.
CHAMBOURCIN: A medium-bodied red wine with a fruity aroma and cherry, spicy complexity.
CHARDONEL: A semi-dry white wine with pineapple fruity character.
CHARDONEL–OAK: A medium-bodied red wine with a fruity aroma and cherry, spicy complexity.
COUNTRYSIDE RED: A light, dry red blend with fruity characteristics.
HUSMANN'S HERITAGE: A semi-sweet light red. Tart in the beginning and light sweetness in finish.
MOONBEAM MELODY: A delicate, semi-sweet white blend with fruity characteristics.
NORTON a.k.a. CYNTHIANA: A rich, full-bodied red wine with a dry character. Similar to Cabernet Savignon, with the spiciness of a Zinfandel.
PORT–RED: A rich, sweet red dessert wine with strong berry flavors.
PORT–WHITE: A barrel-aged white with orange liqueur and honey characteristics.
SAINTRIVER VIEW RED: A sweet red with blackberry and cinnamon characteristics.
VINCENT: A light, delicate, dry red wine with mild fruity characteristics and a cranberry flavor.
SILVER MOON: A dry white wine blending Chardonel and Vidal Blanc.

SWEET CAROLINE: Vidal, Chardonel, and Norton blended for a very sweet dessert-type wine with delicate cherry flavors.

VIDAL BLANC: A dry white wine with fruity flavors. Somewhat like Italian dry wines. Citrus flavors of lemon and grapefruit.

WINE CELLAR CHOICE: A semi-sweet white of Vidal and Muscat.

Oh the view! If there's only three winery stops on the way to heaven, OakGlenn has got to be one of them (Montelle & Les Bourgeois would be my other two requested stops). Enjoy a bottle of wine with friends from one of the Missouri River's best blufftop decks.

The Warnebolds, shown above, have worked tirelessly to honor
Mr. Husmann's timeless contributions to the Missouri wine industry.

The Father of the Missouri Grape Industry

George Husmann was born on November 4, 1827, in Meyenburg, Germany. His father had bought shares in the German Settlement Society of Philadelphia, which founded a colony in the "Far West" where Germans could preserve their language, traditions and values. The colony, named Hermann, was widely publicized, and the Husmanns immigrated to Hermann in 1838.

Martin Husmann began to experiment with grape culture in Hermann, and in 1847 George Husmann planted his first vineyard on his father's farm. Husmann was to become a renowned scientist, writer and educator, and is known today as the "Father of the Missouri Grape Industry."

After a trip to California during the Gold Rush, Husmann returned to Hermann to take care of his widowed sister's property and soon developed a model fruit farm. In 1866 he published his first book, *The Cultivation of Native Grapes and Manufacture of American Wine,* and in 1869 he established *The American Grape Grower,* the only journal on the subject in the United States at that time.

In 1870 he was appointed to the University of Missouri Board of Curators and continued to work with grape growers in the state. During the 1870s, Husmann and others shipped millions of grape cuttings to France, Germany and other countries devastated by the deadly phylloxera infestation.

Today two monuments still stand in France, honoring Husmann and other Missouri grape growers credited with "saving the French wine industry."

In 1879 Husmann was appointed first professor of pomology and superintendent of forestry at the University of Missouri, where he established a nursery, orchards and vineyards. In 1881, he accepted a position in California and contributed significantly to the development of the state's grape and wine industry.

Husmann died November 5, 1902, the day after his 75th birthday.

George Husmann

The George Husmann Pavilion at OakGlenn Winery features a photographic exhibit of the lifetime achievements of its namesake.

The shaded hillside at Stone Hill Winery offers a commanding view of Hermann.
It is the perfect perch to soak in the sun and enjoy a bottle of wine with a friend.

Stone Hill's historic winery offers great wines with views to match, cellar tours and the wonderful Vintage Restaurant. The menu includes German cuisine: German-style schnitzel, sauerbraten and a German sampler platter.

STONE HILL WINERY

1110 Stone Hill Highway, Hermann, MO 65041

(800) 909-WINE (9463)

www.stonehillwinery.com

Hours of Operation:

Monday through Saturday 8:30 a.m. to Dusk

Sunday 10 a.m. to 6 p.m.

HOW TO GET THERE: Take I-70 to Hwy 19 and go south. Or take I-44 to Hwy 19 and go north. Basically, if you travel Hwy 19 between I-70 and I-44 you will run into Hermann. Once there, take Hwy 100 west. Follow the signs.

Established in 1847, Stone Hill grew to be the second largest winery in the United States. The wines were world renowned, winning gold medals in eight world's fairs, including Vienna in 1873 and Philadelphia in 1876. By the turn of the century, the winery was shipping 1,250,000 gallons of wine per year.

Today, it is one of the the the largest wineries in the state and is the third most awarded winery in America. Stone Hill produces close to 40 percent of Missouri's wine. Annual production is 215,000 gallons of wine, which are sold through their three locations: Hermann, Branson and New Florence (the I-70 Tasting Room).

The massive oak posts and beams of the tasting room at Stone Hill Winery are a tribute to time-tested construction. The attached sunroom nearby is a wonderful spot to enjoy your wine regardless of the weather outside.

Wine production reached its peak at Stone Hill around the turn of the century, only to be cut short 20 years later by Prohibition. During this time in Stone Hill's history, the arched underground wine cellars were used to cultivate mushrooms. These cellars are the largest series of underground vaulted cellars in America.

The once grand winery was rescued in 1965 by Jim and Betty Held. Jim says the family started the business with "nothing but determination." Along with their four children, they moved from a nearby hog farm and borrowed $1,500 to finance their first grape crush. They moved in on the second floor and began the long process of restoring the picturesque buildings and vaulted cellars. It took considerable investments of time and money, but rewards and proof of their progress came along the way.

With three of the Held children now holding degrees in enology and viticulture, the winery today is once again earning international attention. In 2004 alone, the winery won 264 national and international wine awards.

At vineyards just outside of town, Stone Hill grows American hybrid grapes to produce wines that are similar to the ever-popular Chardonnay and Sauvignon Blanc. However, the pride of Stone Hill is their Norton.

The Helds and their staff are planning to increase their vineyard from 80 acres to 100 in the future and also add a couple of new varieties of grapes to their repertoire. Along with this growth, the company is preparing to add new vineyard equipment that will allow key canopy management procedures to be carried out in a more timely manner, thereby enhancing overall quality.

Stone Hill is listed on the National Historic Register and offers full tours of its antique cellars and state-of-the-art production facility. Stone Hill has also expanded its tasting room and gift shop. Be sure and stop at the Vintage Restaurant, which specializes in German cuisine and is housed in a renovated carriage house and horse barn.

In addition to their Hermann location, there are two other Stone Hill Winery sites. The New Florence facility, at the junction of I-70 and Highway 19, houses the company's bottle-fermented sparkling wine operation, where visitors may sample and purchase wines in the gift shop. The Branson facility features a fun guided tour of the sparkling wine and cream sherry production, a video viewing room, six tasting rooms and a large gift shop.

The Held family—leaders in the Missouri wine renaissance. Pictured clockwise are Jon Held, general manager; Patty Held-Uthlaut, director of public relations, distribution and special events; Jim and Betty Held, owners of Stone Hill; and Thomas Held, director of sales and advertising.

Vintner Profile:
Dave Johnson

After 27 years of working with the Held family to improve the winery and vineyards, Dave has become the most awarded American winemaker outside of California. That's quite an achievement, not only because of the esteemed competition, but also because few people west of the Rockies have ever even heard of some of the grape varieties grown in Missouri.

Q. What wines do you feel represent Missouri best?

A. I guess you could say Norton is *the* Missouri red. Vignoles is another variety that seems to please the wine judges.

Q. So, have you seen the best of these wines?

A. I've never made a wine yet in which I couldn't see at least a little room for improvement. We have the proper equipment to make it well at the winery, but we can fine-tune it in the vineyards... it will take some time, but we *will* improve both the Norton and the Vignoles.

Q. What are your biggest obstacles?

A. Our weather here makes grape growing a challenge. Another problem here is a lack of a labor force. With a low unemployment rate in Hermann, we *must* mechanize our vineyards as much as possible.

Q. What are you most proud of?

A. Well, it's been gratifying to receive so much attention on wines like Norton and Vignoles, but I'm very happy with the success we've had on our sweet wines. Many other wineries treat their sweet wines like second-class citizens, but I pay as much attention to my Concord and Pink Catawba as I do the Norton.

Dave Johnson, vintage 1979.

Be sure to tour the cellars at Stone Hill—a perfect escape from summer's heat,
and a chance to walk the same hallways trod by winemakers for more than a century.

STONE HILL WINE LIST

Current Offerings:
BLUSH: Stone Hill's version of a White Zinfandel. A bit lighter and more delicate than a traditional rosé. Light and fruity. Gold medal winner at the 2002 Florida State Fair and Pacific Rim International Wine Competitions and the 2003 International Eastern Wine Competition in New York.
CONCORD GRAPE JUICE: Naturally sweet pure grape juice.
CONCORD: Bursting with the sweet, robust flavor of ripe Missouri Concord grapes. Winner of the Gold Medal at the Riverside International Wine Competition in California.
CREAM SHERRY: A luxuriously sweet, fragrant and complex fortified wine. Rich, nutty flavor and aromas of traditional sherry develop during extended aging in old, small oak barrels. Winner of 12 awards in one year alone.
GOLDEN RHINE: A semi-sweet, traditional German-style white wine, with a fruity aroma and flavor. Winner of a Double Gold Medal at the 2003 San Francisco International Wine Competition.
GOLDEN SPUMANTE: Rich, fruity and semi-sweet. Winner of the Gold Medal and Best of Show at the Missouri State Fair and a Double Gold Medal at the Florida State Fair.
HERMANNSBERGER: A semi-dry red wine blended as a sister to the Steinberg. Fruity like a Beaujolais. Gold Medal Winner at the 2004 Los Angeles County Fair.

LATE HARVEST VIGNOLES: Nectar of the gods! Some years a perfect growing season produces extra ripe Vignoles with complex botrutis like the great sauternes of France. Careful selection of individual bunches results in a prized dessert wine with complex honey, peach and floral aromas and flavors that linger on the palate. Stone Hill boasts many "Best of Show" awards from this wine.

MISSOURI CHAMPAGNE: This champagne is naturally fermented in the bottle, riddled by hand in the traditional French method after aging on the yeast. Crisp and delicate, this Brut-style champagne is made from 100 percent Vidal grapes. Gold medal winner at the 2001 Missouri State Fair.

NORTON (Estate bottled): A very dry, full-bodied, oak-aged red wine that has won national and international awards.

PINK CATAWBA: Light, sweet and full of the famous Catawba flavor. Best of Show winner at the 2004 Critics Challenge International Wine Competition and gold at the International Eastern Wine Competition.

PORT: A vintage-style port produced in limited quantities. Matured in oak casks, this rich dark port can be enjoyed now, or left to develop in the bottle for many years. This port was selected as the "Best American Port" by the *Wine Enthusiast Magazine,* proving that ports made from the Norton grape can compete with the best. Bronze medal winner at the California Farmer's Fair.

ROSÉ MONTAIGNE: A semi-sweet rosé that is soft and mellow with a touch of sweetness and a lovely floral aroma. Winner of a gold medal at the 2002 Florida State Fair.

SEYVAL: Cold fermented to retain the varietal character of the Seyval grapes. Dry and full-bodied. Best of Class at the 2002 Los Angeles County Fair Wine Competition and winner of three gold medals in 2004.

SPARKLING GRAPE JUICE: A sparkling, naturally sweet, non-alcoholic grape juice.

SPARKLING RASPBERRY JUICE: A light, non-alcoholic raspberry-flavored juice.

SPUMANTE BLUSH: Bubbling wine with a distinctive pink color and fruity flavor. Winner of double gold at the 2004 San Francisco International Wine Competition.

STEINBERG WHITE: Stone Hill's best-seller. A delicate, semi-dry, German-style white wine vinted from fine European hybrid grape varieties. Winner of numerous awards.

STEINBERG RED: Companion to Steinberg white. Luscious fresh fruit flavors and aromas, very light tannins and a touch of sweetness. A skillful and intricate blend of red and white wines. Winner of a Best of Class gold medal at the Missouri State Fair.

VIDAL BLANC: A dry, white varietal wine that has a delicate fruit and herbal aroma with just a touch of oak. Bronze medal winner at the California Farmer's Fair.

VIGNOLES: A rich, semi-sweet wine that has a natural residual sugar and a varietal flavor. Winner of the gold medal at the San Diego National Wine Competition.

Patty Held-Uthlaut, director of public relations, "thiefs" a sample of an aging Norton from an oak barrel in the historic Apostle Cellar at Stone Hill Winery.

Be Sure to Explore Nearby Cajun Country

While you're out exploring, look for the River's Edge Restaurant and Ferry in Fredricksburg. Located west of Hermann off Highway 100, this ferry ride takes you across the Gasconade River and drops you at a fine Cajun restaurant. The River's Edge Restaurant menu takes you back to the bayou. A wide array of Cajun food and seafood is offered including Cajun catfish, charbroiled shrimp, barbecued ribs, crab legs, swordfish and blackened T-bone steaks. Prices range from $10 to $20. For less than $40, here's the real Cajun deal: The Cajun Crab Boil for two. It includes a pound of crabs, a half-pound of shrimp, a half-pound of crawfish, two baked potatoes, two ears of corn, gumbo and plenty of napkins! River's Edge also make their own sauces, from barbecue to poppy seed salad dressings. Call (573) 294-7207 for more information.

The *Roy J* ferry operates five days a week. Canoe rentals are also available. Call (573) 294-1114 for information.

HOW TO GET THERE: From Hermann, take Hwy 100 west 6 miles to Route J. Take Route J for 8 miles. You'll come to the Gasconade River.

BIAS VINEYARDS & WINERY

3166 Highway B, Berger, MO 63014

(573) 834-5475 or (800) 905-2427

Hours of Operation:

Summer: Monday through Saturday 10 a.m. to 6 p.m.

Sunday 11 a.m. to 6 p.m.

Fall and Winter: Monday through Saturday 10 a.m. to 5 p.m.

Sunday 11 a.m. to 5 p.m.

HOW TO GET THERE: The winery and sales room are located on Route B, one mile east of Berger. From Hermann, take Hwy 100 east 7 miles to Route B, then go north through Berger. Continue 1.5 miles and watch for their sign.

L ocated on a 64-acre farm high atop the bluffs overlooking the Missouri River valley, the laid back atmosphere, gorgeous scenery and friendly folks of Bias Vineyards & Winery make this a favorite stop for both locals and city-escapees.

The entrance to Bias Winery is a mile and a half past Berger, along a circuitous river bottom road. You cross over an old wooden bridge, go across the railroad tracks and up a steep hill. When you see the railroad tracks: Stop, Look and Listen. Two or three trains pass by here each hour, so stop and look both ways.

Despite its seemingly out-of-the-way location, the Bias Winery is hopping on sunny Saturdays and Sundays. Today is a day of rest and relaxation and everyone has taken their cues. The air of joviality is underscored by the 21 wine bottles that are draped with various awards and the meticulously cared for vineyards nearby.

Jim Bias

Cars bearing license plates of Missouri, Illinois, Iowa and New Mexico fill the parking lot. Modes of transportation range from a topless Jeep and a new Beemer to wired-together farm trucks and a horse (no license plate to be seen).

Bias is a small, family-owned winery that intends to stay that way. Jim and Norma Bias established the Bias Winery in 1980. The Bias family started their winery with a five-acre Catawba vineyard. They have since expanded with varieties of French hybrids including Chambourcin, De-Chaunac, Seyval and Vidal.

The Bias family strives to make fresh, clean-tasting wine. Their wines are produced from their own eight-acre vineyard, located only 600 feet from the winery. This allows for prompt harvesting and crushing of the grapes at the moment they reach their peak ripeness. All of the grapes are harvested by hand from mid-August to mid-September. The pressing, fermentation, aging and bottling are all performed on site.

A sign in the tasting room says "Would you like to speak to the man in charge OR the woman who knows what's going on?" Both Bonnie Horstmann and Linda Sitton "know what's going on" and are informative guides to tasting the wide variety of Bias wines. Be sure and try the best-selling favorite, Weisser Flieder (German for white lilac).

In addition to exploring the fine wines of Bias, a walk through the vineyards is a must. These vines are among the oldest, thickest and healthiest you'll see—as thick as your wrist. Many of these vines were planted in 1969. The thick loess soil, good sun exposure, amazing water and air drainage and the meticulous care by Donnie Blanton and Jim's son Jimmy Bias, with help from Bonnie Horstmann and Carol Bradley, make these vines look like something out of *Jack and the Beanstalk*. There is also a small cemetery here dating back to the early 1800s, just below the vineyards near a line of tall cedar trees.

BIAS WINE LIST

Current Offerings:
BERGER RED: A sweet red.
CHAMBOURCIN RESERVE: A dry red.
DE CHAUNAC: A dry red.
FROSTY MEADOW WHITE: Ice wine.
JUBILEE RED: A semi-sweet red.
JUBILEE WHITE: A semi-sweet white.
LIEBESWEIN: A semi-dry white.
NORMA'S BEST: A dry white.
PREMIUM RIVER VIEW WHITE: A dry white.
RIESLING: A semi-dry white.
RIVER BLUFF ROUGE: A semi-dry rosé.
SPARKLING GRAPE JUICE
SPARKLING RASPBERRY JUICE
STRAWBERRY WEISSER FLIEDER: A sweet white.
SWEET AMBROSIA: A sweet white.
VICTORIAN RED: A sweet red.
VIGNOLES: A semi-dry white.
WEISSER FLIEDER: A sweet white.

Annual Events

March: Celebration of the Gnomes
May: Maifest
June: Barbeque Cook-Off
July: Very Berry Wine Trail
September: Chili Cook-Off, Croquet Tournament & Barbeque
October: Oktoberfest
November: Hayrides, Nouveau Day
December: Trim a Tree Party

Gruhlke's Microbrewery
at Bias Vineyards

In addition to growing grapes and producing quality wines, Dennis and Karen Jay have also been brewing beer. Knowing all too well the uncertainties of grape crops and the continuing popularity of beer, Dennis has set out to produce great beer for the masses!

Well, not really. Let's just say Dennis, armed with his Ph.D. in chemistry and years of home brewing experience, thought he had a good idea. Focusing on producing the highest quality beer and making it just right, Dennis has produced small amounts (some 200 gallons) of five varieties of microbrew. Now his efforts are ready for visitors at Bias Vineyards to sample.

But don't expect your beer in a bottle, Dennis's concoctions will travel—at least for the time being—right from the kegs to your glass.

As for the name—Gruhlke, that's another story. The story, according to Karen, is that when Dennis was 12 years old and traveling through New Mexico with his parents, he passed through the town of Gruhlke.

"Dennis told his mother that when he grew up, he was going to name one of his children Gruhlke... Well I changed his mind about that one!" says Karen. "But it worked perfectly for his beer."

As it turns out, Gruhlke is a German gnome and apparently Dennis and Karen have made a deal with him. Karen says, "the gnome agreed to help us brew quality beer if we would put his picture on the label." True to their word, an artist was commissioned to put the gnome's face on Dennis's product.

A Lifelong Passion for the Wines of Missouri

How I Spent My Summer Vacation—1973

by Glenn Bardgett

I fell in love with wine while serving in the Army in Honolulu in 1971. After taking a couple of wine appreciation courses at the University of Hawaii (much the same format and style as the courses that I now give for Meramec Community College in St. Louis), I planned a visit to my family in St. Louis during the summer of 1973. Due to my newfound interest in wine, I had remembered an article on the wines of Missouri written in the *St. Louis Post-Dispatch*, which had been sent to me, that intrigued me. Could it be that a visit to my beloved Missouri and my family could also include a day trip or two to the relatively "new" wine country?

After taking the red-eye flight from Honolulu (an 8-hour ordeal roughly the emotionally draining equivalent of watching one Jerry Springer show), I arrived to visit my family and quickly planned the wine country touring that was to be one of the great highlights of this particular visit.

In those days, we had no Grape and Wine Program, we had under 10 wineries and very little to excite, stimulate and inspire the senses of thirsty lovers of this miraculous product of the grape. It only took a day or so to get all of us out to Augusta, the first stop and closest wine-growing region. When I first stepped into the petite tasting room of the Mount Pleasant winery, I can remember being totally pleased just with the fact that these wines actually had CORKS!!! A good sign, to be sure.

Knowing nothing of the wines or grapes of Missouri (this was even in the pre-Merlot fad days when only a few grapes of California were even talked about), I saw names such as Emigre Red, White, and Rose and a familiar sounding "Missouri Riesling" at Mt. Pleasant. These were explained to me to mostly be blends of something called "French-American Hybrids," another new name to this nearly virgin wino. Along with enjoying the quality of these early attempts of winemaking, I was also impressed with their 10 cents per bottle "buy back" policy. After working to promote recycling on the island of Oahu, this environmental effort impressed me. I even made a trip back out to Mt. Pleasant before returning to Honolulu to turn in the few bottles that I had consumed during my stay and purchase some of their wines to take back to Hawaii with me.

On this second visit, I met Lucian Dressel, founder, owner, winemaker, bottle washer and promoter for the winery. When I finally moved back to St. Louis in 1977, Lucian became one of my great friends in the wine business until he left the area in the early 1990s.

Although today, you can make a full day just in the area around Augusta, in 1973 the next stop was the Stone Hill Winery about 45 minutes away in Hermann. Even in those days, the historical aspects of Missouri's oldest winery were quite impressive. We took the tour, heard the stories of pre-Prohibition grandeur and worldwide distribution and awards given to this onetime "third largest winery in the world" and watched as my appreciation for the wines of Missouri grew by the day.

While such recognizable grape names as Concord and Catawba were gracing the labels here, I also became very respectful of a non-grape wine, Peachy Vino made from fresh Missouri peaches and giving a great deal of pleasure as an after dinner sipper. I thought about my first meeting with this wine a dozen years later when the wine was no longer called Peachy Vino, but simply Stone Hill Peach Wine and how it won the Best of Show award at the Missouri State Fair.

On that initial visit to Stone Hill Winery, I enjoyed the tour, tasting and purchasing of the wines, but at that time, I did not understand how relevant and close to me this winery would eventually become. Although I probably met one or more members of the Held family that day, as usual they were working so feverishly that introductions were not made until many years later. As always, I am sure that all of the four children were in the cellars either giving tours or washing out glasses, bottles, tanks and barrels for Mom and Dad.

This winery was a family devotion and passion and for many many years, they lived above the winery, giving up personal lives and privacy to build a business in days when Missouri wines were not only unknown but actually ignored, disrespected and abused by many local wine drinkers.

There was none of their flagship dry red wine, Virginia Seedling (later to become nationally famous under its better known alter-ego, Norton) available that day, but many bottles of their wines accompanied me when I returned home.

I greatly enjoyed the German cookbook lovingly written by Betty Held. Many of the recipes became household staples and have remained so for more than 25 years. This was truly a day that began a relationship with one of the greatest families I have ever known.

The Held family, led by Jim and Betty, not only succeeded in raising their family (three university trained in winemaking and grape growing and the fourth, an attorney in New York), but they also succeeded in realizing their dream of quality winemaking. They have made their Norton the success story of Missouri red wines, even encouraging wineries throughout the United States to grow this glorious Native American red. I often think of that first visit, when I now stand in the Apostle Cellar and look at the rows of full barrels of their famous Norton. They earned their success.

The final stop on this trip (when my waist was smaller and my hair was darker) was the St. James Winery, opened in 1970. It was obvious even in those early days that this was another family business. Children are expensive as they get older, but a great source of cheap labor when they are young. Founders Pat and Jim Hofherr took their four children to this central Missouri grape-growing region, long famous for Concord grapes, and put up a building to serve the travelling public on what was then a moment in time away from the famed Route 66.

The best selling wine for them then and for many years after was Velvet Red, a sweet Concord grape wine (which nearly single-handedly put their four children through college) that was virtually a condiment for my Mother. Whenever I would look into the refrigerator, I would always see milk and orange juice right next to her half-gallon of Velvet Red.

One of America's leading wine authorities and historians, Leon Adams, wrote that his favorite wine at St. James

was their dry Pink Champagne. I took his advice and many bottles of this very tasty bubbly found their way on the plane with me to enjoy on the beach at Waikiki while watching sunsets and thinking of my trip to my boyhood home.

Today, the Hofherr family is again together, after many years with their three sons in various corners of the country. Within a year, St. James Winery won the Best of Show Award at the State Fair with their Seyval. Today the St. James wines are winning awards locally and nationally, as are many of our state's wines.

For wine lovers, Missouri offers a rare opportunity to easily enjoy top quality winemaking in our own neighborhood. There are so few places on Earth that allow wines to be produced and we are fortunate enough to have one right at home. But the true blessing is not the great wines that we produce in Missouri, but the great families that have dedicated their lives and their efforts to bring us enjoyment from the grape.

Raise a glass of Missouri wine to the passion of our winemaking families. They have earned our support and are, indeed, some of our state's great resources and treasures.

Glenn is a wine advisor for Brown Derby Wine Cellar in St. Louis.

New Haven is like something out of a Norman Rockwell painting.
Park your car and stroll. See where your feet take you.

John Colter, famed mountain man and member of the Lewis & Clark Expedition, spent his final days in the New Haven area. Visit the riverfront memorial, walk the interpretive trail along the river's edge and ponder the river's many explorers, past and present.

EXPLORING NEW HAVEN

Röbller Vineyard & Winery, Bommarito Estate Almond Tree Winery

B&Bs • Eats • Lodging • Parking • Post Office • Restrooms
New Haven Chamber of Commerce: (573) 237-3830

O riginally called Miller's Landing, New Haven was founded in 1836 on the south bank of the Missouri River. In the late 1800s, the town was a busy shipping center and bustled with activity brought by the riverboat traffic. Since then, river traffic has almost stopped—other than an occasional barge or jet-skier from Washington.

Today, a walk through downtown New Haven evokes the feeling you get when viewing a Norman Rockwell painting. In addition to historic homes, the downtown area also has several antique, gift and specialty shops.

Spend the day wandering the historic streets or head to the scenic Riverfront Park for an afternoon picnic in the gazebo. A visit to New Haven isn't complete without doing the "circuit."

Bed & Breakfasts
New Haven Levee House • (636) 239-6190
Aunt May's Farm Guesthouse • (573) 237-2865
Senate Grove Inn • (573) 237-2724

Proprietors Robert and Lois Mueller.

RÖBLLER VINEYARD & WINERY

275 Röbller Vineyard Road, New Haven, MO 63068
(573)237-3986
Hours of Operation:
Summer: Monday through Saturday 10 a.m. to 6 p.m.
Sunday Noon to 6 p.m.
Winter: Monday through Saturday 11 a.m. to 5 p.m.
Sunday Noon to 5 p.m.

HOW TO GET THERE: Röbller is located just off Hwy 100, between Hermann and Washington. Take the Röbller Vineyard Road just east of the water tower. It's a gravel road that comes up quick—be watching for their small sign.

When you visit Röbller Vineyard & Winery, you will find quality French hybrid varietal and traditionally styled blended wines that are sure to please. One Röbller wine you must sample is their Norton. This Native American red wine, with its well-balanced, mellow fruit, spices and soft tannins, is the most popular in their line.

The beautiful, rolling countryside here provides the perfect conditions for grape production while offering a spectacular view for the visitor. Like many vineyards in Missouri, Röbller is a family business. The husband and wife team of Robert and Lois Mueller own and operate the winery, with help from three of their children and other employees.

They produce about 6,000 gallons of wine annually but plan to increase their output with additional planting, bringing the vineyard to 16 acres. Since its beginning in 1991, Röbller was awarded the first Best of Show Governor's Cup for their Norton, along with several other awards that now line the tasting room.

Throughout the year, exciting events are held on the rolling terraces that surround the winery. On the Fourth of July weekend the winery hosts the BBQ and Blues Festival. In early August the energizing sounds of the Reggae Sunsplash Party stream through the air. The highlight of the year is the nontraditional Octoberfest Celebration, which features live blues, jazz and reggae.

Depending on the season, you can watch the crew crushing, pressing, filtering and bottling—and don't forget to bring a kite to fly in the almost continual breeze. At night, the hills offer a great front row seat to a star-filled sky.

Robert Mueller takes a break among the wines aging in oak barrels.

Perhaps their brochure says it best:

I see in my mind a place...
Where carefree is the only state of mind...
Where an afternoon siesta among the fruited vines
is not decay in values, but the rules to live by...
Where the supreme conspiracy is the blurring of reality
by nature's rolling landscape...
Where time and reason become measures from a foreign world...
It is a place you can only find on our map.

The friendly folks at Röbller Vineyard & Winery are proud of the relaxed family atmosphere and are happy to play host to your entire family.

Annual Events

April: Röbllerfest
May: Live Music Saturdays, Maifest
June: BBQ & Blues Festival
August: Reggae Sunsplash
September: Live Music Saturdays, Big Blues & Balloons
October: Octoberfest

RÖBLLER WINE LIST

Current Offerings:

GABRIELLE'S BLUSH
JEU D'EAU
KASSELFEST
LE TROMP
NORTON
SEYVAL
ST. VINCENT

TRAMINETTE
VIDAL
VIDAL BLANC
VIGNOLES
VILLA ROUGE
WHITE STEUBEN

The winery is a family operation staffed only by the Bommaritos and their children.

BOMMARITO ESTATE
ALMOND TREE WINERY

3718 Grant School Road, New Haven, MO 63068
(573) 237-5158
www.bommaritoestatewinery.com
Hours of Operation:
Saturday 10 a.m. to 5 p.m.
Sunday 11 a.m. to 5 p.m.

HOW TO GET THERE: From St. Louis: Take I-44 West for approximately 40 miles. Take Hwy 100 W (Exit 251) toward Washington (right). Travel approximately 27 miles to Grant School Road. Turn left on Grant School Road and the winery will be on your left. From Columbia: Take Hwy 19 Exit 175 toward Hermann/New Florence (right). Travel approximately 15.5 miles and turn left onto Hwy 100/First Street. Travel 8.1 miles until you get to Route W. Turn right and travel 1.6 miles to Grant School Road. Make a left onto Grant School Road. The winery will be on your left.

Established as a vineyard in 1996, Bommarito Estate Almond Tree Winery was bonded as a winery in the year 2000. A small family operation staffed only by the Bommaritos and their sons and daughters, the winery has plenty of room for growth. The relaxing and comfortable tasting room offers a fantastic view of the neatly kept rows of vines. During winter months, a roaring fire is provided to warm up to 30 guests.

With approximately 30 acres, ten of which are already in production, the Bommaritos are confident that as years go by, the vineyards will grow and mature, providing more good spirits for a wider variety of guests. Gazing out across the scenic view of rolling hills and carefully tended rows of grapevines persuades any visitors that a return trip will certainly be in order.

BOMMARITO ESTATE WINE LIST

Current Offerings:

ALMOND TREE BLUSH: A nice pink salmon color and very light fruity flavors.

ALMOND TREE RED: A Bordeaux blending of two wines, Norton and St. Vincent, aged three years in American oak. Color is deep cherry, with nice smooth flavors of fruit and spice.

AMERICAN OAK NORTON: Aged two years in American oak barrels. Spicy, pepper flavors with a hint of currant, quite similar to the characteristics of a Shiraz.

FRENCH OAK NORTON RESERVE: Aged over three years in French oak. A nice vanilla toast with characteristics of a Norton and a hint of cherry or fruitiness.

WHITE SOLERA PORT: A blend of three years harvest of Vignoles. Fortified with grape brandy. A very light dry and fruity port, with a hint of citrus.

EXPLORING WASHINGTON

La Dolce Vita Winery

Amtrak • B&Bs • Eats • Lodging • Post Office
Washington Area Chamber of Commerce: (636) 239-2715
www.washmo.org

W ashington traces its roots back to the early 1820s, when it served as a ferry landing and later as a steamboat landing on the Missouri River. The area was settled by followers of Daniel Boone and early German immigrants. In 1855, John Busch, the older brother of Adolphus Busch, started a brewery here that bottled the original Busch Beer. The area has a wonderful riverfront with boat ramp, a historic downtown full of shops, a centrally located Amtrak train stop, and the only factory in the world that still makes corncob pipes.

When you visit Washington, be sure and visit the Gary Lucy Gallery at the corner of Main and Elm Streets. Lucy's passion in paint is America's inland waterways. His brilliant renditions of Missouri's glory days of river commerce come alive with his acute sense of light and life. If you've already been to Montelle Winery, you'll surely recognize his artwork on their wine labels. Call the Lucy Gallery for more information at (800) 937-4944.

Plan to attend the Washington Art Fair and Winefest, which is held each year on the third weekend in May at the riverfront. About 4,000 people turn out for the tasting of 50 wines from nearby wineries. An admission fee covers the tasting and includes a commemorative wine glass. There is no charge to view the art and enjoy the fair's other entertainment. Call (636) 239-1743 for more information and Amtrak schedules.

Annual Events

March: Chamber's Annual Home Show
May: Art Fair and Winefest
June: Concerts in the Park
August: Town & Country Fair
September: Fall Festival of the Arts & Crafts
November: Holiday Parade of Lights

Bed & Breakfasts

The Guest Haus • (636) 390-8257

La Dolce Vita B&B • (636) 390-8180

Thias House • (636) 239-0153

LA DOLCE VITA WINERY

4 Lafayette Street, Washington, MO 63090
(636) 390-8180
www.ladolcevitawinery.com
Hours of Operation:
Monday through Thursday 11 a.m. to 6 p.m.
Friday through Sunday 11 a.m. to 8 p.m.

HOW TO GET THERE: From I-70 East, turn south on Route 47 (Exit 193). Travel about 23 miles. Turn right on Third Street, then right on Lafayette.

L a Dolce Vita Winery, Restaurant and Bed & Breakfast is located at 4 Lafayette Street (at the corner of Lafayette and Front Streets.) Zachariah and Amelia Foss built this charming three-story stone and frame home in 1846 on the Washington riverfront. It is the oldest frame house in Washington.

In the tasting room at La Dolce Vita (Italian for "The Sweet Life), the winery offers samples of their many award-winning wines. In addition, they offer a variety of wines from other Missouri wineries, and vintages from France, Spain and Germany. Wine is available for purchase by the glass or bottle.

You can enjoy a bottle of their finest outside on the terrace, or on one of their porches while watching the Missouri River slowly roll by in front of you. On the floor above the wine shop is a charming and cozy restaurant. On those gorgeous spring and fall days, dine on the terrace at an umbrella-clad table while enjoying the view. La Dolce Vita offers a daily special in addition to the regular menu items.

The bed and breakfast on the third level has a spectacular view of the Missouri River. The Federal-style clapboard cottage lends itself to a cozy, romantic get-a-way. Soak away your cares in the "his and hers" claw foot tubs. Awake the next morning to a continental breakfast served on the porch or by a sunny window overlooking the river. While staying at the B&B, you are within walking distance to downtown Washington's historic shopping district. La Dolce Vita has all of the ingredients for a great get-a-way. Come and enjoy the sweet life!

LA DOLCE VITA WINE LIST

Current Offerings:
CABERNET SAUVIGNON: A dry red with nice cherry and plum flavors, ample tannins and a hint of sweetness.

HENHOUSE WHITE: A semi-sweet white with a crisp subtle finish.

MISSOURI PORT: A blend with flavors of black fruit, coffee, oak, spice, vanilla, caramel, peanut brittle, apricot, plum, raisin and walnut, all knit harmoniously together.

NORTON: A dry red with qualities of spice and dark fruit and aromas of red and black currants, black cherry, chocolate, and French and American oak.

RIVERFRONT WHITE: A semi-dry white wine with no oak to mask the intense tropical fruit overtones.

SWEET-LIFE RED: A sweet red with aromas of raspberry and cherry and flavors of ripe fruit.

SWEET-LIFE WHITE: A sweet white with a bouquet of honeysuckle and hints of honeydew and lush tropical fruit.

On those gorgeous spring and fall days, dine on the terrace
at an umbrella-clad table while enjoying the view.

NOTES

Chef Brian Manhardt inspects a wine offering from the restaurant's extensive wine cellar.

American Bounty Restaurant

Whereas an architect builds for the future and his or her work may be appreciated by generations, Chef Brian Manhardt has a different challenge. His masterpieces begin in the kitchen and culminate upon the palate—to be enjoyed once and only once.

"Most at a very early age became spellbound by the idea of creating something wonderful that could be enjoyed but once and irrevocably like fireworks," Chef Manhardt said. "The finest food feeds the body and spirit both, and never more so than when it is prepared by those true to their own idea of style and driven by an unquenchable desire to be the best."

The American Bounty Restaurant along the riverfront in Washington, Missouri, serves as the canvas for Chef Manhardt's culinary creations. The offerings reflect his contemporary American style.

"I stay away from the traditional items. I want my patrons to enjoy something new, something that they would not eat at home—rather, something created by a professional chef. I want the menu and the restaurant to be the reason that people go out. So we create many dishes that are unique to us."

For this reason, the dinner menu is light on chicken and pasta dishes and focuses instead on offerings such as blue crab cakes with roasted red pepper and Bolivian quinoa; dry-rub seasoned pork porterhouse with a relish of roasted red peppers, capers with olives and pickled onions; potato and sage encrusted chicken breasts with sun-dried yellow tomato butter, parmesan polenta and fresh vegetables; shrimp, mussels and crab claws in a fresh herb butter with lemon, hibiscus and Caesar toast; grilled strip steak; blackened halibut steak; and sun-dried tomato and black olive pesto–stuffed Portabella mushrooms.

Lunch menu items range from salads to grilled fillets of Atlantic salmon and blue crab cakes in addition to traditional lunch fare.

Chef Manhardt is a graduate of the Culinary Institute of America in Hyde Park, New York. Prior to opening the American Bounty Restaurant with his wife, Manhardt was the executive chef at the Sheraton Plaza Hotel at the Westport Plaza in Maryland Heights, Missouri.

He felt his position there was turning him into more of a manager than a chef, and he longed to get back to his first love—the passion of being head chef.

"I decided to be a chef at the age of 15. When I'm 65 years old, I plan to celebrate 50 years as chef. Working at the Sheraton, it wasn't what I pictured a chef to be. I wasn't involved in cooking anymore. I was a department head, not a full-time or even part-time chef," Manhardt said.

It was, however, an excellent place to hone his management skills. Today at the American Bounty, his staff seldom call in sick or plan to be away during busy seasons. His passion and experience have helped him to develop a group of extremely involved employees. "My employees truly deserve the credit for running the restaurant. I've set it up, but they get the credit for leaving such an outstanding impression."

The American Bounty is the sixth restaurant to be run out of the circa 1858 building. "I believe we've dispelled the myth that a white linen restaurant couldn't survive here," Manhardt said. "I motivate my kitchen staff by teaching them to be better than me. I say 'take my job from me. If you're that good, I'd want you to have it.' "

"We make our own sorbets, so I can show them how the sugars are affected by the freezing process. They learn how much science is involved, and how different acids, heats and juices affect our foods and our palates."

Chef Manhardt also cites another reason for his continued success.

"From the day we began at American Bounty, our philosophy has remained the same. We have always believed in delivering a superior product. We have never bowed to the pressures of changing that 'to make ends meet.' That hasn't been an option. We don't believe in change, wait and wonder.

"We have always worked with quality certified Angus beef, 100 percent Columbian coffee, fresh herbs and fresh chicken and pork. It takes us all day to prepare for the evening's presentation."

The American Bounty has been given an Award of Excellence for Superior Wine List by *Wine Spectator Magazine* for four straight years.

"We take our wine service every bit as seriously as our food service," says Manhardt. "That's something that you don't encounter in every restaurant."

Along a cobblestone street, the historic restaurant is just minutes from several area bed and breakfasts. The restaurant includes settings for 44 inside the main dining area, with 30 more upstairs, and seats an additional 36 on the patio.

Located in the heart of Missouri wine country, the American Bounty Restaurant makes an excellent stop for lunch or dinner. It is located steps from the Amtrak stop at the riverfront, at 430 W. Front Street in Washington, Missouri. For more information, call (636) 390-2150.

PHOENIX WINERY & VINEYARDS

1840 Highway 50, Owensville, MO 65066
(573) 437-6278
www.phoenixwinery.com
Hours of Operation:
Monday through Saturday 10 a.m. to 6 p.m.
Sunday Noon to 6 p.m.

HOW TO GET THERE: From St. Louis: take I-44W to US-50W toward Union/ Jefferson City and travel approximately 80 miles until you reach Drake. When you reach Drake, the winery will be less than one mile ahead.

Guenther Heeb was born and raised in one of the finest wine regions in Germany along the Rhine River. The Heeb family's history of making wine goes back two hundred years. Guenther spent many years resisting the urge to return to doing what he loves best, but as the millennium approached, so did his determination to revive the family tradition of creating fine wines.

Phoenix Winery and Vineyards proudly produces wines in an old-fashioned way, much as they are still produced in Germany. Their wines can be enjoyed in the tasting room or on the covered patio. In November 2005, the Heebs opened their International Food and Gift Shop, where visitors can purchase sausages and cheeses or browse for that perfect gift for a loved one. All featured items are of international origin.

A unique feature of the winery is their exclusive dining club. Visitors who are interested in dining in the Edelweiss Restaurant are encouraged to sign up to be a member. There is no charge for membership, but it is exclusive in order to ensure adequate staff and accommodations for diners. With a menu that features genuine German and European dishes such as schnitzel, lasagna and Hungarian Goulash as well as hearty American ribeye, T-bone or KC Strip steaks, it is a mouthwatering opportunity you won't want to pass up.

PHOENIX WINE LIST

Current Offerings:

BLACKBERRY	GOLDEN SEPTEMBER
CAYUGA	HIMMELS–TROEPFCHEN
DRAKER ROSE	PINK PASSION
DRAKER STEINGARTEN	SCHILLER WINE
DRAKER VOGELSBERGER	VALIANT
EDELWEISS	

The open air pavilion at Wenwood Farm serves as a
site for summer concerts featuring local musicians.

WENWOOD FARM WINERY

1132 Brick Church Road, Gasconade County, MO 65014
(573) 437-3443
www.wenwoodfarmwinery.com
Hours of Operation:
Summer: Monday through Thursday 10 a.m. to 6 p.m.
Friday & Saturday 10 a.m. to Sunset
Sunday 11 a.m to 6 p.m.
Winter: Monday through Saturday 10 a.m. to 5 p.m
Sunday 11 a.m. to 5 p.m.

HOW TO GET THERE: From Hwy 50, go south on Hwy A from Mt. Sterling 4.6 miles. Turn east on Brick Church Road. Travel one mile to the winery. From Hwy 28 at Owensville, take Hwy Y northwest out of town (Y only goes one way). Travel to the end of Y, and turn north (right) on Hwy A. Go 3 miles, turn east (right) on Brick Church Road and travel one mile to the winery. From Hwy 28 at Bland, take Hwy A to the north (A only goes one way) and travel approximately 10 miles to Brick Church Road. Go right, and travel one mile to the winery.

In 2001, wine production began at Wenwood Farm Winery, a former dairy farm that has been in the Neese family for four generations. Laura Neese and her husband, Tom Kalb, live in the old farmhouse on the 400-acre farm that Laura

visited as a child, when her grandparents lived there. The couple has had plenty of experience working at wineries in the past, with Laura having worked several years at Hermannhof Winery, and Tom gaining experience working at a fruit and berry winery in his native state of Wisconsin as a teenager, and later working at Stone Hill Winery and Bias Winery in the early 1990s.

The farm that once produced award-winning cattle is now producing award-winning wines. Wenwood Farm Winery offers a unique winery experience, preserving the Neese family's heritage in any way possible. According to Laura, they were a "good old German family" that never threw anything away. There is a lot of history to be found in the tools, photos and even old deeds that were found on the property and incorporated into the winery's decor. Laura has even utilized her past experience with milk production, asserting that the processes of milk and winemaking are similar in several ways, including the necessity for cleanliness and the use of stainless steel tanks. The couple even utilizes some of the old milk chillers for the cold stabilization process in making their wines. Interestingly, the winery's tasting room was once a calf barn, the wine production area was once the dairy barn, and the event pavilion once served as the bull barn. The couple does not currently maintain vineyards. They purchase local grapes for their wines.

This family-friendly winery offers a number of special events during the summer months. The open air pavilion serves as a site for summer concerts featuring local musicians. Winter events include hay rides, dinners and Christmas gatherings. The winery offers a special menu during every event, with Laura using Wenwood

Farm wines in most of the recipes. Sausages, cheeses and soft drinks are available anytime. Check the website for upcoming events.

WENWOOD FARM WINERY WINE LIST

Current Offerings:

BAUERNHOFAN RESERVE: Aged in Missouri oak, rich with vanilla, chocolate and dark berry tones.

BAUERNHOFAN: A light-bodied dry red wine, slightly fruity.

CREEK BED RED: A sweet red Concord and silver medal winner.

FRAGARIA: A sweet blush reminiscent of spring-time berries.

FROHLICHWEIN: A white holiday spice wine.

KIRSCH: Semi-sweet with vibrant color and a kick of cherry. Gold medal winner.

KRAN ROSE: A semi-dry white grape transformed into a rosé. Hints of cranberry. Silver medal winner.

LANDSITZWEIN: A crisp, clean and citrusy dry white. Winner of Concordance Gold Medal.

NOUVEAU: A traditional Beaujoulais-style red wine, released on the third Thursday of November—Nouveau Day!

REDBUD RIDNOUVEAU: A seasonal semi-sweet red. Available during the Redbud Festival, the third Saturday in April.

TREULESE: "Faithful vintage" in German, this sweet German-style wine has won gold medals.

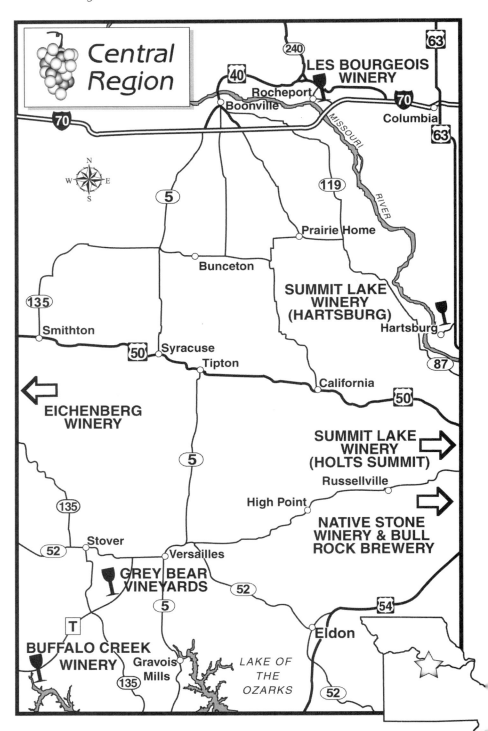

CENTRAL REGION

This region includes seven wineries. With its central location, the wineries in this region make for an ideal daytrip destination from almost anywhere in the state. Les Bourgeois Winery commands one of the best views in the state. Towering limestone bluffs, the bend in the Missouri River and the Katy Trail meld their lines into a beautiful outdoor scene.

And be sure to visit Stover. Buffalo Creek Vineyards & Winery has a tasting room with a gorgeous view overlooking the Lake of the Ozark's Big Bend. Nearby, Grey Bear Vineyard's tasty wines and their inspiring environmentally conscious design makes for a great stop. In neighboring Cole Camp, stop by Eichenberg Winery, located in the original blacksmith shop of this historic German town. Summit Lake Winery in Hartsburg offers a unique experience in a quintessential Missouri River town. Closer to Jefferson City, wines from Summit Lake Winery and a bit of Lewis & Clark history and some good microbrew at Native Stone Winery & Bull Rock Brewery are sure to please.

The stately columns are a centerpiece of the M.U. campus.

EXPLORING COLUMBIA

B&B • Eats • Entertainment • Lodging • Museum • Post Office
Columbia Convention and Visitors Bureau: (800) 652-0987
www.visitcolumbiamo.com

Columbia is more than a progressive college town. This growing city offers residents and visitors a surprising array of dining, shopping and recreational opportunities. Columbia's special mix of old with the new along with the beauty of its tree-lined streets makes the city a favorite stop for those exploring Missouri's wine country. Located 12 minutes east of the Les Bourgeois Winery &

Bistro on the bluffs of the Missouri River in Rocheport, Columbia makes a great daytrip destination. Be sure to explore downtown, just north of the University of Missouri, where dining and shopping options are nearly limitless. Whether looking for artwork or a piece of vintage clothing, chances are you will find it here. Annual festivals, special events and community activities are the rule in Columbia. Contact the Columbia Convention and Visitors Bureau for a complete schedule of events and a list of hotels, or stay at the University Avenue B&B, (800) 499-1920.

Enjoying a shower of bubbles downtown.

Tim Flynn and George Liggett, proprietors of
The Nostalgia Shop—one of Columbia's most unique specialty shops.

For more than thirty years, George Liggett and Tim Flynn have operated the Nostalgia Shop in downtown Columbia. Today, the result of their combined efforts is a shop that is truly unique.

Their store specializes in life's finest vices—cigars, spirits and wines. Their elegantly appointed shop offers a sensory experience that is remarkably inviting. If you're searching for a fine cigar or a special bottle of scotch or wine, this is a great place to stop.

Let yourself go... linger in their two immense humidors—long corridors packed to the top of their 14-foot ceilings with an assortment of cigars that have been waiting for you—some for more than 25 years. If fine wines and spirits are more your taste, you can select from a collection of hundreds of varieties that line the walls, perched upon handcrafted wood cabinetry or atop antique tables.

The Nostalgia Shop offers more than the best cigars and spirits. Liggett and Flynn flavor their collection with a helping of expertise and friendly advice. They add the true sense of nostalgia, giving customers insight into their world of special treasures.

In the late 90s, Liggett and Flynn teamed with chef Tony Hudson to offer another touch of class to Columbia—The Grand Cru—an upscale restaurant featuring both French and continental fare, each served in its own unique atmosphere. It is located only minutes from downtown.

While exploring downtown Columbia, be sure to make time for a visit. *The Nostalgia Shop,* 819 East Walnut, (573) 874-1950.

EXPLORING ROCHEPORT

Les Bourgeois Vineyards

Antiques • B&Bs • Bikes • Crafts • Entertainment • Eats
Post Office • Katy Trail State Park
www.rocheport.com

Rocheport offers many amenities for the Katy Trail user and is a popular starting point for many Sunday saunterers. Here you'll find many historic homes, nationally renowned antique shops, craft shops and cafés. One of the bed & breakfasts is a restored 80-year-old schoolhouse, which was recently named one of the "Top 10 Most Romantic B&Bs in the United States."

French for "port of rocks," Rocheport is better known today for its pleasant shopping district and historic flavor. With a population of 208, Rocheport entertains as many as 30,000 visitors annually. The local museum, (573) 698-3210, is an ideal place to recapture some of the early pioneer spirit. Open seasonally on weekends, it features artifacts and an extensive collection of black-and-white historical photographs.

The blackened ceiling of the Rocheport train tunnel is another reminder of the area's past. You can't say you've ridden the Katy Trail until you've passed through the MK&T tunnel, a 243-foot-long train tunnel built in 1893.

The towering limestone bluffs beside the Missouri River reflect another important aspect of Rocheport's history. The Moniteau Bluffs are considered sacred by several tribes. "Moniteau" is a French derivative of "Manitou," the Indian word for Great Spirit, hence the naming of Moniteau Creek.

The bluffs southeast of town bear a faded remnant of a Native American petroglyph. This is visible from the trail a few miles east of Rocheport above the Lewis and Clark Cave, otherwise known as Torbett Spring. The maroon-colored petroglyph of a "V" with a dot is right beside the bottom edge of the left bow of a prominent fracture impression. The crescent moon and dot symbol is thought to signify water, thus indicating the water source below for fellow travelers.

The Lewis and Clark Expedition reported many "uncouth" murals and symbols upon the bluffs here, but couldn't examine them due to a severe infestation of rattlesnakes. Many were under overhanging bluffs that were summarily blasted off in later years to prevent train accidents.

Located on the Missouri River at the mouth of the Moniteau Creek, Rocheport grew rapidly as steamboat traffic increased. In 1849, 57 steamboats made 500 landings at Rocheport. That's more than one a day!

Although fires in 1892 and 1922 destroyed many historic buildings, Rocheport was placed on the National Register of Historic Places in 1976.

Don't miss out on Cooking School Gourmet Weekends in Rocheport. Dixie Yates of the Yates House B&B and Mary Schlueter of the Amber House B&B, both experienced chefs, offer gourmet cooking classes, fine dining and a luxury weekend getaway. The experience lasts from Friday to Sunday and is "hands-on," with students preparing the recipes for the final, candlelit dinner. Students also receive a folder with the menu and recipes, as well as two nights' lodging and two wonderful breakfasts. Reserve your space by calling (573) 698-2129 or visit www.yateshouse.com.

Most eateries and shops are generally open Tuesday through Sunday. Try to plan your trip so that you can dine in Rocheport. The restaurants are outstanding. Be sure to visit the Rocheport General Store, which serves lunch and dinner and offers live music most weekends.

Take a rest day in Rocheport and paddle the Missouri River with Mighty Mo Canoe Rental, with an area naturalist and river historian as your guide along this incredibly scenic portion of the river. (573) 698-3903. www.mighty-mo.com.

The Katy Trail Bed & Bikefest is a popular stop for cyclists, since it's right on the trail, has a hot tub, and offers a full breakfast. Stay in the 1880s historic home, or stretch out in the spacious, Adirondack-style carriage house. Families are welcome. (573) 698-BIKE. www.katytrailbb.com.

Bed & Breakfasts
Amber House B&B
(573) 698-2028

Katy Trail B&B
(573) 698-BIKE

Schoolhouse B&B
(573) 698-2022

Yates House B&B
(573) 698-2129

Bike Rental
Trailside Cafe &
Bike Rental
(573) 698-2702

Biking through the old MK&T Railroad tunnel
is one of the highlights of the Katy Trail.

Diners enjoy a bird's eye view of the Missouri River Valley, under
the outstretched chrome wings of Les Bourgeois' one-of-a-kind goose.

The 150-seat, oak-beamed bistro sits atop the bluffs overlooking the Missouri River.

LES BOURGEOIS
VINEYARDS & WINERY

12800 Hwy BB, Rocheport, MO 65279

(573) 698-2300 or (573) 698-2716 or (800) 690-1830

www.missouriwine.com

Hours of Operation:

I-70 Winery & Gift Shop—Daily 11 a.m. to 6 p.m.

Blufftop Bistro—Tuesday through Saturday 11 a.m. to 9 p.m.

and Sunday Brunch from 11 a.m. to 3 p.m., closed on Mondays

Outdoor winegarden—Daily noon to sunset., March through October

HOW TO GET THERE: Les Bourgeois has three locations, all right outside Rocheport. The winery and gift shop are just off I-70 at Exit 115; the new bistro and the original A-frame are just 1 mile north of I-70 on Route BB. Rocheport is 12 miles west of Columbia.

A t Les Bourgeois Vineyards, Bistro & Winery you will find wonderful wine and great food coupled with a panoramic view of the Missouri River.
"We've come a long way since 1985, when we had our garage declared a bonded winery, and used the A-frame as a tasting room," said founder, Curtis Bourgeois. "In those days, we did everything at our home, including pasting on the labels while we watched TV. We named our first wine 'Jeunette Rouge'—a

Cajun word for a woman that means not quite old, not quite young, just right."

From a first year run of 500 gallons, to the opening of a tasting room in their A-frame in 1986, the Bourgeois family has turned what started out as a part-time hobby into the third largest winery in Missouri, producing more than 100,000 gallons in 2005 alone. These days, the garage is reserved for the sporty convertible, and a seasonal peak of close to 65 people fill out the ranks at the bistro, winery and vineyards.

"It's the employees that have grown with us that have made it possible for us to advance so quickly and well," said Curtis Bourgeois II, the eldest son. As manager, he continues to expand upon the foundation his father has built.

"I think Les Bourgeois is so successful because we've all worked so hard," said Dr. Bourgeois, "and because we entered the market at the same time this part of the country was demanding a drier California-type wine."

In addition to hard work and timing, family support has also played a vital role in the winery's success. Two of the Bourgeois' four children fill important roles at the winery: Curtis Malcolm is the general manager and Stephen is the architect who designed the new bistro.

A local newspaper's "Best of Boone County" contest voted Les Bourgeois as the best place to take out-of-town guests and the top place to buy wine. Responding to this kind of popularity, the Bourgeois' moved their tasting room from the A-frame on the bluffs to a larger location a mile away, just off the I-70 Rocheport Exit. Today, this building houses the Bourgeois' winemaking facilities, tasting room and gift shop. The A-frame remains a favorite for locals and college students alike.

Chicken and White Bean Soup
by Sous Chef Ben Clay

Ingredients
4 onions • 6 banana (or green) peppers • 3 cups dry white beans 4 quarts of chicken stock • 4 lbs of chicken breast • 1/2 lb Pepper Jack cheese • 2 bay leaves • salt and pepper

Directions
Sweat the onions, peppers and bay leaves. Use chicken breast to make stock. Clarify (strain stock). Chop chicken. Cook white beans and combine.

In 1996, the winery expanded again by building a larger bluff-top wine garden and bistro. A long, winding walkway leads visitors to the 6,000-square-foot timber frame structure—crafted from 80-year-old red and white oak, some of which is Missouri oak. This 150-seat bistro is just a mile north of I-70 on Route BB, beside their 5-acre vineyard. Here, Les Bourgeois' wines, made from native cultivars and French hybrid grapes, are complemented by salads, soups and hearty provincial fare.

In 1998, the winery purchased a 180-acre farm just on the south side of I-70 at the Rocheport exit. In 2000, 22 of those acres had been planted in grapes. Seven acres are now dedicated to Chardonel grapes, five acres to Vignoles, and 10 acres to Vidal. Future plans include an expansion of the I-70 location. It will include a larger tasting room and gift shop and a production and storage area. The goal is to ultimately create an artists' park where potters, woodworkers, ironworkers and other craftspeople will work in full view.

Les Bourgeois is the perfect place to end a day of biking on the Katy Trail or antiquing in Rocheport. Chief winemaker Cory Bomgaars says Riverboat Red is the most popular wine and that the dry, white Chardonel has won the most awards, including gold medals at the Missouri Wine Competition and the California Jerry Meade International Wine Competition.

Four guys and a pig. From left to right, Nick Pehle, vineyard manager; Jacob Holman, assistant winemaker; Drew Lemberger, cellar master; and winemaker Cory Bomgaars.

Shown above, the Bourgeois family, in the early 1980s: Front, left to right, Marsha, Doc & his late wife, Martha. Back, left to right, Curtis, Karen & Stephen.

How the A-frame Came to "B"
by Jan Parenteau

In the late 1960s, Ed and Hazel Williams were walking along the old Missouri Bluff Road when they found a perfect site for a cabin they had been thinking about building. It took a while for Ed to persuade Gussie Nolte, the old bachelor who farmed the land, to sell him 11 acres of it for a country home and garden.

What Ed had in mind was a far cry from the old 1850s traditional home at the corner of Second and Clark in Rocheport where his mother, Ada Williams, had lived for many years. Ed was intrigued with an interesting new design called an A-frame. He and Hazel thought it would be a perfect weekend home—a place to get away from the hustle and bustle of their busy city lives and perhaps someday they would be able to build their dream home a little closer to the road.

It was from the buildings being torn down on North Eighth in Columbia that Ed salvaged the materials he needed to build their cabin. The necessary 24-foot beams came from the basement of an old distributing company and the back door was from Cottle's Grocery. The plate glass for the front came from other buildings along Eighth. After the glass had been cut to his specifications Ed hauled it to the site very carefully on a boat trailer piled high with old mattresses.

"It was a wonderful retreat place," said Hazel Williams, "but at that time, it was also a place of scorpions and rattlesnakes and we had two small children. We also worried about the bluffs even though there was a fence." The fence was something they felt would soon be conquered by their inquisitive son, David.

They debated about selling the land, torn between letting go of their dream and an ever-increasing workload in Columbia. "We'll put a price on it so high no one will ever buy it," Ed said. It sold in a week!

Since that time, the A-frame has sheltered the family of Curtis and Martha Bourgeois while they built their home on the bluff. "Well... only for part of the family," said Curtis. "We had four children. The older three lived in a mobile home which we pulled to the site and the youngest child lived with us in the A-frame."

From 1983 to 1986, David Vaught and Shade Morris, both present residents of Rocheport, spent their bachelor years as roommates in the A-frame. "The bathroom facilities were a little tight," David said with a laugh. "We're talking about men well over six feet, a tiny tub and a sloping ceiling." The problem was resolved by an outside shower with hot and cold running water, which served them faithfully year round.

Several people have owned this tiny home and land since Ed and Hazel parted with it. Curtis Bourgeois sold it once and then bought it back to house his new hobby, winemaking. Today, people from everywhere come to the A-frame and its surrounding garden picnic area to enjoy the ambiance provided by the magnificent view of the Missouri River and the many fine wines of one of Rocheport's most popular businesses, Les Bourgeois Winery & Vineyards.

From Rocheport Chronicles

What started out as a weekend refuge put together piecemeal has become one of mid-Missouri's most popular attractions.

Perhaps the only thing better than making wine for a living... playing with life-size Lincoln Logs. Here, Alan Judy (standing) and his crew, oversee the framing of the bistro. Six months of meticulous cutting were necessary to create the entirely wooden frame.

There's more than good food waiting for you at Les Bourgeois' bistro. The architecture is as spellbinding as the river view just beyond the floor-to-ceiling windows. Exposed oak timbers, crafted by Heirloom Handcrafting of Macon, are the highlight of this building.

The bistro is one of the only modern-day examples of "authentic" timber framing used on such a large scale. There isn't a single nail in the entire substructure of this restaurant. Master timber framer Alan Judy used all-wood mortice and tenon connections, rather than metal bolts, to build the bistro's frame. Judy spent 6 months in his shop planing, cutting and finishing the timbers before the first beam was raised in May of 1996. This complex, zigzagged joinery is then further reinforced with wooden pegs.

And the tricks don't stop there. A ground source heat pump provides the heating and cooling. A 100-gallon-a-minute well uses the earth's cool underground temperatures to regulate the bistro's climate. Architect and son Stephen Bourgeois returned from Colorado to design and oversee this ambitious project.

As you admire the architecture, be sure to notice the chrome goose near the crown of the vaulted ceiling. It was crafted by Shawn Guerrero of Crested Butte, Colorado. The goose has long been the mascot of Les Bourgeois, but never before has the winery's logo been "reflected" in recycled chrome bumpers. I was told the chrome goose raised a bit of skepticism before alighting onto its permanent perch, but that once there, everyone said, "Oh, wow. It's perfect."

LES BOURGEOIS WINE LIST

Current Offerings:
BRUT: Made with the Vidal grape in the "methode traditionale."
CHARDONEL: A dry, lightly oaked, 100 percent Chardonel sparkling wine.
FLEUR DU VIN: A semi-dry red blend of St. Vincent and Cayuga grapes.
JEUNETTE ROUGE: Fruity character and light body make this a refreshing, northern Italian–style dry red. Composed of Chambourcin, Grenache and Cabernet.
LABELLE (formerly Vidal): A semi-dry German-style white with lush floral aromas and tropical fruit flavors, blended from Vidal and Muscat.
NORTON PORT: A fortified dessert wine made with Norton grapes.
PINK FOX: Distinct grape flavors in this semi-sweet blush.
PREMIUM CLARET: A dry red with a deep color, spicy fruit aromas and earthy flavor of the Norton grape with a blend of Colorado Cabernet. Limited release.
RIVERBOAT RED: A sweet red blend with fragrant fruit tones.
RIVERBOAT WHITE: A sweet white wine with honey and ripe melon flavors. This is a traditional Labrusca American-style wine.
SOLAY (formerly Seyval): A dry, crisp white with a citrus aroma. Made from Seyval, Vidal and Vignoles.
VIGNOLES–TRAMINETTE: A sweet dessert blend. Part of the Collector's Series.

Mark Geiger, a Columbia resident and professor at William Woods University, inspects the remains of an old cellar at the Boonville Wine Company. Geiger's great-great-great-grandfather William Haas established the winery, which closed in 1874.

History Section:
A LOOK BACK IN BOONVILLE

by Sara Ervanian

If Mark Geiger could have his way, he would reclaim the land that his great-great-great-grandfather owned here and replant the family crop: Catawba grapes. Then, the mild-mannered professor from Columbia would make wine just like his ancestor, vintner William Haas, did at Boonville Wine Company on the banks of the Missouri River in Boonville shortly before the Civil War.

At that time, grapes were the biggest-paying cash crop in Missouri, Geiger said, better even than tobacco or hemp. Haas was selling his Catawba wine for between $2 and $2.50 a gallon, or about double the price of wine made by his fellow vintners downriver in Hermann.

The German immigrant also brewed beer in his 80-square-foot stone brewery built on the hills west of town, on privately owned land not far from what is known today as Harley Park. The brewery closed in 1874 and never reopened. Geiger would like a chance to sample a bit of his past.

"That's my pipe dream," Geiger said with an air of reverie. "To buy back the land and plant a vine or two."

Since January, Geiger has been combing through old newspaper articles, circuit court cases, land transfers, military records and epitaphs to piece together a profile of Haas, his business and his family, which included a wife, Marie, and nine children. So far, Geiger has managed to extract an extraordinary amount of information despite the fact that he's never uncovered a photograph of his ancestor, nor has he found a surviving wine bottle, label or logo from the winery/brewery. "The Haases are as vanished as the Sumerians," Geiger said.

What Geiger has managed to uncover about Haas paints a picture of an industrious, energetic and intelligent man born to working-class parents in 1800 in Halwitzheim, Germany. The family emigrated to the United States in 1830 and settled in Watertown, N.Y. Three years later, Geiger said, Haas founded the first brewery in Chicago when the town was still a village with a population of 150. The brewery grew to become the largest in Chicago before the Civil War. It burned in the Great Fire of 1871 and was never rebuilt.

In 1840, however, Haas sold his interest in the Chicago brewery, Geiger said, and moved to St. Louis. In 1846, he moved to Boonville and bought 7.92 acres of land for a brewery. Beer was brewed at the site the first year and wine production began in 1849, Geiger said. The four-story brewery included two levels above ground (the pressroom and sleeping rooms for the workers) and two levels below ground (a fermenting room and six wine cellars).

Today, the remains of the stone brewery resemble the ruins of a forgotten castle tangled in the brush and trees, invisible from the nearby railroad tracks. At its height, Geiger said, the Boonville Wine Company encompassed 115 acres, including Harley Park.

Haas died in 1862, which was the first in a series of circumstances—the Civil War, a collapsing Missouri wine industry, grapes that were vulnerable to disease and heirs unsuited to carry on the family business—that led to the closing of the company 12 years later. "It was all very unfortunate," Geiger said.

Boonville folk singer and historian Bob Dyer would like to see the brewery ruins preserved as a state historic site. "To me," he said, "the ruins are an important and significant site in the history of the state, not just Boonville."

Reprinted from the Columbia Daily Tribune

EXPLORING STOVER
Buffalo Creek Vineyards & Winery

Eats • Parking • Post Office • Restrooms
Chamber of Commerce: (573) 377-2608
www.stovermissouri.org

Stover is named after John Stover. In 1875 this retired colonel-turned-congressman succeeded in establishing a post office in western Morgan County. There was already a church, a school and several businesses.

As the Rock Island Line Railroad Company moved into the densely wooded area, the small village seemed poised for a bright future. But when the railroad was unable to get a few right-of-ways, it had to bypass the small village. Fortunately, the company soon decided to locate a depot with switching yards a few miles away, so Stover businesses simply relocated to be beside the economic vein. This new area was so heavily wooded that "Stumps" was briefly considered for the name of the new village. However in 1903 "Newstover" was recorded as the official name in the Morgan County court. Two years later the "New" was dropped.

In 1902, the village was home to about 15 residents. The unpaved streets, with deep wagon ruts, were nearly impassable. Flourishing businesses included livery stables, a general store, a blacksmith and wagon-making shop and a saloon. In 1907, Stover's saloons closed for a four-year period when people in the county voted to make the sale of alcohol illegal. Stover's population today is around 1,000. Along with a few restaurants and gas stations, Stover has a number of quilt shops.

Buffalo Creek Vineyards and Winery are owned and operated by James and Olga Stephens. Jim started the vineyards and winery in 1994. Olga's roots in the Russian "Napa"(Crimea) bring a European perspective to their wine styles. Seyval, Ruby Cabernet, Vignoles, Foch, and Concord vines are all grown in the nearby vineyards.

The deck at Buffalo Creek overlooks the
Lake of the Ozarks at "Big Bend," Mile Marker 70.

BUFFALO CREEK
VINEYARDS & WINERY

29003 Possum Trot Road, Stover, MO 65078
(573) 377-4535 or (888) 247-1192
www.buffalocreekwinery.com
Hours of Operation:
Monday through Saturday 10 a.m. to 6 p.m.
Sunday 11 a.m. to 6 p.m.

HOW TO GET THERE: Buffalo Creek Vineyards & Winery is located south of Stover on the Lake of the Ozarks. Follow Hwy 135 out of Stover for 6 miles to Morgan County Road T. Turn right on T, and go nine miles to the winery. Buffalo Creek is located on a pastoral hill overlooking the Lake of the Ozarks. The last two miles will be on gravel road. Pass the vineyards and continue until you see the winery's sign, turn left and continue up the hill.

After his early retirement from electrical engineering in March 1988, James Stephens began what would become Buffalo Creek Vineyards & Winery. Fueled by his love of the outdoors and of good wine, he spent the next seven years starting a vineyard and building a winery. At first he just planted a few vines on half an acre. As these vines bore healthy fruit, he planted more and built trellises. For two years he sold his harvests to other wineries. Finally, in March of 1995, he opened Buffalo Creek Vineyards & Winery. Buffalo Creek now includes almost 20 acres of beautiful Ozark vineyard.

In 1997, Stephens expanded his business considerably. He purchased a larger piece of land closer to the lake and converted an existing barn into a new winery and tasting room. From the deck outside the new place, perched atop a 170-foot bluff, Stephens says you can see for four miles up and down the lake. Stephens has a boat dock on the water, with accommodations to take people to the new winery and back to their boats.

James is a self-taught vintner. He read various books and attended seminars put on by the state's Grape and Wine Advisory Program in Mountain Grove. Viticulture advisor Sanliang Gu helped him a lot along the way, says Stephens, who refers to him warmly as "Guru Gu."

Hard work and patience have paid off at Buffalo Creek. In 2004, 3,000 gallons of several wines were produced, including Seyval, Vignoles, Concord, Foch and Ruby Cabernet. Visitors should taste some of Buffalo Creek's Persimmon wine, which Stephens makes from the local wild persimmons. Other selections can be chosen in the tasting room before heading out to the picnic area to enjoy the sausage, cheese and crackers that are also available.

Buffalo Gal, a blend of Seyval and Foch grapes, won a gold medal at the 2006 Lone Star International Wine Competition in Texas, and a silver medal at the 2005 VinoChallenge International in Georgia. The wine bouquet and flavor are berry-like, light, smooth and semi-sweet.

BUFFALO CREEK WINE LIST

Current Offerings:
BUFFALO GAL: Berry-like, light, smooth and semi-sweet.
CONCORD: A fruity, semi-sweet wine.
FOCH: A medium-bodied wine with an herbal bouquet and slightly pungent finish.
MUSTANG: A full-bodied wine with a soft vanilla-like finish.
OSAGE CHIEF: Sweet with pear and citrus flavors and a smooth finish.
PEACH: Rich in aroma and character.
PERSIMMON: Made from the plumlike fruit of the persimmon tree.

QUERCUS ALBA: A new style of Concord, aged in white Missouri oak. A slight sherry-like flavor.

RUBY CABERNET: A dry red wine with rich vanilla oak flavors.

SEYVAL: A clean, crisp medium-bodied wine with an herbal, fresh flavor.

SHOW ME RED: A blend of Foch and Concord, which has taken on its own berry flavor.

VIGNOLES: The Queen of Missouri wine, aged with French high-vanilla oak.

70 MM: A semi-sweet blended wine made with Foch and Concord wine. Bright and soft with fruit and a slightly tart finish.

Harvest time at Buffalo Creek Vineyards & Winery.

David and Marschall Fansler moved their Colorado-based winery to Missouri in 2005.

GREY BEAR VINEYARDS

25992 Highway T, Stover, MO 65078

(573) 377-4313

www.greybearvineyards.com

Hours of Operation:

Monday through Friday 11 a.m. to 6 p.m.

Sunday Noon to 4 p.m.

HOW TO GET THERE: Located on Hwy T just four miles south of Hwy 135 in Stover.

David Fansler started his first winery, Rocky Hill Winery, in 1993 in Montrose, Colorado. Some time later, he and his wife, Marschall, came across a small Missouri vineyard in a real estate brochure, and on a whim they headed to the Show Me State. Seventeen driving hours landed them in Sedalia, where they visited the vineyard and saw the quality potential and the good condition of the house and grounds. They decided that the property was a perfect place to semi-retire and they closed on it in March 2003. They moved their winery to Stover. They renamed it Grey Bear Vineyards and opened for business in March of 2005.

Before entering the wine business, David attended college in Illinois and went on to try his hand at farming and gun-smithing. He served 18 years with the Montrose County Sheriff's Posse in Colorado and is currently a First Responder and Volunteer Fire Fighter at Station 2 in Stover. He also owned a restaurant for five years, but working until 1:30 in the morning left him little time to enjoy his success. He began growing grapes in 1990 and in the fall of 1993, closed the restaurant, opened the winery and never looked back. He attended the University of California at Davis and studied chemistry, enology and viticulture and took classes on growing grapes and winemaking.

"There's a challenging learning curve in this business," David says. "You have to experiment. Each winemaker has his or her own style. No one makes a bad wine; there are simply some that you like better than others."

The wines David made in Colorado earned four gold medals, two silvers, and a bronze from 1993 to 2004.

"We've done pretty well," he says.

Grey Bear has 4.5 acres in vineyards and rents another couple of acres of vines nearby. Fellow grape growers will help supply more grapes for their production and they will also be utilizing grapes from their former Colorado operation. Future plans for the vineyard include a fire pit, a bubbling water feature and a pond in front of the winery.

The structure at Grey Bear was built when the couple moved to the vineyard as well. It is a state-of-the-art, Deltec Home design. The premises also feature alternative energy sources such as photovoltaic panels and a wind generating system to help reduce the winery's environmental impact. The building at Grey Bear is the only one of its kind in the area. Homes like the Fanslers' are typically

The unique, round design of the building at Grey Bear Vineyards
provides guests with plenty of elbow-room.

found along ocean coastlines because they are able to withstand hurricane force winds. The structure consists of 20 panels, each eight feet long, and a basement that holds the winery, tasting room and gift shop. The basement area is constructed of seven inches of reinforced concrete sandwiched between three-inch layers of expanded polystyrene insulation. The design is efficient and unique, with the round design of the building providing an interior space absent of structural bearing walls, giving visitors plenty of elbow-room and a one-of-a-kind experience.

GREY BEAR WINE LIST

Current Offerings:
BEAR CLAW: A dry, chocolate Cabernet Sauvignon.
BLACK DAHLIA: Cabernet sauvignon. Dry with lots of tannins.
BLACKWATER: A Merlot. Dry and fruity, a great sipping wine.
BLUE RIDGE: A sweet blueberry foch.
BUCKSKIN: A dry, crisp, smooth and delicate Chardonnay.
BUSHWACKER: A Riesling/Gewurz blend with a raspberry finish.
CHICKS & TIGGERS: A sweet blush.
CROSS TIMBERS: A semi-sweet blackberry foch.
DEER TRAIL: A sweet apple wine.
INDIAN MAIDEN: A soft and sweet strawberry wine.
KOKOPELLI: A semi-dry foch Concord.
MCWINE: A sweet blend of Vignoles and Merlot.
OZARK RIDGE: a fruit/Riesling blend, peach and apricot finish.
PRIDE OF OSAGE: A semi-sweet chocolate cherry Cabernet.
SMOKE MOUNTAIN: Norton. Dry and full-bodied.
TIGHTWAD: A sweet, smooth cherry wine.
TRAIL OF TEARS: A semi-dry Norton Concord.
VIGNOLES: Queen of the whites. Softly sweet.

BUSHWACKER
American
White Table Wine
A smooth and easy sipping sweet white that's great with cheese, crackers & good friends. Perfect for a campfire, a slow boat ride or wiggling your toes at the TV. Try some.

PRODUCED AND BOTTLED BY GREY BEAR VINEYARDS LLC, STOVER, MO
ALC. 11.4% BY VOL.

Come tour our one of a kind Winery with Vineyards that wrap around Hwy T just 4 mi south of 135 in Stover. Call 573-377-4313 for times.

BUSHWACKER

EICHENBERG WINERY

103 North Olive Cole Camp, MO 65325
(660) 668-3511
www.eichenbergwinery.homestead.com
Hours of Operation:
Friday 3 p.m. to 6 p.m.
Saturday 11 a.m. to 6 p.m.
Sunday 1 p.m. to 6 p.m.

HOW TO GET THERE: From Sedalia, take 65 South to 52 East, approximately six miles. Go one block past four-way stop in Cole Camp, turn left and you're there. From Kansas City, take 70 East to 65 South to Sedalia, and the directions are the same as above. From Columbia, take 70 West, to 65 South, then same as above.

R odger Luetjen grew up playing in his grandfather's vineyard on the family farm north of Cole Camp. He came to love the taste of the grapes that had come with his family from northern Germany. When Rodger became a grandfather, he began to dream of giving his grandchildren the opportunity to experience the family's long tradition of grape growing. In the spring of 1996, Rodger planted the first grapevines in the rocky soil on the rolling hills of his property in Cole Camp. In 2000, the first crop was harvested, and a batch of "Diamond" wine was made. The wine was so enjoyable that the next step became

obvious. Over the next few years, Rodger and his wife, Theila, bought adjoining land and planted more grapes until they had three acres planted with 10 different varieties. The Luetjens wanted a name for their winery that would reflect their property's gently rolling hills that are riddled with numerous varieties of oak trees. After conversations with other local members of the German Club, they decided on "Eichenburg," which loosely translated, means "Oak Hills." The historic winery building, located in the town's original blacksmith shop in the heart of Cole Camp, was purchased in 2001. There, Rodger crafts the wine himself, bringing each variety to a perfect finish while Theila assists in production.

The Luetjens' entire family pitched in to turn the winery into a beautiful downtown attraction. Visitors can enjoy sipping one of 10 wine varieties in the gardens, under the shelter or in the tasting room. A proudly displayed photograph of the family greets visitors to the tasting room from beside the bar. Together and with the help of family friends, they've transformed an historical downtown building into a warm, friendly atmosphere where one can enjoy fine wines, food and fun.

EICHENBERG WINE LIST

Current Offerings:
BACO NOIR: A light, spicy red.
CONCORD: "The little black dress of wines."
ELVIRA: Refreshing with a slightly citrus finish.
EVE'S SIN: A semi-sweet wine with a distinct apple flavor.
LIEBERSAFT: A light white with a slightly citrus finish.
NORTON: A full-bodied red, lightly oaked.
ROSAWEIN: A blush with pink grapefruit or strawberry finishes.
SEYVAL: A light, semi-sweet white.
TRIPLE CREEK: A lightly oaked, semi-sweet red.
WEISWEIN: A true off-dry blended white.

EXPLORING JEFFERSON CITY

Lodging • Eats • Bikes • Post Office
Jefferson City Convention & Visitors Bureau: (800) 769-4183
www.jeffcitymo.org

A tour of Missouri's capital city offers many insights into early pioneer life. Located right on the Missouri River, Jefferson City's sites are directly tied to the evolution of river trade and the story of Lewis & Clark. Visit the Capitol's State Museum and be sure to take the guided tour that includes famous Thomas Hart Benton murals. Tour the Jefferson Landing State Historic Site, where steamboats brought immigrants who settled the area. The nearby Runge Conservation Area has trails and great kid-friendly wildlife displays. The North Jefferson Katy Trail trailhead is located directly across the Missouri River. A ten-mile pedal west will bring you to Hartsburg, or pedal east 12 miles to visit tiny Tebbetts, where you will find the Turner Katy Trail Shelter hostel, (800) 575-2322.

Bed & Breakfasts

Huber's Ferry B&B
(877) 454-2979

Jefferson Inn B&B
(800) 530-5009

Mae's Grandview B&B
(573) 659-9160

Cliff Manor B&B Inn
(877) 538-9616

The Capitol's State Museum offers an excellent overview
of the many faces and forces that shaped Missouri.

Fellow Missouri guidebook authors Diana Lambdin Meyer (left) and Katie Van Luchene take a break at Central Dairy Ice Cream in Jefferson City.

Let's face it, there's nothing better than a triple scoop of Mocha Blaster ice cream to help your brain process all of this history stuff. So stop at Central Dairy Ice Cream, a Mid-Missouri institution, serving ice cream since 1936. If you are one of those Seize-the-Moment people, order the Rock 'n Roll—eight scoops of your four favorite ice creams with four toppings and nuts. It costs less than the price of a movie ticket and has enough calories to power a Third World country. They also serve hot dogs and other fixings. At 610 Madison Street. (573) 635-6148.

Cara and Larry Stauffer's renovated farmhouse serves as Native Stone's tasting room.

NATIVE STONE WINERY & BULL ROCK BREWERY

4317 Native Stone Road, Jefferson City, MO 65109

(573) 584-8600

www.nativestonewinery.com

Hours of Operation:

April through October

Thursdays through Saturday 11 a.m. to 9 p.m.

Sunday 11 a.m. to 6 p.m.

HOW TO GET THERE: Located 10 minutes northwest of Jefferson City. From Jefferson City, take Hwy 50 west to Hwy 179, exit right. Go approximately nine miles on Hwy 179 north/west. Pass over Meadow Creek Bridge. Native Stone is on your right.

In 1804, Lewis and Clark passed through Jefferson City on their voyage of discovery. Along the way, they noted a large riverside limestone formation with a scenic view. Known as "Bull Rock," the landmark is now part of a vast, picturesque estate owned by Cara and Larry Stauffer. The sprawling farm is home to Native Stone Winery & Bull Rock Brewery.

The Stauffer family acquired the land in the 1960s and named it "Native Stone" in honor of an award-winning play written by Jim Steerman and based on the lives of the Stauffer family's ancestors. In 1997, Cara and Larry planted their first acre of Norton vines. Today, the vineyard has seven acres of grapes that are producing a variety of award-winning wines.

The wine tasting room, restaurant and gift shop are all located within a unique 1800s farmhouse that the couple has renovated. With seating for 60 inside and covered decks and sunny patios that will seat another 100 outside, Native Stone has plenty of room for special events. With rolling hills and manicured lawns, it's also a wonderful place for a daytrip or a relaxing weekend getaway. For beer fans, Bull Rock Brewery offers a variety of styles made from grains that are ground mere minutes before brewing. The result is beer that is always fresh and tasty. Four styles are kept on tap and are rotated year-round, giving the opportunity for new tastes with each visit.

In celebration of the Lewis & Clark Bicentennial, the Stauffers opened a hiking trail to Bull Rock. The two-mile round-trip hike is fun and easy for all ages. It's not unusual to encounter turtles, ducks, blue heron, deer and even the occasional soaring eagle along the trail. Top-notch Lewis & Clark signage is sprinkled at just the right intervals along the hike to allow you to take a breather in the shade without looking like you need it. The trail chronicles the Corps of Discovery's journey through Missouri and is open from 11 a.m. to 4 p.m. on Fridays, Saturdays and Sundays.

The Bull Rock Historic Site offers a shaded vantage point from which to view
this scenic stretch of river that Lewis & Clark traveled 200 years ago.

NATIVE STONE WINE LIST

Current Offerings:
CAPTAIN'S RED: A sweet blend of Catawba, Chambourcin and Norton grapes,
with fruit flavors and aromas.
CHAMBOURCIN: Hand-picked from Lakeside Vineyard. A light dry red. Bronze
medal winner at the 2005 Missouri Governor's Cup.
CHARDONEL: Harvested by hand and aged in Missouri oak. A crisp, dry white.
ESTATE BOTTLED NORTON: Hand-picked from the Barrows Bluff Vineyard and
aged in Missouri oak. A hearty red. Silver medal winner at the 2004 Missouri
Governor's Cup.
LEWIS AND CLARK'S SWEET DISCOVERY: Hybrid Traminette grapes crafted
into a delicate, floral semi-dry white.

BULL ROCK BEER LIST

Current Offerings:
HOLIDAY ALE
IRISH RED
KOLCH
RASPBERRY ALE
SPICED ALE
STOUT
WHEAT

Summit Lake Winery's SoBlue is a popular sweet white wine
with peach, strawberry and kiwi fruit characteristics.

SUMMIT LAKE WINERY

1707 South Summit Drive, Holts Summit, MO 65043

(573) 896-9966

www.summitlakewinery.com

Hours of Operation:

Sunday through Thursday 11 a.m. to 9 p.m.

Friday & Saturday 11 a.m. to 10 p.m.

HOW TO GET THERE: From Hwy 54 N: In Holts Summit, take the Center Street Exit. Turn right onto Center Street then left onto Summit Drive. Travel for 2.5 miles. The Summit Lake Winery entrance is on the left. From Hwy 54 S: Take the Summit Street Exit 1.5 miles north of the Missouri River, and go left onto Summit Drive. The Summit Lake Winery entrance is the second right.

L ocated less than three miles off of Highway 54 in Holts Summit is one of Central Missouri's newest wineries. Summit Lake Winery opened its doors in 2002 and quickly became a favorite stop for many, thanks to its great outdoor dining. Summit Lake Winery has a bistro menu that includes Tuscan wraps, shrimp scampi, bistro brats and more. Enjoy your meal on the outdoor garden terrace with a great view, or indoors near the huge stone fireplace. They offer wine samples in their tasting room, as well as a wide variety of foreign and domestic beers. A conference room and smaller gathering rooms are also available.

SUMMIT LAKE
WINE LIST

Current Offerings:

CHARDONEL: A dry wine done in traditional Chardonnay oak style.

EBERBACH RED: A sweet red wine with rich blackberry characteristics.

KINGDOM BLUFF: A semi-sweet German white wine with apple-like crispness.

LEGEND: A medium-bodied red with fruity aroma and a touch of spice.

MISSOURI PORT: A blend of Norton grapes fortified with alcohol while fermenting. A sweet dessert wine with aromas of pepper and truffles.

NORTON: A deep, complex, oak-aged dry red.

SOBLUE: A popular sweet white wine with peach, strawberry and kiwi fruit characteristics.

ST. ANDREW: A semi-dry, blended red wine made from the Norton and St. Vincent grapes. This wine is named after the local Catholic parish. Summit Lake Winery donates a dollar to the parish for each bottle sold.

SUMMIT MIST: A sweet white wine. Soft and delicate with a fresh floral finish.

VIDAL BLANC: A dry white wine with a crisp rich finish.

VIGNOLES: A semi-sweet, full varietal wine with a fruity nose and a touch of spice.

EXPLORING HARTSBURG
Summit Lake Winery

B&Bs • Eats • Historic Homes • Katy Trail State Park • Lodging
Parking • Post Office • Restrooms
Post Office: (573) 657-2300

H artsburg is an interesting little river town to visit. You won't find an amusement park or other major-league attraction to help you spend your time and money. Natural resources like the Katy Trail State Park, and yes, one of Missouri's newest wineries, are the major attractions here.

More than 100 residents call Hartsburg home. Hartsburg is probably best known for its annual Pumpkin Fest. It is a Mid-Missouri tradition that has grown in popularity each year. Hartsburg has a world-class bike shop that offers bike rental and much, much more (mochas, gifts, gear and even hand-built bikes). The Globe Hotel B&B is another cornerstone of Hartsburg's charm. This hundred-year-old hotel is truly unique. Grab a bite to eat at the local cafe. And now, with the addition of Summit Lake Winery, this small town has become another great Missouri wine country destination.

Bed & Breakfasts
Globe Hotel B&B • (573) 657-4529

Hartsburg Inn • (573) 657-0071

Bike Rental
Hartsburg Cycle Depot • (573) 657-9599

SUMMIT LAKE WINERY

Route A & Highway 6, Hartsburg, MO 65039
(573) 657-0467
www.summitlakewinery.com
Hours of Operation:
Thursday through Saturday 11 a.m. to 9 p.m.
Sunday 11 a.m. to 4 p.m.

HOW TO GET THERE: Hartsburg is approximately halfway between Columbia and Jefferson City on Hwy 63. From the junction of I-70 and Hwy 63 at Columbia, head south on 63, past the airport, and look for the Hartsburg sign on the right. Turn right and follow this road for several miles. Once you drop down the hill and see the Hartsburg population sign, turn right immediately after passing the Hartsburg Post Office. The winery is on the right.

Proprietor John Ferrier and crew have resurrected what was formally known as Thornhill Vineyards and Winery and reopened it under the Summit Lake Winery name and logo. A block from the Katy Trail State Park at 15 Main Street, Summit Lake in Hartsburg carries a unique offering on the menu (pastas, pizzas and quesadillas), along with all of your favorite wines. Summit Lake Winery–Hartsburg is available for private events Sunday evenings and Monday, Tuesday, and Wednesday during the week.

The Dauphine Hotel in Bonnots Mill

When visiting Mid-Missouri, Bonnots Mill is a must-visit. Hemmed in by steep hills and bluffs along the Osage River, Bonnots Mill offers visitors a nice reward for taking the back roads: an historic inn, two restaurants and a nice vantage point that overlooks the confluence of the Osage and Missouri Rivers (at the Bonnots Mill Parish Hall).

This is my favorite roadtrip destination on motorcycle trips. Take the lazily winding and curvaceous Highway 179 from up near Boonville down to Jefferson City, enjoy the stops, then scoot about 20 miles east to spend the night at the Dauphine Hotel. Please note this is generally considered a Thursday through Sunday town. Call the inn for more information: (573) 897-4144.

Bonnots Mill is the successor to two previous villages, French Village and Cote Sans Dessein, both of which succumbed to the river. The first European settlement in the area, Cote Sans Dessein, began as a trading post for French-Canadians dealing with Osage, Shawnee and Delaware Indians.

The Dauphine Hotel has been welcoming travelers along the Missouri River since 1875. The hotel started as a two-room farmhouse built by an American settler in the 1840s. The location was at a French settlement called Dauphine (its name prior to becoming Bonnots Mill). The founder of Dauphine, Felix Bonnot, came from France in the 1840s and eventually purchased the farmhouse and land. In 1870, he sold the house and land to relatives of his wife, Lucienne Party. The Partys then built the Dauphine Hotel, which was open for business in 1875 and is one of Missouri's oldest lodging establishments.

The Dauphine Hotel is listed on the National Register of Historic Places and is part of the Bonnots Mill National Historic District. The Dauphine Hotel offers six guest rooms, each furnished with antique dressers and iron beds original to the hotel. A full country breakfast is served in the large family-style kitchen as well as the adjacent dining room. Innkeepers Sandra and Scott Holder pride themselves on offering a comfortable and very casual atmosphere in one of the most authentic old hotels west of the Mississippi.

The Dauphine is the only hotel in the tiny town of Bonnots Mill, originally servicing river travelers and farmers bringing grain to the mill, and later railroad traffic. Salesmen called "drummers" would arrive via steamboat or the railroad and stay at the Dauphine. They would sell their wares in an open market on the street in front of the hotel.

The Partys eventually sold the Dauphine Hotel and about half a dozen owners passed through its doors until the Verdot family purchased the hotel in 1890. Adelaide and Alex Verdot and their four daughters, Constance, Lizzy, Louise and Annie, lived in the Dauphine. Alex was a county judge and had a number of other businesses while the women ran the hotel. Little changed on the outside of the Dauphine in 120 years. Adelaide died in the early 1920s and Alex in 1928. By that time, one daughter, Constance, was married and had moved to Kansas. The three remaining sisters continued to live in the hotel and operate it.

By 1930, they made the decision to shut down the Dauphine as a regular hotel, although they occasionally rented rooms to long-term boarders. The reason for the closure was twofold: U.S. Highway 50 was finally paved by 1930, which diverted most traffic away from Bonnots Mill. Furthermore, the Great Depression was in full swing by then, so what little commerce and traffic that had passed through town virtually ceased to exist.

The three sisters, or "the Girls" as they were known by most area residents, lived in the hotel for the remainder of their lives. They never married and all lived well into their 90s. The last sister died in 1970 and their nephew purchased the Dauphine Hotel. Unfortunately, many of the original antiques were either sold or given away. However, many items original to the Dauphine remain, namely the iron beds and the dining room table, which probably predate the Verdots' ownership.

In 1979, Bob and Barbara Bregant purchased the Dauphine and began a 15-year renovation that resulted in all of the upstairs bedrooms, the kitchen and the dining room being refinished. Scott and Sandra Holder purchased it in 1994. Guests will be hard-pressed to find another B&B as authentic and yet as comfortable as the Dauphine Hotel.

(877) 901-4144
www.dauphinehotel.com

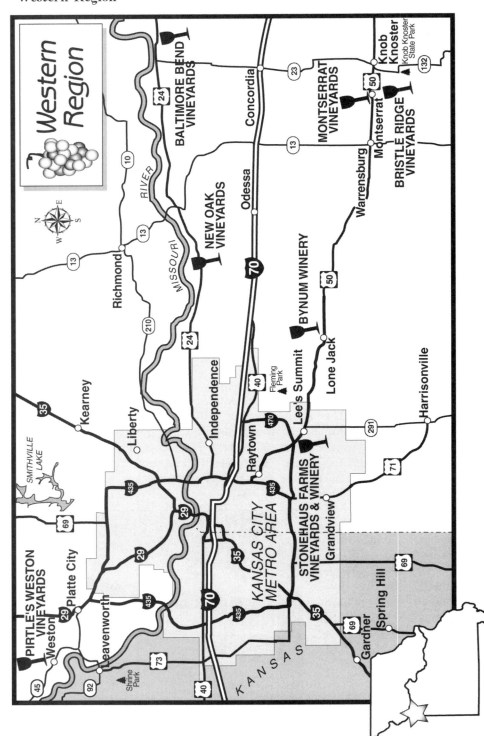

WESTERN REGION

Cattle herds and corn rows are associated with western Missouri agriculture more than grape vines—but vineyards are out here, too. Currently there are seven. Just outside Knob Noster, Bristle Ridge Vineyards & Winery has one of the oldest vineyards in production in the state and one of the most scenic settings you can find. Nearby Montserrat Vineyards offers a fantastic view to accompany unique wines. Bynum Winery in Lone Jack offers a different feel, along with some good wine. Pirtle's Weston Vineyards, just north of Kansas City, has all the historic atmosphere of a Missouri river town. Stonehaus Farms in Lee's Summit offers great wines in a comfortable setting. Baltimore Bend Winery near Waverly offers a relaxed atmosphere and several fruity wines. New Oak Vineyards exhibits an Italian influence and has a 10-acre lake.

EXPLORING KNOB NOSTER

Bristle Ridge Vineyards & Winery, Montserrat Vineyards

Eats • Gas • Lodging • Parking • Post Office • Restrooms
Knob Noster Chamber of Commerce (First Community Bank): (660) 563-3011
www.knobnostergov.com

The town of Knob Noster lies 70 miles east of Kansas City on Highway 50. Knob Noster is home to Whiteman Air Force Base, named to honor pilot and 2nd Lieutenant George Whiteman, a Sedalia native, who was killed during the Japanese attack on Pearl Harbor.

This base is home to 13 B-2 Spirit bombers, otherwise known as Stealth Bombers. It is not entirely uncommon to see these sleek black crafts sliding silently through the air. In fact, with their jagged wingspan stretching 172 feet and a cabin height of only 17 feet, this plane looks more like a UFO than an aircraft (and I should know). This sleek design helps the craft evade enemy radar.

The Air Force press release explains it best: "The B-2's low observability is derived from reduced infrared, acoustic, electromagnetic, visual and radar signatures. These signatures make it difficult for the sophisticated defensive systems to detect, track and engage the B-2." If you've gotta have one, raid your penny jar and bring an extra $1.3 billion along—and it only comes in black.

Whiteman Air Force Base is also responsible for the vast network of now defunct Minuteman II missile silos and launch control centers spread out over 5,300 square miles of central Missouri. These products of the Cold War, completed in 1964, are now being "imploded," according to the Public Affairs office.

Back at the base, there is a museum of the Launch Control Facility for the ICBM. "Spirit" tours can be arranged (in advance only) by calling (660) 687-6123.

Not far from the Air Force base, along State Road 132, lies Knob Noster State Park. This beautiful park is full of silver maples, burr oaks, pin oaks and white oaks, along with a buttonbush shrub swamp. The park is perfect for camping, fishing, horseback riding, hiking and mountain biking. It is also equipped with restrooms, showers and laundry facilities. A nominal fee is charged for camping. Also part of the park is the Royal Oaks Golf Course, a public course managed by Whiteman Air Force Base.

So where did the name Knob Noster come from? Upon its founding in 1846, Knob Noster took its name from two prominent mounds on a nearby prairie. Noster in Latin means "our," so the translation is "our mounds." Shortly after its founding, the town moved closer to the newly completed Missouri Pacific Railroad. Only one year after the move, the wooden buildings on Main Street burned to the ground. These buildings were replaced, constructed from locally produced bricks.

The knobs are an important landmark and are the subject of several interesting legends. Some locals tell of a great battle between two Native American tribes, after which, the mounds were erected as a burial monument for those slain in the battle. Another legend tells of lost Native American treasures buried in the mounds. Several treasure hunters have tried their luck digging in the mounds but most have met with little success. One group of treasure hunters did manage to make an interesting find. They uncovered several human skeletons and a variety of artifacts from an early mound-dwelling tribe.

Lodging

Econo Lodge
(660) 563-3000

Central Hotel
(573) 237-8540

Eats

Bill Sharp's Bar-B-Q
(660) 747-9011

Panther's Steakhouse
(660) 563-3930

Buck's Hilltop Lounge
(573) 237-9003

Shamrock Cafe
(573) 237-5484

BRISTLE RIDGE
VINEYARDS & WINERY

98 NE 641, Knob Noster, MO 65336

(660) 422-5646

www.brvwine.com

Hours of Operation:

Saturday 10 a.m. to Dusk

Sunday 11 a.m. to Dusk

HOW TO GET THERE: From Sedalia go west on Hwy 50, past Knob Noster. Bristle Ridge is located about four miles outside town in Montserrat. At Montserrat follow the signs a half-mile south to the winery. You can also take US 50 from Kansas City. Look for the signs at Montserrat about four miles east of Warrensburg.

Bristle Ridge Vineyards & Winery is a small family-owned winery that produces a wide variety of French hybrid wines. Established in 1979, Bristle Ridge was the first winery in Johnson County. With their large variety of wines, you will undoubtedly find something to please your palate.

Their wines range in sweetness from subtle dry whites to bright sweet reds. In the fall they also make hard cider—a perfect treat for cold winter nights.

A three-story building that originally served as a water tower in the 1950s now houses the winery and tasting room. Bristle Ridge's panoramic hilltop view once served as a lookout for Civil War soldiers. It is a great spot for an afternoon picnic. Breads, cheeses and summer sausage can also be purchased at the winery. Be sure and bring the kids along to enjoy some of Bristle Ridge's grape juice.

BRISTLE RIDGE WINE LIST

Current Offerings:
BURGUNDY
DIAMOND
DeCHAUNAC
MONT ROSE
MONTSERRAT RED
SAUTERNE
SEYVAL BLANC
SEYVAL BLANC OAK
VILLARD NOIR OAK

Dr. Phillip Weinberger operates Montserrat Vineyards.

MONTSERRAT VINEYARDS
104 NE 641, Knob Noster, MO 65336
(660) 747-0466
www.montserratvineyards.com
Hours of Operation:
Monday through Sunday: 11 a.m. to 8 p.m.

HOW TO GET THERE: From Kansas City, go 50 miles east on Hwy 50. From Sedalia, go 20 miles west on Hwy 50. Located six miles east of Warrensburg and four miles west of Knob Noster. From Hwy 50, look for the "Welcome to Montserrat Park" sign to the south, across the railroad tracks. Follow the gravel road straight. You will see the vineyards on the left after going through the stop sign.

When David and Maxine Pearson purchased property in Knob Noster, it was overgrown with old fencing and brush. The Pearsons immediately went to work, clearing the property and planting wheat. They planted their first two acres of grapes in 1981 and later introduced blueberries. As they continued to add more and more varieties of grapes and berries, they began to casually refer to the farm as "Blueberry Hill Farm."

In 1994, Dr. Phillip Weinberger purchased Blueberry Hill Farm with the intent of building a new home. The farm continued operation as a fruit farm offering blueberries, blackberries, raspberries, gooseberries and even asparagus. The grape varieties included Vidal, Seyval, Stueben, Niagara and Catawba. In 1997, Weinberger made the decision to remove the berries and replace them with additional grapes. With Norton grapes added to the already existing acreage, Montserrat Vineyards became a licensed, bonded winery in 1998. Today it produces approximately 2,000 gallons of wine annually from more than five acres of vines. Montserrat Vineyards' wines have won bronze medals at the Indiana International Wine Competition.

MONTSERRAT WINE LIST

Current Offerings:
CHAMBOURCIN: A medium-bodied, dry red.
DAMIFINO: A medium-bodied, semi-sweet blush.
JOLIE BLONDE: A full-bodied, semi-sweet white.
MONT BLANC: A medium-bodied, semi-dry white.
NORTON: A full-bodied, dry red.
TRAMONTO: A medium-bodied, semi-dry rosé
TRE' BELLE: A full-bodied, sweet white.
VIDAL BLANC: A full-bodied, dry white.

On your journey down Highway 50, stop by Powell Gardens, just 30 miles east of Kansas City. This 915-acre botanical garden features a perennial garden, a rock & waterfall garden, terrace beds, a conservatory, a wildflower meadow, an herbarium and more. For a small fee, you can explore fantastic natural landscapes for hours on end. The garden is open daily except major holidays. Call (816) 697-2600 for more information.

EXPLORING LONE JACK
Bynum Winery

Eats • Parking • Museum • Post Office • Powell Gardens • Restrooms
Lone Jack Civil War Museum (816) 697-8833
Friends of Historic Lone Jack (816) 805-1815
www.historiclonejack.com

Upon its founding in the mid-1840s, Lone Jack was named for a single blackjack tree, which marked the location of a spring on the prairie site. A marble monument in town marks where Confederate and Union forces engaged in some of the fiercest hand-to-hand combat of the Civil War. The Lone Jack Civil War Museum documents this battle and several others that occurred in the area. About 600 people live in Lone Jack today, and it's growing fast as people from Kansas City and Lee's Summit move out to the country.

Martin Rice was a poet laureate from Jackson County. His poems deal with many issues, including Civil War battles.

Here's a stanza from his poem, "The Cruel War Is Over."

'Tis done—
the bloody strife is over,
the storm of war has passed—
We hear the marching tramp
no more,
of men in armor massed.

From *Rural Rhymes & Talks*
& Tales of Olden Times, 1904

BYNUM WINERY

13520 S. Sam Moore Road, Lone Jack, MO 64070
(816) 566-2240
Open each day from noon to 5 p.m.
Mondays & Wednesdays close at 4 p.m.

HOW TO GET THERE: From I-70, east of Kansas City, head south at Exit 28, Oak Grove, on Route F. At 50 Hwy go left a short bit. Then make a right onto Sam Moore Road.

With a background in food chemistry, winemaking and vineyard operation, Floyd Bynum has developed the unique wines of the Bynum Winery. His wines are produced from Villard Blanc, Villard Noir, and Concord grapes. Bynum also creates fruit wines from cherries, apples and other fruits.

The Bynum family has had a rich history in the area around Lone Jack since 1836. The first Bynums were English settlers. Floyd Bynum's great-grandmother was a Native American who married a Bynum. His great-great uncle George Shawhan was famous for producing Shawhan Whiskey from the 1870s to Prohibition. Through the generations, many of the Bynums worked in agriculture. With a degree in agricultural education and a masters in school administration and supervision, Floyd is carrying on the family legacy in Lone Jack.

When you visit the winery you may meet Mr. Bynum himself while trying his selection of fine wines. When you're actually able to meet the maker of the wine you're about to taste for the first time, it adds an intimacy to the experience. This is part of the charm of visiting the smaller wineries. At the winery you will also find several unique gifts including a small selection of Watkin's Spices and crafts.

Powell Gardens is four miles east of Bynum Winery. The garden is open year-round and is the perfect complement to a trip to Bynum Winery.

BYNUM WINE LIST

Current Offerings:
APPLE WINE: A sweet, delicate finish of smooth, ripe apples.
CHERRY WINE: Almost like eating a cherry pie.
CONCORD: An old-time favorite.
FOXY RED: A semi-dry, light Bordeaux-style wine with a beautiful color.
MISS MEADOW LARK: Semi-dry, with hints of oak and vanilla.
RED TAIL: A dry, Bordeaux-style wine with intense flavor and color.
VIDAL BLANC: Semi-dry, cool, crisp and fruity flavor.
VIGNOLE BLANC: A dry, full-bodied wine with a smooth finish.
VILLARD BLANC: Available in sweet or dry. Crisp, smooth flavor.
WHITE DOVE: Sweet, smooth flavor, a delicate palate with hints of oak and vanilla.

Martin Russ, the resident "toy man" at Missouri Town 1855 leads tours at one of the most interesting living history sites in the state. Whether your interest is to see the antebellum home, log cabins and log church, the sheep, the blacksmith shop or toys from the 1800s, this is one stop you will want to make.

EXPLORING LEE'S SUMMIT

Stonehaus Farms Vineyard & Winery

Antiques • B&B • Eats • Historic Sites • Museums
Parking • Post Office • Restrooms
Chamber of Commerce: (816) 524-2424 or (888) 816-5757
www.lschamber.com

Lee's Summit is a balance of the old with the new. This community features a restored historic district that features quaint shops and regionally recognized cuisine, tree-lined streets, Victorian homes and eight lakes that adjoin the community. The Jackson County park system maintains more than 20,000 acres of public land within a short drive of Lee's Summit.

Lee's Summit is also home to Longview Farm, originally built as a summer home and gentleman's farm for lumber baron Robert Long. Many feel Longview Farm is the world's most beautiful farm. Long's daughter, Loula Long Combs, polished her equestrian skills at Longview and became known worldwide. Today, the original mansion, barns and outbuildings are being restored and are now used for special events. Call (816) 761-6669 for more information.

Be sure to visit Missouri Town 1855, a 30-acre historic community, with more than 35 buildings dating from 1820 to 1860. Living history interpreters re-create a lost era. Missouri Town is at Fleming Park on the east side of Lake Jacomo.

Stonehaus Farms' Festhall is perfect for weddings.

STONEHAUS FARMS

24607 N.E. Colbern Road., Lee's Summit, MO 64086

(816) 554-8800

www.stonehausfarms.com

Hours of Operation:

Daily Noon to 6 p.m.; January through February, weekends only.

HOW TO GET THERE: From I-70 Exit 20, take Hwy 7 south for six miles to Colbern Road. Go west (right) one mile to the winery. Or, from I-70 Exit 15A, take Hwy 470 south for six miles to Exit 10A (Colbern Road). Then go east 3.8 miles. Or, from 470 East take the Lee's Summit Exit 9. The sign will read Douglas/Colbern Road Exit. Then go east 4.5 miles to the winery.

Amid rolling hills, pastures and a tasteful residential area, Stonehaus Farms Vineyard & Winery boasts a truly unique location. Just 20 minutes from downtown Kansas City, the winery provides a serene country setting. Enjoy a panoramic view of the farm's vineyard or taste wine in the garden room.

After retiring as a personnel administrator from General Motors, Ken Euritt and his wife, Carol, began working to open the winery. First came special training in winemaking and viticulture through Missouri State. Today, Ken, Carol, and their three sons, Brett, Craig and Doug, are all involved with the business.

Early wine production consisted of fruit wines. While the winery today has a full range of award-winning grape wines, it continues its popular selection of fruit wines. It employs a vertical trellising system in its vineyards, which assures the best conditions for growing Cynthiana grapes. It allows improved air flow and reduces the leaf-thinning necessary to maximize sunlight to the fruiting zone. Hence, a Cythiana with lower acids and pH and a great black cherry flavor.

Recently a Festhall was opened to accommodate special events. This hall seats up to 250 people and is frequently used for wedding receptions.

STONEHAUS FARMS WINE LIST

Current Offerings:

APPLE CRANBERRY: A festive wine with tart finishes.

APPLEBERRY: A semi-sweet wine blended from apples and elderberries.

CHARDONEL: A clean, fresh dry white.

CHAMBOURCIN: A dry red French hybrid aged with French oak, medium toast.

CONCORD: A Native American variety with fruity flavor.

CYNTHIANA: A full-bodied dry red, rich and spicy with pronounced berry flavors. Aged with French oak, medium toast.

PORT: Produced exclusively from estate Cynthiana.

PRAIRIE ROSE: A proprietary blend, semi-sweet white. It's Germanic style is similar to the Riesling.

STROTHER RIDGE: 100 percent Elderberry. A unique and powerful flavor.

TRAMINETTE: A white French hybrid lives up to its Gewurztraminer heritage. Intense fruit aroma and rich finish.

Stonehaus Farms, once known for its specialty fruit wines, now offers grape wines as well.

Visit a wee bit o' Ireland in Weston. Bob Reeder, an Irish folk musician, has been taking audiences "back to the homeland" for close to 20 years at O'Malley's 1842 Irish Pub, (816) 640-5235. This classic Irish pub is tucked down in the cellars of the American Bowman Restaurant, at the corner of Short and Welt Streets.

EXPLORING WESTON
Pirtle's Weston Vineyards

Antiques • B&Bs • Eats • Post Office • Restaurants • Museum
Weston Information Center: (816) 640-2909
www.westonmo.com

Located just 20 minutes north of Kansas City on Highway 45, Weston is a great little town that has retained many of its historic homes and buildings. In the 1800s Weston was an important port of call along the Missouri River, until the river changed course and left the town landlocked.

The town was founded in 1837, after 2 million acres of Missouri's northwest corner were opened to pioneer settlement by the Platte Purchase. Weston quickly grew to become the second largest port in Missouri, as its population surged to around 5,000 citizens.

In addition to its river access, Weston was also an important departure point for wagon trains headed west. Steamboats would arrive at the port loaded with pioneers ready to venture into the western territories. They would leave stocked with locally grown tobacco and hemp to trade farther out West.

Even today, huge tobacco barns still in use dot the rolling hills as Highway

45 takes you past large farms and stately country mansions. It's easy to distinguish a tobacco barn from a hay barn by the thin vertical vents or windows that often stretch several stories high. These special windows help regulate the tobacco drying process.

Hemp and tobacco supported Weston's economy during its heyday as a river town. They remained successful crops until the 1857 flood took the meandering Missouri River elsewhere. Without its river access, the town's economy suffered. The population shrank nearly as fast as it had risen only 20 years before.

The town remained practically untouched for nearly 100 years. Many of the aging buildings and homes have now been restored and the business district is rising again to its previous grandeur. In 1972, Weston was designated a Historic District and placed on the National Register of Historic Places.

Today, Weston's business district includes a variety of stores sure to please, like The Town Mouse and Plum Pudding. Weston is also home to Snow Creek ski area, a winery and many museums. The town of 1,440 is dotted with several pre–Civil War homes and a good selection of bed & breakfasts. If you enjoy exploring the rolling countryside and quiet, lovingly restored towns, Weston is for you.

McCormack's Distillery is also nearby. Founded in 1856, this business is the oldest producer of bourbon west of the Mississippi. The Weston Historical Museum is also highly recommended. Their number is (816) 386-2977.

Bed & Breakfasts

Benner House
(816) 640-2616

The Hatchery
(816) 640-5700 or
(888) 640-5701

The Inn at Weston Landing
(816) 640-5788

The Lemon Tree
(816) 386-5367

Annual Events

March: Weston Pub Crawl
April: Annual Antique & Collectible Flea Market
May: Annual Antique, Art & Garden Show
June: Citywide Garage Sale, Wheel to Weston, Kids Day
July: Weston Jaycees Annual July 4th Celebration
September: Lewis & Clark Run/Walk
October: Applefest, Irishfest
December: Candlelight Homes Tour

Readers of *Midwest Living Magazine* voted Weston
one of the top ten antiquing towns in the Midwest.

Pirtle's is housed in an old church building, seen here in the window reflection of The Vineyards Restaurant, across the street. If you're looking for a cozy dining spot, this is it.

PIRTLE'S WESTON VINEYARDS

502 Spring Street, Weston, MO 64098

(816) 640-5728

www.pirtlewinery.com

Hours of Operation:

Monday through Saturday 10 a.m. to 6 p.m.

Sunday 11 a.m. to 6 p.m.

HOW TO GET THERE: Located in downtown Weston, about 20 miles northwest of Kansas City off I-29 or I-435 north.

The winery and cellars at Pirtle's Weston Vineyards are housed in a restored German Lutheran Evangelical church constructed in the 1860s. The French hybrid grape varieties that produce the Pirtle wines are grown in the 13-acre Pirtle vineyard in Camden Point. Varieties include Villard Noir and Leon Millot. Along with their fine grape varietals, the vintner, Scott Pirtle, also

Pirtle's Weston Vineyards has something for everyone, including replicas of hand-blown glass goblets used for drinking mead in Viking and Celtic regions of northern Europe.

makes wonderful apple wine from apples grown in local orchards. Platte County is famous for its apple production, and Pirtle's apple wine is sure to please. Pirtle also produces mead, also called honey wine. Mead was one of the first wines ever produced, reportedly being enjoyed long before grapes were even being cultivated.

The word "honeymoon" originated from an English tradition involving mead. Mead was considered a love potion so, according to tradition, newlyweds were to drink mead from "moon to moon" (one month). Mead is a great after-dinner wine. With some cheese and fruit it makes an appetizing combination. Mead is moderately sweet and should be served chilled.

Pirtle's Winery also sells replicas of the hand-blown glass goblets used for drinking mead throughout the Viking and Celtic regions of northern Europe. This was a time when even your most right-hand Norseman could try to poison you, so the glasses have no base, which prevents you from putting the goblet down before your cup is empty.

According to Jim French, author of *Meads, Maids and Mayhem,* the original goblet was found in Birka, Sweden, the Viking's major trading post to the East, and is believed to date from the 7th Century.

Be sure and visit Pirtle's wine garden where you can relax and enjoy a bottle of Pirtle wine while munching on some sausage, cheese, Tuscan loaves and fruit.

PIRTLE'S WINE LIST

Current Offerings:

APPLE WINE: Made from Missouri apples, fermented in whiskey barrels.

BLACKBERRY MEAD: Made from blackberries and honey. Gold and silver medal winner.

CHAMBOURCIN: A premium dry red with a hint of oak.

MEAD: A sweet dessert wine. Winner of the bronze medal at the Pacific Rim International Wine Competition and a gold medal at the Indiana State Fair.

MELLOW RED: A soft fruity red with lots of great flavor and aroma. Bronze medal, Indiana State Fair.

RASPBERRY MEAD: Made from honey and raspberries in a blush wine style. Silver medal, Indiana State Fair.

SPARKLING MEAD: This mead has earned numerous awards, including gold medal at the Indiana State Fair, gold medal at the Pacific Rim International Wine Competition, and the bronze medal at the Louisiana County Fair.

SEYVAL: Dry and crisp with hints of citrus and melon. Silver medalist.

WESTON BEND WHITE CAYUGA: Light, fragrant and semi-dry. Made from grapes grown in Platte County.

Richard Livingston operates the winery with his wife and their two children.

BALTIMORE BEND VINEYARDS

27150 Highway 24, Waverly, MO 64096
(660) 493-0258
www.baltimorebend.com
Hours of Operation:
Wednesday through Saturday 11 a.m. to 6 p.m.
Sunday: 1 p.m. to 6 p.m. Closed major holidays

HOW TO GET THERE: From I-70 take Exit 58 at Concordia, go north on State Road 23 to Hwy 24. Go west three miles to the winery. From Kansas City on Hwy 24, "The Bend" is located 15 miles east of Lexington.

In November of 2003, Waverly's first winery opened its doors. Owners Richard and Kathleen Livingston operate the winery with the help of their two children, Scott Livingston and Sarah Schmidt. Schmidt graduated from the University of Missouri-Columbia majoring in agriculture journalism, and after writing a few stories about wineries, she began to encourage her parents to enter the industry. Her efforts were fruitful (no pun intended), and Baltimore Bend now produces more than a dozen wines made from Cynthiana, Chambourcin, Cabernet Franc and Chardonel grapes.

The family planted two acres of grapes in 1997 and made their first wine in 1999. They now devote six acres to grapes and plan to increase to 10 in the near future. They harvest the grapes and bottle the wine in a small winery just a half-mile from their fields. They hope to eventually construct a winery next to the fields with a wine deck and tours of the entire process.

Baltimore Bend gets its name from a bend of the Missouri River where, according to legend, a steamboat called the "Baltimore" ran aground.

BALTIMORE BEND VINEYARD WINE LIST

Current Offerings:
ARROWHEAD RED: A sweet Concord wine.
C^2: A dry red blend of Cynthiana and Chambourcin.
CHAMBOURCIN: A medium-bodied dry red.
CHARDONEL: A dry full-bodied white wine.
CIRRUS: A semi-sweet white.
CONCORD GRAPE JUICE
CYNTHIANA: A full-bodied dry red.
ENCORE: A medium-bodied red blend.
JOLI VIN: A semi-sweet blush.
JUBILEE: A sweet, crisp apple wine.
JUST PEACHY: A luscious, sweet peach wine.
LAST MINUTE: A semi-sweet red blend.
RED SPARKLING GRAPE JUICE
SWEET BEGINNINGS: A Catawba-based sweet white.
TREY BLANC: A semi-sweet white blend.
WHITE SPARKLING GRAPE JUICE

Kathleen Livingston strolls through the vineyard, located just a half-mile from the winery.

Be sure to tour the 1853 Anderson House, once called "the largest and best arranged dwelling house west of St. Louis." This house was also home to a bloody three-day battle during the Civil War.

EXPLORING LEXINGTON

Lodging • Eats • Shopping
www.historiclexington.com

L exington, founded in 1822, was the original headquarters of Russell, Majors & Waddell, the primary outfitters and suppliers of goods along the Santa Fe Trail. These three men later helped to found the Pony Express in St. Joseph, Missouri.

Today, Lexington is best known for the prestigious Wentworth Military Academy, the more than 130 antebellum homes located here and the Lafayette County Courthouse.

When you visit the courthouse, look for the Union Army's Civil War cannonball still visibly wedged into the top of the structure's column (having missed General Sterling Price's headquarters across the street, when originally fired September of 1861). Today, a variety of antique shops and bed & breakfasts make this a popular weekend getaway from Kansas City.

Explore a Civil War battlefield that preserves the remnants of the original trenches and the graves of unknown Union troops on this 100-acre site. Tour the 1853 Anderson House, once called "the largest and best arranged dwelling house west of St. Louis." The home is better known for the three days of strife that occurred here in 1861, when it was a fiercely contested prize in a battle between the Union Army and the Missouri State Guard.

A visitors center explains the events of September 1861, and why the "Battle of the Hemp Bales" lifted southern spirits and dampened the North's hopes of an easy victory in the struggle to control Missouri. The spirits of several soldiers are said to still linger here.

Bed & Breakfasts

Annie's B&B • (660) 232-1480

Bridge Water B&B • (660) 259-2822

A Civil War cannon ball is stuck in a pillar of the Lexington Courthouse. Today, cannons have to be checked at the front desk before entering.

Actors, like the femme fatale shown above, perform murder mystery plays a few times a month at the New Oak Vineyards event hall.

NEW OAK VINEYARDS

1164 Flournoy School Road, Wellington, MO 64097

(816) 240-2391

www.newoakvineyards.com

Hours of Operation:

Monday through Friday Noon to 6 p.m.

Saturday 10:30 a.m. to 6 p.m.

Sunday Noon to 6 p.m.

HOW TO GET THERE: Go 35 miles east of Kansas City, 5 miles north of I-70 on Hwy 131, then two miles east on Route FF.

Tim and Barb Gasperino always dreamt of having a career in agriculture. Raising a crop, producing a product and maintaining control of their own operation seemed like a great idea. In 1997, they began planting grapes. The couple harvested their first crop in 1998, and New Oak Vineyards was established in Wellington, near the historical town of Lexington. Named for the mighty oak trees that influence Missouri wines, the vineyard is now producing 5,000 gallons of nine wines from 10 acres of grapes.

The Gasperinos' goal is to offer people a relaxing atmosphere. The winery exhibits an Italian influence, as Tim's ancestral roots originated in northern Italy. A patio overlooking a nine-acre lake is a unique place to sit and sip a glass of wine.

Eventually, they hope to have the capacity to seat up to 80 people near the lake and to offer live music. There is an event hall that seats 150 people and is available for weddings, showers and meetings. This is where the winery hosts murder mystery dinners. A few times a month, murder mystery plays are put on by professional actors and are accompanied by a home-cooked meal. The food, wine and laughter all flow freely during these entertaining events. They satisfy Tim's philosophy that two things are good for people—wine and laughter.

Another unique feature of New Oak Vineyards is that it is the only winery in the state that doesn't use paper labels on the wine bottles. They have the logo and other information silk-screened on. Tim designed the graphic logo himself, then sent it to New York to be transferred to a silk-screen template. The printing is done in Canada, and the bottles are shipped back to New Oak to be filled. Some of the wines are then sent to Frederick's Wines & Spirits in Lexington or Patricia's Foods in Odessa, but most are sold through the Gasperinos' winery located in the vineyard.

NEW OAK WINE LIST
Current Offerings:

APPLE	NEW OAK WHITE
CHAMBOURCIN	NORTON
CHARDONEL	SEYVAL
CONCORD BLUSH	ST. VINCENT
GIUSEPPE	VIGNOLES
NEW OAK BLUSH	VINO ROSA
NEW OAK RED	

A wedding in the vineyard.

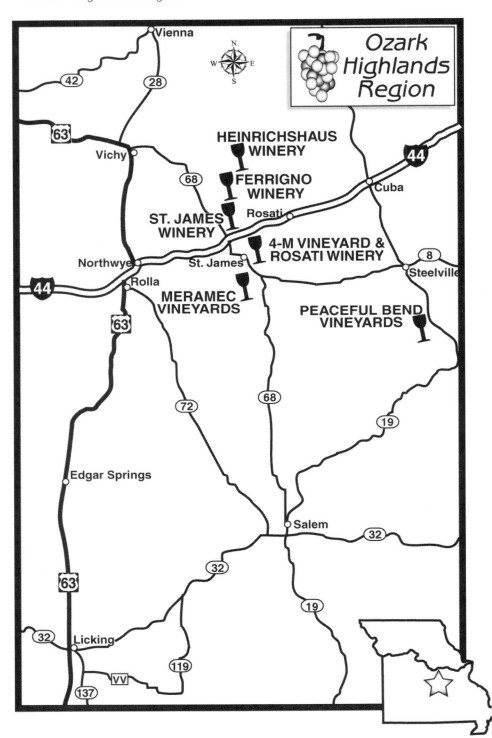

OZARK HIGHLANDS REGION

The Ozark Highlands region has a long winemaking tradition. By the 1870s, there were vineyards in nearby Rolla and Dillon. Italian immigrants settled in the St. James area and planted their own vineyards. By 1922, there were 200 vineyards in the region with more than 2,000 acres in production.

Many vineyards were under contract with Welch's grape juice operation located nearby in Arkansas. When these contracts came to an end, many vineyards went out of business, and others began growing grape varieties more suited for winemaking.

Buying grapes from roadside stands is still a tradition here, and it's hard to get lost on these rolling country roads without seeing several magnificent vineyards. Be sure and leave plenty of time for exploring Maramec Spring Park, too.

EXPLORING ST. JAMES

Ferrigno Vineyards & Winery, 4-M Vineyard & Rosati Winery,
Heinrichshaus Vineyard & Winery, St. James Winery, Meramec Vineyard

B&Bs • City Park • Eats • Lodging • Parking • Post Office • Restrooms
Tourist Information Center: (573) 265-3899 • www.stjamesmissouri.org

Sitting in the middle of perfect soil and weather for growing grapes, the Ozark Highlands region was designated an official viticultural area in 1987.

The St. James area was first settled in 1826 when an Ohio banker sent Samuel Massey to the area in search of minerals. Massey found enough iron ore to start the Maramec Iron Works at the site of the Maramec Spring. Land was soon purchased along the prairie nearby to start a settlement that was initially called Jamestown. However, once the locals learned that another Jamestown already existed in Missouri, they changed their name to St. James.

In the early years the iron was shipped by river and used to make cooking utensils and farming implements. Later, when the railroad came to town, St. James continued to grow as the demand for iron ore increased. By 1876, however, production slowed and the works closed shortly thereafter.

Today, the remains of the iron works and the 1857 cold-blast furnace stand like forgotten ruins in the jungles of Central America. The ruins are preserved right next to Maramec Spring in Maramec Spring Park, located six miles south of town on Highway 8. In addition to the spring and the iron works, this beautiful park offers trout fishing, camping and hiking. There are also two museums. For more information call Maramec Spring Park at (573) 265-7387.

While in St. James, you'll find shops and eateries throughout town, especially along West Springfield and North Jefferson Streets. Just 12 miles west on I-44 lies Rolla, home of the University of Missouri–Rolla along with several fine restaurants, shops and taverns that make the St. James area not only the perfect daytrip destination, but a great vacation spot.

Just north of St. James on Highway 63, there's a great road to explore. It's located directly across from a pull-off with a "Scenic Overlook" sign. A "Road closed 6 miles ahead" sign on the east side of the road marks your arrival. Highlights include a Vichy fire tower, an old cemetery, Spring Gap Conservation Area with hiking trails and primitive camping and some gorgeous views. The road dead-ends right before the Gasconade River.

Bed & Breakfasts
The Painted Lady
(573) 265-5008

Both Ferrigno Vineyards & Winery and
Rosati Winery also operate B&Bs.

Visit Maramec Spring Park to feed the trout (above) and explore the 1857 cold-blast furnace (left). Other nearby highlights include hiking trails, state parks and the Vichy fire tower (far right).

Annual Events

April: Winery Bike Ride
June: Summerfest Car Cruise
September: Grape & Fall Festival
October: Old Iron Works Days
December: Festival of Lights

The winery is a family business, operated by Pat Hofherr and her three sons.

ST. JAMES WINERY
540 Sidney Street, St. James, MO 65559
(573) 265-7912 or (800) 280-WINE
Hours of Operation:
Monday through Saturday 8 a.m. to 7 p.m.
Sunday 11 a.m. to 7 p.m. Closes at 6 p.m. in winter

HOW TO GET THERE: Take I-44 to St. James. Head north on Hwy 68 and take the first right onto Route B (the north service road of I-44). Follow Route B for half a mile to the winery. The winery is easily visible from I-44.

In 1970, James Hofherr and his wife, Pat, started their winery in the Ozark foothills outside St. James. Mr. Hofherr had worked as a brewmaster for the Falstaff Brewery and as a winemaker for Bardenheier's Wine Cellars and Post Winery. The family tradition lives on today as Pat and her three sons, Andrew, John and Peter, run one of the most technologically advanced wineries in the state.

St. James Winery produces over 23 wines and juices to meet a variety of tastes. The wines, aged in premium European and American oak barrels, continue to win awards vintage after vintage. St. James has become one of the most nationally and internationally awarded wineries in the state. In 1997, St. James Winery won an unprecedented eight gold medals at the Missouri State Fair, including the

Governor's Cup award. In 2005, three St. James wines took the top awards in the "Best of Category" at the Missouri "Best of the Bunch" Wine Competition.

"Our Norton has even won best red wine at an international competition," Peter said. "There are only a few Missouri wineries that have won this honor."

The St. James wines are produced from vineyards nearby. The Native American and French hybrid grapes used to make the St. James wines all grow well in this prime area. The winery produces upward of 140,000 cases of wine per year, and they are continually planting new vineyards to keep up with the growing demand for their wines. The crew manages approximately 160 acres of vineyards.

When you visit the St. James Winery you can sample the excellence of their wines for yourself. You might also like to visit their large gift shop, which features gourmet edibles, souvenirs, wine-related books and a large selection of home winemaking supplies. The staff is happy to let you taste from their wide variety of wines, or show you the facility while answering any questions you might have. Be sure to ask about some of their favorite recipes, ranging from bean soup to wine jelly.

St. James offers great wine and great roads for motorcycle touring. St. James Winery, located on Highway 44, is a popular stop while enjoying the Ozark scenery.

St. James wines continue to win awards vintage after vintage.

ST. JAMES WINE LIST

Current Offerings:
BLACKBERRY: A sweet berry wine made from 100 percent blackberry juice.

CHAMBOURCIN: Flavors of red cherries, freshly roasted coffee and bittersweet chocolate complement a silky texture and smooth tannins.

CHARDONEL: Soft and creamy, rich in flavor. A nose of lemons, oak and spice.

CONCORD GRAPE JUICE: A naturally sweet, 100 percent juice with no sugar or preservatives added.

COUNTRY RED: A full-bodied semi-dry red blend of American and French hybrid. A gold medal winner.

COUNTRY WHITE: A semi-dry, cold-fermented Catawba. Earned Best of Class in the 1998 San Diego National competition.

CYNTHIANA: Intense aromas of blackberries and blueberries with undertones of cocoa and hickory.

FRIENDSHIP SCHOOL BLUSH: Fruity character with a smooth finish.

FRIENDSHIP SCHOOL RED: Black cherry characteristics and a medium body.

FRIENDSHIP SCHOOL WHITE: Fresh, light and fruity.

LATE HARVEST CHARDONEL: Flavors of wild honey and fresh apricots give this rich, dark golden wine a wonderfully aromatic nose.

LATE HARVEST VIGNOLES: A dessert wine with intense tropical fruit characteristics and hints of honey. Named Best Dessert Wine in Missouri in 2002.

MUSCATTO: A refreshing citrus and tropical fruit wine with a floral nose.

NORTON: A dry wine aged in American and Hungarian oak. Winner of more than twenty gold medals.

PINK CATAWBA: A sweet Catawba blush. Winner of two gold medals.

RESERVE CHARDONEL: Butterscotch and nectarine flavors mingle with a complex oak character.

RESERVE NORTON: Luscious aromas of cherry and cocoa with notes of vanilla and blackberry.

RIESLING: A fruity, semi-dry wine with floral aromas and a hint of apricots. Cold fermented to maintain balance.

SEYVAL: A dry white wine with grapefruit and citrus flavors

SPARKLING BLUSH: A festive wine with a spicy aroma and taste.

VELVET RED: A sweet Concord. Winner of four gold medals, including a double gold at the San Diego National competition.

VELVET WHITE: A sweet Niagara. Gold medal winner at the Riverside California Fair.

VINTNER'S SELECT CHARDONEL: Rich in citrus and fresh apple flavors.

VINTNER'S SELECT SEYVAL: A semi-dry white wine full of tropical fruit flavors. Gold medal winner.

VINTNER'S SELECT VIGNOLES: A special wine made in a German style. Semi-dry. Governor's Cup winner.

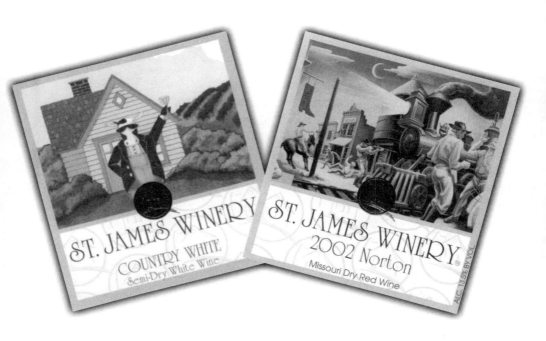

An old dairy barn serves as the winery and tasting room at Ferrigno Winery.

FERRIGNO VINEYARDS & WINERY

17301 State Route B, St. James, MO 65559

(573) 265-7742 or (573) 265-8050

Hours of Operation:

Monday through Saturday 10 a.m. to 6 p.m

Sunday Noon to 6 p.m.

Weekends only during January, February and March.

HOW TO GET THERE: Take I-44 to St. James. Turn north on Hwy 68 and take the first right onto Route B (the north I-44 service road). After passing St. James Winery, follow Route B for just over four miles. The winery will be on your left.

The rustic scenery and fine wines of the Ferrigno Winery (pronounced Fur-EEN-yo) exemplify the romance and flavor of Missouri wine country. The winery and tasting room are housed in an old dairy barn surrounded by 12 acres of beautiful vineyard. With its covering of well-weathered wood and a welcome sign mingled among the antiques near the entrance, the barn welcomes you with an atmosphere of hospitality.

The winery's covered deck offers a view of the vineyard to the west. This is the perfect place to enjoy a relaxing afternoon with friends or a romantic sunset with someone special.

The handcrafted wines of the Ferrigno Winery are made entirely from Missouri-grown grapes. The entire process, from crushing grapes to aging the wines is done on the Ferrigno estate. All of Ferrigno's wines are aged in stainless steel tanks with the exception of the dry red wines, which are aged in barrels made of Missouri white oak. The majority of the wines are sold directly from the winery. Dick and Susan Ferrigno have one goal that guides their winemaking: "to produce clean, flavorful wines of premium quality and distinctive regional character."

Dick Ferrigno is a host who works hard to make his winery a special place to visit. The winery is open for private dinners, wine tastings and receptions in its heated wine garden room. You might also like to prepare a picnic from the deli or browse the wine-related gifts that line the tasting room. You can even turn your visit into a memorable overnight stay at Ferrigno's Bed & Breakfast. A stay in the guesthouse or in the private loft above the winery is accompanied by complimentary wine and breakfast.

FERRIGNO WINE LIST

Current Offerings:
CHAMBOURCIN RED: A dry, oak-aged red varietal with medium body, deep color, rich fruit flavors and a spicy nose.
CONCORD: A classic, sweet, dessert-style red wine.
GARDEN BLUSH: A semi-sweet rosé. Light with a wild grape flavor.
GARDEN RED: A light, semi-sweet red.
GOLDEN HARVEST: A sweet white wine.
PRIMAVERA: Semi-dry with a zesty springtime flavor and a hint of sweetness. Floral and spice overtones of the Missouri Riesling grape.
SEYVAL: A semi-dry varietal. Clean and pleasantly tart, with a delicate fruit flavor.
VINO DI FAMIGLIA: A semi-dry red blend with a mellow fruitiness.

When you visit Heinrichshaus, you will likely get a chance to meet Heinrich himself and his charming and vivacious wife, Gina.

HEINRICHSHAUS VINEYARD & WINERY

18500 State Route U, Saint James, MO 65559

(573) 265-5000

Hours of Operation:

Monday through Saturday 9 a.m. to 6 p.m.

Sunday Noon to 6 p.m. Closed Wednesday.

HOW TO GET THERE: To visit Heinrichshaus Vineyard and Winery take I-44 to Hwy 68 at St. James. Follow Route KK four miles to Route U. Go north on U for three miles and look for the entrance to the winery.

Founded on the belief that affordable, high-quality wine can be produced in Missouri, the Heinrichshaus Vineyard & Winery has been producing wine since 1978.

Nearly all of the Heinrichshaus wines are made from French hybrid and Native American grape varieties. Heinrichshaus wines have won many gold, silver and best-of-show medals. Heinrich's specialty is dry wine but you may find a semi-sweet or semi-dry to suit your tastes. You might also try one of Heinrich's experimental wines that are available from time to time.

When Heinrich Grohe emigrated to the United States from Germany in the 1950s, he found Missouri wines to be quite different from those he knew in Europe. In order to find a wine that he could enjoy with his meals, Heinrich began experimenting with Missouri grapes. After honing his skills with the native grapes, Heinrich and his family purchased a tract of land and began planting the Heinrichshaus Vineyard. In the early years of grape production, he sold his grapes to other wineries, but all the while plans for the Heinrichshaus Winery were in the works. Construction began in 1978 and one year later the doors of the winery were opened to the public.

When you visit Heinrichshaus, you will likely get a chance to meet Heinrich himself and his charming and vivacious wife, Gina. If a relaxing picnic sounds good, head to the terrace where you can spend a carefree afternoon in the shade, enjoying the flowers and the cool breezes. Picnic baskets are encouraged.

In the spring, the Grohes host a "taste the new wines" celebration, and all are invited. In the autumn, they invite you to join them in celebrating the harvest's end and perhaps taste some wines in the making when fermentation is in progress. Check the website or call the winery for more information.

HEINRICHSHAUS WINE LIST

Current Offerings:

CHAMBOURCIN
CHARDONEL
CYNTHIANA

PRAIRIE BLANC
VIDAL
VIGNOLES

vintage 2002

heinrichshaus

Missouri

CYNTHIANA

*A full-bodied dry red table wine
made from the Cynthiana grape.*

XXV

Fine Wines Since '79

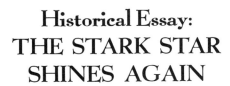

Historical Essay:
THE STARK STAR
SHINES AGAIN

by Phyllis Meagher

*"Dear Sir: We beg to call your attention
to a most promising new Grape we have secured... "*

So began a letter written January 9, 1902, by William Stark, treasurer of Stark Brothers' Nurseries & Orchards Co. of Louisiana, Missouri. "We will invest a great deal of money in this variety," he continued, "which may be called Stark for the present... Certainly no grape is more beautiful and attractive."

The path that led me to Mr. Stark's letter began with a neighborly comment not long after I bought my 15-acre Concord vineyard in St. James.

"That last row isn't Concord," said Lou Tessaro. "It's the late grape. You'd better let me prune it. You can't let as many buds as with Concord or you'll overload it."

He was right. The late grape was different. (Lou was always right, I learned, and not just about grapes—there would be many more Lou lessons for this neophyte country dweller.) It bloomed later, produced big, shouldered bunches and ripened a good month after the Concords were off the vines.

The late grape was also susceptible to black rot, and it seemed to push new growth from everywhere, even mid-trunk. Suckering was serious business with that row. And, true to folklore, we harvested that row after the first frost.

My curiosity aroused, I questioned my elderly neighbor Mr. Stoltz, who had over 100 acres of grapes, including some 20 varieties. "The late grape is the Stark Star," he said. He thought it had been developed by one of the old grape experimenters of the last century, maybe Munson.

A call to Roy Renfro of the Munson Memorial Vineyard in Dennison, Texas, ruled out that possibility. But some additional sleuthing turned up historical records about the Stark Star grape. Louis Zellner of Granby, Missouri, reported in the 1904 report of the State Horticultural Society of Missouri that the Stark Star "ripens about the 1st of October, but does not fully mature until frost has stripped the leaves from the vines."

That sounded familiar. By now, I was fairly sure of two things. My grapes were the Stark Star, and I was hooked on Missouri grape history.

Missouri history is resplendent with grapes. Then, as now, grapes fascinated, intrigued, puzzled and excited Missourians. At the turn of the century, nearly everyone was trying to find suitable varieties for eating and winemaking that grow well in our climate.

Varieties were cross-bred, sent to experimental stations and nurseries, set up in commercial plots with "successful and responsible vineyardists," planted and observed by professionals and amateurs alike.

Mr. Stark's attention-getting letter was well received. The Stark Star was sent as far away as the Geneva Experimental Station in New York, where written logs still exist of bloom, growing conditions and harvest dates for the next 17 years.

Some varieties, either because of their inability to flourish in our climate or because of their uninteresting wine and juice qualities, passed from current interest. Others didn't survive the Volstead Act. Sometimes, even in places like my vineyard where old varieties were tended, their histories were lost... or almost.

The Stark Star trail, which led from Missouri to Arkansas and back to Missouri, started with Professor Joseph Bachman, an immigrant from Lucerne, Switzerland, who settled in Altus, Arkansas, in 1881. He was eulogized in the *American Fruit Grower Magazine* in 1928 as "one of the most expert grape culturists in the U.S." The grape that was to become the Stark Star was one of Professor Bachman's first successes. He crossed the Cynthiana (also called Norton's Virginia Seedling) and Catawba and won a silver medal with the grape at the St. Louis Exposition in 1904. He then sold the rights to the grape to Stark Brothers' Nursery, who introduced it commercially.

While both its parents are still familiar to today's consumers of Missouri wine and juice, the Stark Star made a brief, brilliant flash on the scene and then disappeared. But, like a comet, the Stark Star reappears every so often to take a bow.

Its first reappearance in our time was as a dessert wine and then a port, produced by Lucian Dressel of Mount Pleasant Winery in Augusta after he discovered this new/old grape in St. James.

The fall of 1994 was the first crush at Adam Puchta Winery. I delivered a load of Stark Stars to the winery on a crisp, sunny afternoon in October. There's something to be said for the Stark Star's late ripening. Picking on a nice, cool October day is a delightful reward for making it through our hot August harvest.

It was the sort of mid-October harvest day that inspired Mark Twain to say that to be in Missouri in October is to know heaven. Handling crush along with their first Octoberfest crowds was a little tricky for winemaker Tim Puchta and his wife, Vicki. At small wineries like theirs, the salesroom staff and the cellar rats are one and the same. We all pitched in to crush the grapes while Spencer, the seventh generation Puchta, observed from his stroller.

The grapes were beautiful, dark blue, almost black. Juice was pumped from the crusher and destemmer on the patio to a jacketed stainless steel tank in the arched stone cellars. This was an experimental batch of only a few hundred pounds of grapes, so crushing didn't take long. Clean-up, on the other hand, did.

Tim is a fanatic about cleanliness. Henry Ford said genius is 2 percent inspiration and 98 percent perspiration. Tim Puchta's corollary is that after getting good fruit, winemaking comes down to 2 percent inspiration and 98 percent sanitation.

The Stark Star underwent a slow, traditional fermentation at about 64 degrees. Tim used *prise de mousse* yeast and left skin contact for three or four weeks. Tim noted that the juice has a very pleasant aroma, a trait noted by winemakers nearly 100 years ago.

"I was surprised the wine came up with a light color, as nice and dark as the skins were," Tim said. "We extracted every bit of pigment from the skins, yet I feel there's still not enough pigment and plan to blend a little more to achieve the color I want."

A pretty blush color is something winemakers work to achieve when making a blush wine. Since the Stark Star by itself produces the perfect blush color, Tim is thinking how he will vinify the grape next year. He may also ferment at a little warmer temperature to see if he can't "blow off some heaviness."

This year, Tim is making a light, Chianti-like red wine. To tone down the heavy Labrusca character, he blended in two French hybrids—Bellandais, a Seibel French hybrid, and Seyval Blanc—and he plans to sweeten it a little.

"There's a lot of nose, but not a lot of taste when it's totally dry," he observed.

Adam Puchta Winery's Stark Star is made to drink young.

And yes, Mr. Stark, we want to learn more about your "beautiful and attractive grape." With the Stark Star already pushing buds for its 100th-year crop, I believe some tasting and discussion is required.

Gentlemen, you have our attention.

From Wine Country Journal Magazine

4-M VINEYARD & ROSATI WINERY

22050 State Road KK, St. James, MO 65559

(573) 265-8147

Hours of Operation:

Farmers' Market open daily from daylight to dark

HOW TO GET THERE: Located on historic Route 66. Take I-44 to Route F (Exit 203), go west on the south service road for two miles and you're there. The winery is four miles from St. James, nine miles from Cuba and 15 miles from Rolla.

Owned and operated by Marvin and Donna Rippelmeyer, the Rosati Winery is a standing reminder of the early Italian heritage of Rosati. The building was originally constructed in 1922 by the Knobview Coop to help grape growers ship their goods by train to the St. Louis markets and beyond. In 1933, wine production began at the site, and today, the early vats and stately oak barrels remain as monuments to their efforts.

Now, the Rosati Winery produces Concord grape juice and a selection of Missouri wines. The Rosati Winery also has a country store that sells a variety of handcrafted Ozark products. Picnic supplies are available for you to enjoy an afternoon in their quiet wine garden. Rosati also features a large meeting room for catering and special functions and an adjoining bed & breakfast. A vineyard and horse farm tour can also be arranged for a nominal fee (minimum of six persons). 4-M Vineyard's Farmers' Market, featuring fruits, juices and crafts is one mile west of the winery.

A look at the winery at Meramec Vineyards, from a grape's point of view.

MERAMEC VINEYARDS

600 State Road Route B, St. James, MO 65559
(877) 216-WINE or (573) 265-7847
www.meramecvineyards.com
Hours of Operation:
Monday through Saturday 10 a.m. to 5 p.m.
Sunday Noon to 5 p.m.

HOW TO GET THERE: Located halfway between St. Louis and Springfield at St. James, Exit 195 on I-44. Go 3/4 mile east on the north outer road Hwy B.

Meramec Vineyards' classy setting encourages visitors to stop and enjoy award-winning estate-grown and made wines. Browsing the attractive gift shop with its gourmet food and wine-related items can fill up an entire afternoon. The Art Gallery contains works from nationally recognized local artists. The Bistro d'Vine has been mentioned in *Southern Living Magazine* and serves European-style lunches. Enjoy "tasting plates" with wine in the bistro, covered courtyard or in the garden. Check out the garden's Bocce court as well.

Bistro d'Vine Dressing

Ingredients

1 cup extra virgin olive oil • 1/3 cup lemon juice • 1-2 tbs balsamic vinegar (blackberry, pear, fig or raspberry) • 1 tsp. salt • 1 tbs minced garlic • 1 tsp. sugar (or substitute) • 1/4 tsp. pepper (white or coarse black) • 1 tbs dried basil (crushed) • 1 tbs dried parsley

Directions

Whisk or place in a jar and shake until consistent. It's best if it sets overnight before use. If you prefer, add dried Dijon mustard (cranberry mustard is great).

Owner Phyllis Meagher stands in the gift shop at Meramec, brimming with fine gifts and the work of local artists.

MERAMEC WINE LIST

Current Offerings:

BISTRO GOLD: A dry white wine both subtle and crisp.

BISTRO WHITE: An off-dry light-bodied white with floral overtones and sweetness in the finish.

BISTRO RED: A medium-bodied dry red wine with subtle fruitiness and a long dry finish.

CATAWBA BLUSH: A light semi-sweet wine from the tangy native American Catawba grape.

CLASSIC CONCORD: A semi-sweet wine made 100 percent from the quintessential American grape.

NEW WORLD RED: A blended, sweet, fruity red.

NEW WORLD WHITE: A sweet white with the fruity taste of the Niagara grape.

NORTON: A dry, full-bodied, deep-colored, aromatic red wine with complex fruit flavors.

SILVIO'S RED: A red wine with a slightly sweet finish to complement its fruity character.

SWEET CAT: Made from the tangy native American Catawba, this version is finished sweet.

Notes on Silvio's Red
by Phyllis Meagher

We have a slightly fruity red wine unique to us called Silvio's Red. It is made from a blend of Stark Star and Norton. The Stark Star was developed in the late 1800s by Professor Bachman of Altus, Arkansas, and introduced at the St. Louis World's 1904 Fair by the Stark Brothers Nursery, where it won a medal. Our wine is named after the real Silvio who worked in the grapes his whole life, the last twelve of which he tended the vines at Meramec Vineyards. To us, he is the epitome of the grape grower and in his memory we named this wine. He took on the Stark Star row, put it on a Geneva Double Curtain (GDC) trellis system, propagated more vines and expanded the planting. The Stark Star adds a certain fruitiness to this wine.

The Norton, *vitis aestivalis,* is a grape native to North America. The Norton grape was found (by a Dr. Norton) in Virginia prior to 1830. It is renowned as Missouri's powerful and complex red. Missouri put it on the map both in the 1800s and again in the current modern epoch of winemaking. It adds an underlying structure and richness and a subtle complexity to our Silvio's Red. We make this wine with a slight residual sugar that complements its fruitiness.

EXPLORING STEELVILLE

Peaceful Bend Vineyards, Winery & Guest Cottage

B&Bs • Eats • Lodging • Parking • Post Office • Restrooms • Shopping
Steelville Chamber of Commerce: (573) 775-5533
www.steelville.com

Originally settled in the 1830s, Steelville was originally named Davey. Later, the town was renamed in honor of James Steel, an early settler. The name was on the mark because the town eventually became an important center for the mining of high-grade iron ore.

The town is surrounded by national and state forest land that is intersected by several streams and rivers. There are several opportunities for hiking and mountain biking in the surrounding forests, and the area's rivers are great for floating and fishing.

The 1990 census named Steelville the National Population Center. This designation means that if the entire population of the United States was placed on a flat map of the country (assuming they all weighed the same and no one moved), the map would balance at a point 9.7 miles south of Steelville.

Local attractions include a country music show, a bluegrass festival, camping, dude ranches, golf courses, riding stables, RV parks, riverside resorts, caves, a trout park and several antique shops.

Bed & Breakfasts

Frisco Street B&B
(573) 775-4247

Wildwood Springs Lodge
(800) 554-3746

Annual Events

April: Dogwood Festival
May: Summerfest and Car Show
June: Spring Junk-A-Rama, Mid America Rendezvous
July: Freedom Festival
September: Harvest Festival
October: Fall Junk-A-Rama and Quilt & Doll Show
November: Veteran's Tribute
December: Children's Christmas Pageant

PEACEFUL BEND VINEYARD, WINERY & GUEST COTTAGE

1942 Highway T, Steelville, MO 65565

(573) 775-3000

www.peacefulbend.com

Hours of Operation:

Tuesday through Friday 10 a.m. to 5 p.m.

Saturday 10 a.m. to 6 p.m.; Sunday Noon to 5 p.m.

HOW TO GET THERE: From I-44 take Exit 208 at Cuba. Go south on Hwy 19 for eight miles to Hwy 8. Go west two miles on Hwy 8 to Route T. Turn right on T and go two miles. Peaceful Bend is on the left. Watch for the signs. (The Cuba Hwy 19 turnoff is just a one-hour drive west of I-270.)

The motto at Peaceful Bend Winery isn't "bigger is better." Rather, proprietors Clyde and Katie believe "smaller is better." Both bring extensive experience to their new endeavor from a large Missouri winery, and they are pleased that their new winery is a size they can put their arms around.

They look forward to building a winery that represents their combined experiences. This year's production will be approximately 15,000 gallons of wine.

"We've been doing better with our quality dry wines, and that is the direction I would like to see us go." Clyde said.

Clyde, Katie and their trusty
companion "Hey Jude."

Although Clyde and Katie have been involved with the Missouri wine scene for some time, rolling up their sleeves and operating a winery of their own has allowed them to appreciate the much broader network of support that exists in Missouri for small wineries.

"A lot of people have helped us out. We've gained a lot of knowledge from other small wineries, because we're small too. There's a kind of sharing, almost cooperative atmosphere," Clyde said.

As for their new home and workplace, the two of them are still reeling from the whirlwind that landed them here.

"I had no concept that this would happen. I heard the winery had closed, but the thought of the two of us making it our own was too farfetched to conceive. We really owe it to Judy and George DuBose, the previous owners since 1995, and George Weese, who owned the property. They really bought into our dream of making this place go."

In addition to rejuvenating the vineyards and reopening the winery, Clyde and Katie renovated and opened a cozy guest cottage on the property. This cottage has two bedrooms.

So far, more than 90 percent of visitors have been tourists. Many of those who make it to Peaceful Bend do so by floating by the wine booth that is set up along the banks of the Meramec River.

In addition to the new owners' dedication to producing quality wine, the location of Peaceful Bend will play a large part in attracting visitors and selling the wines. Most of the wines are named after area creeks and rivers—even the winery is named from a bend in the Meramec River located just a short hike from the main tasting room.

In addition to traffic coming in by highway, the Gills have been surprised at the number of floaters that come to the winery by canoe and stop in for a bottle of wine before heading farther downriver.

The move to Steelville and the reopening of Peaceful Bend has been a challenge. The decision was not an easy one to make, but the lure of the established winery and the appeal of a change in lifestyle to be played out on 72 beautiful acres was something Clyde and Katie couldn't allow themselves to pass up.

As for the history of Peaceful Bend, Dr. Axel Arneson, in conjunction with the University of Arkansas, Fayetteville, planted the first parts of the vineyards at Peaceful Bend in 1965. The original research project's objective was to determine the best grape hybrids to grow in Missouri. This study helped to lay the foundation for the renaissance of Missouri's post-Prohibition wine industry.

In 1972, the winery was built, patterned after the traditional family wineries of southern Europe. Dr. Arneson envisioned a rural operation that encompassed every aspect of winemaking, from the grapes to the bottle. The viticulture site is excellent and the beautiful Ozark location makes it a popular stop for visitors.

Clyde and Katie are recapturing the dream of Dr. Arneson. Equipped with all the necessary equipment required to produce quality wine, combined with the new owners' experience and skills, a backdrop is set for a wonderful winery experience. And these two know what they are doing. Prior to purchasing Peaceful Bend, Clyde had been the cellar master at Stone Hill Winery in Hermann since 1994. He apprenticed with renowned winemaker Dave Johnson, from whom he learned winemaking skills from *methode champagnoise* to state-of-the-art techniques. Clyde played a major role in Stone Hill's production of more than 150,000 gallons a year, the largest output of any Missouri winery at the time. Before joining Stone Hill, Clyde worked in the California wine industry.

Katie had been vineyard manager at Stone Hill Winery since 1996. She managed an 80-acre vineyard, among the largest in the state, supervising crews in the production of five types of grapes. She earned a bachelor of science degree from Michigan State University in horticulture, where she studied viticulture and enology under the leading cold-climate researcher—Stan Howell. Her manager at

The Peaceful Bend vineyards.

Spark, the newest addition to the vineyard, enjoys a "Peaceful" afternoon cat-nap.

Stone Hill, Jon Held, earned the Grape Grower of the Year award in 1994 and served as her mentor.

"Our goals are to produce world-class wines and provide a memorable winery experience," Clyde said.

In the vineyard they plan to increase production and expand the winery's eight acres of French-American hybrid grape varieties, the first hybrids grown in Missouri, as well as to create cottage-style gardens where visitors can linger.

Clyde and Katie encourage guests to stop by the winery's sales and tasting room, tour the vineyard, explore nature trails and enjoy a picnic along the Meramec. Peaceful Bend also offers bed and breakfast accommodations and special events throughout the year.

Peaceful Bend is located 1.5 hours southwest of St. Louis in the popular Steelville area, just eight miles south of I-44. Nearby attractions include four other area wineries, Maramec Spring, resorts, campgrounds and RV parks, a golf course, antique shops, caves and much more.

PEACEFUL BEND WINE LIST

Current Offerings:

CHARDONEL: A barrel-fermented dry white. Fruity with a creamy texture. Silver medal winner.

CONCORD: A sweet red wine bursting with the aroma of fresh Concord berries.

COURTOIS: A crisp, dry white wine. Made primarily from Chardonel grapes. Bronze medal winner.

FORCHE RENAULT: A soft-bodied red blend with an array of complex fruit and spice flavors.

HARVEST MIST: A semi-dry white wine. A hybrid blend with a light texture and a hint of sweetness.

HUZZAH VALLEY: Pronounced WHO-zaw, this is Peaceful Bend's most popular wine. A sweet rosé with a fruity nose.

MERAMEC: An ultra-premium dry red made from a blend of Chambourcin and Norton grapes.

NORTON: A robust red. The native grape fermented to bring out its spicy character.

SWEET RIVER WHITE: A sweet white with a delicate acidity.

WHITTENBURG: A smooth and fruity semi-sweet white wine from five varieties of French and American hybrid grapes. Silver medal winner.

The sounds of the ocean and shorebirds emanate from Steelville, the population center of the United States. Here, full-time hobbyist James Barksdale is busy freeing a bird form from a curved piece of sugar pine.

Small coastal shorebirds are the main carving interest for Jim. He researches his pieces by poring over volumes on decoys and bird identification books by Audubon and Roger Tory Peterson. His bird colors are not only correct, but historically correct as well.

Today his carvings serve as ornamental fixtures in homes, but they are modeled after hunting decoys that were heavily used in the 1800s up and down the East Coast, until the 1912 passing of the Migratory Bird Act.

Jim's lifelike seabird decoys authentically rekindle this bygone era. Sandpipers, avocets, yellowlegs, curlews, woodcocks and dowitchers are familiar decoys, painted in subdued hues of grey and tan. Jim also puts holes in his decoys, simulating the wear these decoys received.

"These decoys were used to draw in the birds. The hunters actually shot the birds on the ground. So, the decoys got as many shot in 'em as the birds did."

Jim carves both full-bodied birds and "flatties," which are thinner silhouettes of the birds, easier for hunters to carry and store.

In his Antique Series, Jim follows age-old traditions of using readily available materials in his decoys, such as tack eyes, cut-nail bills and distressed finishes. "Some have a nail for a beak... this one's got a bent gutter nail for a snout."

"I can do the same bird, the same pose, but they never turn out the same." Jim carved his first piece of wood some 45 years ago, but it wasn't until 15 years ago on a trip to Branson that he picked up the idea of carving shorebirds.

"That's always the first thing people ask, 'Are you from the coast?' Well, I've lived in Missouri all my life. Everybody's doing ducks. I just really enjoy the variety of shorebirds... my driftwood pedestals also make mine stand out." Recently, his work was recognized nationally in *Midwest Living* magazine, and his work is sold at L.C.'s in Steelville and at Bluestem Missouri Crafts in Columbia.

Special Section:
THE UBIQUITOUS WINE BARREL

Missouri's abundance of white oak in the Ozark Highlands Region makes our state an important manufacturer of oak barrels. Although only three cooperages within the state continue this ancient barrel-making trade, their efforts define many subtleties of Missouri's finest wines.

The most obvious reason barrels have been the traditional choice for storing wine is that they can be rolled from place to place. A barrel's special shape also allows it to absorb most impacts without smashing. But the major reason barrels play such an important part in winemaking history is not so readily visible.

Premium white and red wines are frequently matured in oak barrels to impart subtle flavors to the wine and add a healthy finish. Just as dominant grape varieties provide standards for wine production, white oak has endured as the wood of choice for barrels. In addition to the resilient nature of white oak, the wood contains natural sealants, called tyloses, that help to prevent leakage. For wine, tight barrels are essential—they simply must not leak!

Though the shape of the barrel, or cask, has remained relatively unchanged for close to 3,000 years, the wine casks used today are constructed to much more precise specifications. In fact, casks used by Missouri wineries are required to be accurate within a few tenths of a gallon. This precision is required in order for vintners to be able to produce premium wines that meet their exacting standards.

Just as the vintner is following meticulous steps toward creating award-winning wine, the cooper is also following exacting specifications honed by generations of craftsmen. The first, and perhaps the most important, step is the selection of the oak. Oaks that yield premium barrels are sound, have straight grains and are fairly free of knots and branch stubs. Second, the wood is milled, yielding bolts, or roughed-out barrel pieces. These are then refined to become the staves of the barrel. Staves are the thin pieces of wood, typically four inches or less in width, that form the body of the barrel.

As the barrel is raised, or begins to take shape, the staves are cupped to make them adhere. The staves are then assembled into metal truss hoops. Once in place, the barrels are heated over a small fire to set the shape of the cask.

Next, the barrels are charred on the inside. A torch shoots flames through the barrel until the right degree of charring is attained. This critical step is variable. Often the buyer of the barrel predetermines the degree of charring, which will greatly affect the finish of the wines stored within it.

Then a small groove, called a croze, is machined into the barrel so that it will accept the end pieces, called headings. Headings are then put on. These are most often flat-cut from oak timber then attached using flagging, a form of grass that helps to seal the seams. With the ends in place, the truss hoops are removed and permanent hoops are added. Next, the bung hole, or filling hole, is drilled through a selected stave and *voilà*, a barrel is born.

EXPLORE BARRELS OF FUN
A Producer of World Famous Oak Barrels

The Barrels of Fun store in Lebanon offers three attractions in one. The store offers barrel and wine giftware and provides guided walking or cart-driven tours of the barrel factory of the World Cooperage Company. Tours run every half-hour, the last one going out at 2:30 p.m.

The crafting of barrels is a fascinating process, typically regarded as an art. Although technology has been revolutionary in recent years, the most crucial elements of the craft are much the same today. First introduced in northern Europe around 400 B.C., wooden barrels were adapted by Romans for transporting wine. Today, the barrels must still be leak proof, free of glue, paraffin, liners, nails or any other such substances that would react with the wine and must facilitate a breathing process that will allow evaporation of alcohol and water, concentrating the wine. World Cooperage Company uses only white oak because of its extra toughness, resilience, strength and character. The large thick rays help the barrels remain dimensionally stable whether wet or dry.

The Boswell family has been dedicated to producing high-quality oak barrels for four generations. Founded in 1912 by T.W. Boswell, Independent Stave Company was initially focused on producing white oak staves and heading for cooperage. At that time, the demand for the barrels was primarily for storage and transport of household goods and liquids such as flour and oil. By the 1950s, Boswell had expanded into the bourbon barrel business, which led to the establishment of the wine barrel division, World Cooperage Company. The company is now managed by Brad Boswell and Amie Boswell Dewane, who carry on the tradition of commitment to quality. This commitment has turned a single man's small business into the largest cooperage company in the world.

The barrel division has three cooperages, located in Missouri, Kentucky and France. Combined, the facilities can produce more than 4,000 barrels a day. The Kentucky cooperage focuses on bourbon barrels and the location in France provides European winemakers with different barrel types. The Lebanon facility is the only one that produces both bourbon and wine barrels. Made from the premium fine grain timber unique to the Ozark Mountains, the barrels produced here account for more than 50 percent of the barrels made in the entire world. The staves have an average of two or three more growth rings per inch than those made elsewhere, earning them worldwide renown as the tightest American oak available.

Missouri's wine barrels are more than just storage and transport containers— they impart color, aroma, flavors and harmony. Visitors to Barrels of Fun may witness firsthand the crafting of a product that is so essential to the flavoring and finishing of their favorite Missouri wines.

Opposite page: A cooper, or barrel maker, demonstrates the ancient art of barrel making at the barrel factory of the World Cooperage Company in Lebanon.

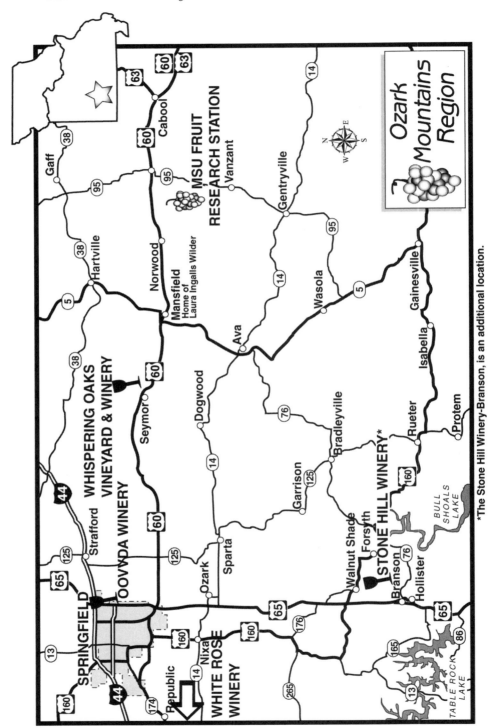

OZARK MOUNTAINS REGION

This region includes the White Rose Winery of Carthage, Whispering Oaks Winery in Seymour, OOVVDA Winery in Springfield, and Stone Hill's Branson Winery. Missouri State University's Fruit Experiment Station in Mountain Grove is also in this region. This is where much of the grape and wine research for the state takes place.

Once home to some of the state's wealthiest early industrialists,
Carthage retains some of Missouri's best-preserved early homes.

EXPLORING CARTHAGE

White Rose Winery

Antiques • B&Bs • Eats • Gas • Lodging • Parking • Restrooms
Carthage Convention and Visitors Bureau: (866) 357-8687
www.carthage-mo.gov

In 1841, Jasper County was created and named in honor of Revolutionary War hero Sergeant William Jasper. Rich in history and natural resources,
Carthage was chosen as Jasper County's permanent county seat.

Different bands of Native American Indians were removed from the area in
1825 to Kansas Territory by treaty. In 1837, many Osage returned due to the poor
conditions in Kansas. Missouri Governor Liburn Boggs called on the state militia
to expel them again. The event was known as the Osage War. A marker is located
at the southwest corner of the Jasper County Courthouse Square in Carthage.

A wealth of limestone, zinc and lead and an abundance of timber, prairies
and fertile river bottom land fueled an industrial boom in Carthage during the era
leading to the Civil War. The citizens of Carthage (and all of Missouri) were bitterly
divided over slavery. The bitterness erupted into what became known as the
Battle of Carthage. Many citizens fled the area. They returned after the war to find
their town in ruins. Industrial and agri-businesses began to reestablish themselves

after the Missouri Western Railroad arrived in 1872. The later addition of a second railroad, the Missouri-Pacific, sparked yet another industrial and commercial boom in the 1880s. The area also became well-known for its abundance of "Carthage marble." Many buildings and homes constructed of Carthage marble are still standing and immaculately preserved, making a tour of the town a treat.

The early construction of some of Carthage's most notable homes and other buildings transformed the community. It is a magnificent place to tour the grand estates of some of the state's early industrial leaders. A driving tour of Carthage reveals a wealth of Victorian and early 20th Century architectural styles. A survey in the 1970s nominated two districts of Carthage to the National Register of Historic Places. Visitors to picturesque Carthage can walk, cycle or drive the districts and enjoy some outstanding examples of these early architectural designs.

Nearby: While in Carthage, swing into the Route 66 Drive-In Theatre, then take a drive down the famed transcontinental highway to Lebanon to explore the Route 66 Museum or the Barrels of Fun Store.

Lodging

Days Inn • (417) 926-3152

Mountain Grove Motel • (417) 926-6101

The Triangle • (417) 926-6101

The drive-in theater on Route 66 is a popular stop for travelers.

Visitors to White Rose Winery will enjoy the unique setting that
includes majestic gardens and a relaxing fountain.

WHITE ROSE WINERY

13001 Journey Road, Carthage, MO 64836
(417) 359-9253
www.whiterosebed-breakfast.com
Hours of Operation:
Thursday through Tuesday 11 a.m. to 8 p.m.
Wednesdays by appointment only.

HOW TO GET THERE: From Hwy 71, take Hwy 96 east through Carthage, past
Kellogg Lake to County Road 130. Turn left and immediately turn left again onto
Journey Road. Turn immediately right through the stone gate and drive up the
lane and around the house to the portico entrance.

For Jim O'Haro, winemaking was a hobby that he dabbled in occasionally
for the last forty or so years. In the past, Jim had worked as a computer
engineer. He helped design spacecraft that can be seen at the Smithsonian.
He also worked in hydroponics, the satellite business, apartment rehabilitation,
and finally, cemetery management. The cemetery job brought him to historic
Carthage, where he and his wife, Jan, fell in love with a 100-year-old Irish estate
made of Carthage marble. They began to realize their longtime dream of retiring to
run a bed & breakfast. They purchased the estate and soon began operation as the
White Rose Bed & Breakfast.

Jim continued his hobby of winemaking and planted a few acres of
grapevines near the B&B. With his background in science, Jim had kept meticulous

written records of which formulas worked best for him as well as changes that took place in his wines over time. With winemaking, nothing is an exact science, but Jim's background has contributed to his understanding of the chemical processes involved in fermentation and aging. Jim says that from 2,500 to 3,000 chemical processes are going on. These processes don't end once the wine is in the bottle, either. Jim is the first to admit that winemaking is both an art and a science, and for him, it turned from a hobby to a passion. The wines he crafts are hand-picked, sorted, de-stemmed, crushed, fermented, racked, fined and bottled without the use of pumps or other modern technology. The only machinery used is an old press.

Shortly after offering their first wines to customers of the B&B, Jim and Jan realized the need for a winery to fill the enormous market in the southeast corner of the state. In 2005, White Rose Winery produced about 1,000 gallons of wine from approximately four acres of vines. Being the only operating winery in this area, they still believe that there is a local demand for much more than they can provide. In hopes of helping to meet that demand, the O'Haros are working with a friend who hopes to obtain the necessary licensure to open another winery in the area.

Visitors to White Rose Winery will enjoy the unique setting that includes majestic gardens and a relaxing fountain. Lunch and dinner are served in the White Rose Restaurant. This recent addition to the operation specializes in "Irish Pub Grub." Offerings include Bally Canally Chicken (baked in Guinness and honey), seafood fettucine, reuben sandwiches, classic Irish soups and a delectable dessert menu. A day of "drinking in" the magnificent scenery and historic architecture of Carthage can be topped of with a unique Irish dinner, a bottle of fine wine and a comfortable night's stay at the White Rose Winery, Restaurant and Bed & Breakfast.

Jim O'Haro utilizes a background in science, extensive recordkeeping and, most of all, years of experience to produce the quality wines offered at the White Rose Winery.

WHITE ROSE WINE LIST

Current Offerings:

CABERNET FRANCE: A wine with deep shades of red and purple packed with intense fruit flavors and a long finish of dark chocolate, vanilla and ripe cherries.

CAYUGA WHITE: A light dry wine bursting with lemon and honey flavors.

CHAMBOURCIN: Aromas of fresh berries and fruits with hints of cinnamon and chocolate and intense flavors of raspberries, blackberries and herbal notes.

CHARDONEL: A full-bodied and crisp dry white with a complex nose of butter and oak, ripe apple and pear.

CLARET: A light red that is festive in color and taste.

LADY IN RED: A semi-sweet wine with aromas and flavors of dark fruit.

MARECHEL FOCH: Named for a WWI hero, this wine has deep character, deep color and low tannin. Spicy cherry aroma and a spicy plum finish.

NORTON: Deep and inky in color. Complex flavor and plum fragrance.

ST. VINCENT: Aromas and flavors of dark fruit in a Bordeaux-style wine with earthy, herbal notes on the nose.

ST. VINCENT NOUVEAU: The first bottling of this new vintage. Light and luscious with soft tannins.

SPRING RIVER RED: A unique blend with aromas and flavors of plums, raspberries and vanilla.

SPRING RIVER WHITE: A dry blend with citrus overtones, a spicy aroma and the taste of pears and apples.

STRAWBERRY: A light dry wine with a soft nose of strawberry and citrus and a mouthful of berries and lemon.

SWEET LADY IN RED: A sweet full-bodied wine in Bordeaux style with aromas and flavors of dark fruit.

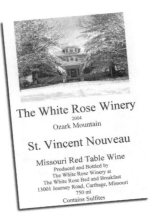

The White Rose Winery
2004
Ozark Mountain
St. Vincent Nouveau
Missouri Red Table Wine
Produced and Bottled by
The White Rose Winery at
The White Rose Bed and Breakfast
13001 Journey Road, Carthage, Missouri
750 ml
Contains Sulfites

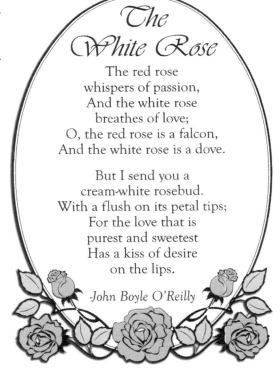

The White Rose

The red rose
whispers of passion,
And the white rose
breathes of love;
O, the red rose is a falcon,
And the white rose is a dove.

But I send you a
cream-white rosebud.
With a flush on its petal tips;
For the love that is
purest and sweetest
Has a kiss of desire
on the lips.

John Boyle O'Reilly

EXPLORING BRANSON

Stone Hill Winery–Branson

B&Bs • Bikes • Crafts • Eats • Lodging • Parking • Post Office • Restrooms
Branson Area Chamber of Commerce: (417) 334-4136
www.branson.com

Branson was nothing more than a quiet Ozark hamlet until the early 1900s. With the publication of the novel *Shepherd of the Hills*, however, things began to change. This book, written by Harold Bell Wright, flooded the community with curiosity seekers interested in the Ozarks. Visitors' camps housed many of these early tourists.

The completion of the Ozark Beach Dam near Forsythe in 1913 greatly increased recreation on the newly formed Lake Taneycomo. Then, in the 1950s, Table Rock Lake was formed by another dam. Fishermen and boaters increased their visits and haven't ceased since.

The 1960s brought another new attraction to Branson—one that was to change the town beyond its wildest dreams. When Hugo and Mary Herchend opened their small attraction atop Marvel Cave and called it Silver Dollar City, little did they realize what they were giving birth to. Next came the production of "Shepherd of the Hills," which was located on the site where the characters in Wright's novel originated.

With these two pillars of attraction firmly established, other acts followed. The first music act to hit the town was called The Baldknobbers. Their success in staging an Ozark country repertoire led to the infusion of additional acts.

Several regionally famous acts increased the number of visitors to Branson, but it wasn't until the Roy Clark Celebrity Theatre opened in 1983 that the town really began to attract national attention.

Today, there are scores of things to do in Branson. From music and drama to rides and recreation, you'll find more to do here than you could possibly accomplish in a single day's visit.

The Branson Visitors Center is the best place to get started before exploring Branson. From Highway 65, take the Highway 248 Exit and follow the signs. The visitors center and chamber of commerce are right next to one another. Their friendly staff will provide you with all of the maps and information you may need. As for places to stay, there are more hotels in Branson than you can shake a stick at. Contact the Chamber of Commerce number listed above for a complete listing.

Reprinted from Daytrip Missouri.

STONE HILL WINERY–BRANSON

601 State Highway 165, Branson, MO 65616

(417) 334-1897

Hours of Operation: Monday through Saturday 8:30 a.m. to dusk

Sunday 11 a.m. to 6 p.m. Tours start every 15 minutes.

HOW TO GET THERE: Stone Hill Winery in Branson is located on Hwy 165, two blocks south of Hwy 76 west.

Stone Hill's Branson winery offers one of the best free tours of any winery. You are led through the history of winemaking with interesting videos and memorabilia, and bottlers give demonstrations that, in addition to being informative, are also very entertaining. After the tour, the tasting room has samples of Stone Hill's award-winning wines. Each sample is presented with interesting background information and serving hints. There's plenty of grape juice for the kids (and adults), and an expansive gift shop.

Five-foot-high oak barrels that were housed in a St. Louis monastery, and thus survived Prohibition, now rest in Branson's Stone Hill location. Other than the winemaking and wine tasting demonstrations, there are no vineyards or large-scale wine production facilities here. As one tour guide says, "All we can grow on the hills here are rocks." If this visit piques your interest in Missouri wine country, a visit to Stone Hill in Hermann is definitely in order. Please see Stone Hill's Hermann entry for their wine list.

Leonard Kaminski, a.k.a. Santa, has been a fixture at Stone Hill Winery's Branson location since 1992 (when he's not attending to business at the North Pole). Visitors will enjoy his demonstration of making two spumantes: a golden and a blush.

WHISPERING OAKS WINERY

520 Lucky Road, Seymour, MO 65746

(417) 935-4103

Hours of Operation:

May through December 11 a.m. to 7 p.m.

January through April: Wednesday through Sunday Noon to 6 p.m.

HOW TO GET THERE: From Seymour, take US 60 east, turn left (or north) on Star Road. Turn right on Metney Hollow Road and continue to Severs Road. Turn right (or east) on Severs Road, go a mile and the winery is on the left.

When retired teachers Larry and Miriam Green began planting grapes on their farm near Seymour in 1997, the plan was to raise the grapes for sale to the state's wineries. The Greens' first plants came from a grower in Mountain Grove, along with a few from Gloria Winery. Two vineyards were created, one just off Severs Road and a larger one just west of the first. The project was a success and their grapes were healthy and flavorful. Wineries were buying grapes at a good price, and 21 years of teaching math at Seymour told Larry that opening a winery of his own was the next natural step.

Growing up in an Italian neighborhood where most of the families made their own wines, Larry had always been interested in winemaking. His recent retirement had given him the time and the means to pursue his interest. Miriam, also retired, taught art at Seymour for 35 years. She was a willing assistant in helping Larry realize his vision of being the "best lil ole winemaker around." In 2004, 11 acres of vineyards yielded about 10,000 bottles of wine, and the couple opened their winery just off of Highway 60.

The Greens joined the Missouri Grape Growers Association together, and Larry has attended numerous classes on grape growing and winemaking to help him perfect the craft. Their son, Nathan, is the only full-time employee, while their daughter, Rachael, helps part-time. The family estimated between 20 and 30 tons of grapes to be harvested in 2005. It's not unusual for their harvests to be so bountiful that the Greens recruit visitors to help pick grapes and then send them home with a few pounds to keep for themselves. This family-run winery offers a friendly atmosphere and a convenient location for visitors to enjoy.

WHISPERING OAKS WINE LIST

Current Offerings:
CATAWBA: A sweet white wine bursting with a medley of grape-filled flavor.
NORTON: A dry red wine. Full-bodied and complex with some fruity overtones.
ST. VINCENT: A dry red wine with delicious cherry overtones.
VIDAL BLANC: A semi-dry white wine. Light, refreshing, delicate flavor.
VIGNOLES: A semi-sweet white wine, somewhat Riesling in character.
WHISPERING OAKS RED: A sweet red wine, very fruity in nature.
WHISPERING OAKS ROSE: Light-bodied and crisp.
WHISPERING OAKS WHITE: A sweet white blend of a variety of white grapes.

Whispering Oaks Winery, a family-run establishment,
offers a convenient location and a friendly atmosphere.

OOVVDA WINERY

5448 N. Berry Lane, Springfield, MO 65803

(417) 833-4896

www.oovvda.com

Hours of Operation:

Tuesday through Saturday 11 a.m. to 8 p.m.

Sunday 2 to 8 p.m.

HOW TO GET THERE: The winery is located just three miles north of I-44 at Exit 80B(1), one-quarter mile west of the intersection of H and AA at the flashing red light on the south side of the road.

This new addition to the wineries of the Ozark Mountains Region is a small, family-owned and operated winery. Brian and Fran Overboe, owners and proprietors, are third and fourth generation winemakers, with family roots that trace back to 1192 in Norway. The acronym OOVVDA stands for Overboe's Own Viking Vintners Distinctive Alcohols. When pronounced quickly, the winery's name comes out sounding much like "uffda," the Norwegian word that translates into English as "oops," "uh-oh," or "good grief." Despite the humor, the Overboes take serious pride in their family's Viking heritage as well as the family history of making wine.

OOVVDA Winery offers many types of fruit wines, each available in a full range of sweetness from dry to sweet, depending on each customer's individual preferences. OOVVDA wines are made from the best fruits available, including estate-grown raspberries and cherries. Currants were also recently planted. The Overboes are proud to use only the highest quality, fresh Missouri fruits. The fruit is selected, picked, washed and prepared by hand. The estate fruits that are used are pesticide-free, with only the cherry trees getting an annual spray of dormant oil in the wintertime.

Fran adds, "Our philosophy is that there is enough fruit that we can share it with the birds, so we do not spray the raspberries—we prefer to let the birds take care of the pests! And all the fruit we pick is fruit that we would eat—it is clean and pretty, not to mention very tasty."

The winery opened its doors to the public in 2004 and is now serving an assortment of fresh fruit wines. The Overboes' two sons, Mason and Damon, were relieved to learn that their parents were opening a winery, as they were getting tired of eating all of the jelly that Brian was making from the berries grown on their five-acre farm. In fact, the two boys stepped up to the plate and helped their parents get the winery up and running, with Mason designing the website and Damon designing and printing the winery's custom labels.

They offer custom finishing, which means that you can have wine bottled to your individual preferences and accordingly labeled as "Made and Bottled by OOVVDA, Inc. of Springfield, MO for (your name or occasion here)." OOVVDA can customize your wine with little additional expense, making a wine for your personal cellar and enjoyment.

OOVVDA WINE LIST

Current Offerings:
BLACK BERRY
BLACK RASPBERRY
BLUEBERRY
CHERRY
PEAR
RED RASPBERRY

EASTERN REGION

The Eastern Region highlights only two wineries. Eagle's Nest Winery is located in Louisiana, a short drive north of St. Louis. Villa Antonio Winery is located a short drive south of St. Louis. Given this area's prodigious growth as a regional tourism destination, I expect that future editions of this book will see more wineries in this region.

Georgia Street is lined with Victorian storefronts,
and on the east end, there is a fantastic view of the Mississippi River.

EXPLORING LOUISIANA

Eagle's Nest Winery, Inn & Bistro

Antiques • Bikes • Canoes • Lodging • Museum
Post Office • Parking • Restrooms • Eats
Louisiana Visitors & Convention Bureau: (888) 642-3800
www.louisiana-mo.com

In 1808, French settlers began building a town that would soon be the shining star of northern Missouri. Louisiana was built Victorian-style on the sloping hills where the Mississippi River runs between Missouri and Illinois. As a trading post, Louisiana was so named because of its close ties to New Orleans. Rich with cultural history, Louisiana is now enjoying a sort of modern renaissance. What the Missouri Department of Natural Resources calls "the most intact Victorian Streetscape in the state" has undergone a transformation that has helped the town embrace its heritage. It's the perfect place to capture a glimpse of Victorian elegance mingled with Cajun flair.

In 2001, what was known as *The Provenance Project* began along Route 79, designated by the state as the first Scenic Byway. The route between Louisiana, Clarksville and Hannibal, Missouri, became known as "Fifty Miles of Art." Residents were given incentives for filling the existing Victorian buildings in the area with studios and galleries or other such establishments. Drawing more artisans to the area was a major theme of the project. Many of the artists and private citizens that invested their own resources into restoring historic buildings became eligible for public funds as well. The success of the project has been overwhelming. Be sure and take a drive down Route 79 and check out the numerous galleries and studios that now line the way. Annual studio tours are held during the last weekend of April and the first weekend of November. For more information, contact *The Provenance Project* at (573) 221-1033.

There are many galleries to be explored in Louisiana these days, including "Reflections of Missouri" by John Stoeckley, co-founder of the Eagle's Nest Winery. John is a pen-and-ink artist that has lived in Louisiana for more than 20 years. His gallery is located on Ninth Street. He and his wife, Karen, were the first to undertake a restoration project, investing much of their own time and resources to renovate four adjacent buildings on Georgia Street, creating the Eagle's Nest Winery, Inn & Bistro. Located on the corner of Georgia and Fourth Streets is their son's colored pencil art gallery, the Clark Stoeckley Gallery. There are many local artisans that perform live by appointment or by chance, including woodworkers, glassworkers and ironworkers. Louisiana is also known as the "Route 79 Mural City," proudly displaying more than twenty murals in the downtown area.

Also located in Louisiana is the St. Louis University Lay Center for Education and the Arts. There, artists and fans alike can get lost in the serenity of over 350 acres of hills, meadows, lakes and streams featuring two sculpture gardens. One of these gardens is called Story Woods. It is designed to stimulate the imaginations of children with its wonderful combinations of art, literature and nature.

Visitors to Louisiana will want to check out one or all of the town's six parks, or take a Pike County Tombstone Tour, visiting up to fifteen historic cemeteries. Victims of Indian massacres, Revolutionary and Civil War soldiers, statesmen, legislators and community leaders are buried here. There are also Protestant, Catholic, Jewish, African-American, community and family cemeteries. Riverview

Cemetery contains more than 14,000 graves, all overlooking the Mississippi River. For more information call the Pike County Tourism Commission: (573) 324-2077.

Located only an few hour away from I-70, Louisiana beckons for an entire weekend of exploration. A lot has been going on in the town and the surrounding area in recent years. The area is not only a dream-come-true for artists, but a weekend getaway for all.

Nearby: While in the area, be sure and visit the Clarence Cannon National Wildlife Refuge. Over 200 species of birds visit the 3,750-acre refuge each year. Visitors are welcome daily from sunrise to sunset. Spring and fall are the best times for viewing wildlife. Bald eagles are common to the area year-round, and during mating season as many as 1,000 may be seen. The refuge is located on County Road 206 in Annada, about 20 miles southeast of Louisiana.

Bed & Breakfasts

Applegate B&B
(573) 754-4322

The Eagle's Nest Inn
(573) 754-9888

Louisiana Guest House
(573) 754-6366

Meadowcrest
(573) 754-6594

Orthwein Mansion
(573) 754-5449

Riverview
(573) 754-4067

The Great Escape
(573) 754-3222

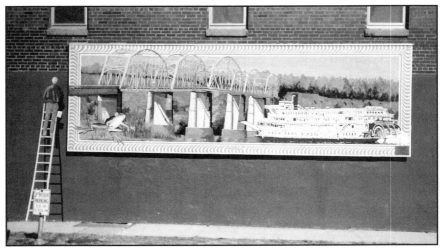

One of more than twenty murals located in Louisiana. This one of the Delta Queen, on Fourth Street, is by John Stoeckley, co-owner of the Eagle's Nest Winery, Inn & Bistro.

The Eagle's Nest occupies four adjacent historic buildings on Georgia Street.

EAGLE'S NEST WINERY, INN & BISTRO

221 Georgia Street, Louisiana, MO 63353

(573) 754-9888

www.theeaglesnest-louisiana.com

Call for hours.

HOW TO GET THERE: Located on the Illinois border just off of Hwy 54, Louisiana is north of St. Louis. It's just 12 miles northeast of Bowling Green, at the junction of Hwys 54 and 61. From Hwy 54, turn right onto MO-79/N Third Street. Travel less than one-half-mile and go left on Georgia Street.

After living in the small, historic river town of Louisiana for almost twenty years, John and Karen Stoeckley were becoming sad to see windows in the downtown area being boarded up as businesses closed and moved elsewhere looking for better opportunities. They became involved in a movement known as *The Provenance Project.* According to Karen, "We wanted to get more of our high school and college kids to stay in town after graduation. When they were done with school, our young people were all moving away."

The Stoeckleys felt the need to do something that would help revitalize the Victorianesque downtown district and attract people and businesses back to the area. The movement was also an effort to draw more artists and artisans to the region, rejuvenating Louisiana's downtown area and transforming the region into

At the Eagle's Nest Winery, Inn & Bistro, the Victorian architecture
(as well as numerous works of art) can be enjoyed both inside and out.

a charming and romantic mini-destination for visitors from St. Louis, Kansas City and points in between. Thus far, the plan has worked like a charm.

"A lot of good things are happening," Karen said.

In what became a regional effort at preservation and rejuvenation, the Stoeckleys undertook the first major project on their own, when they recognized the need for a winery in the northeastern part of the state. In just a few years, they have transformed four historic buildings in the downtown district into a charming winery, accompanied by the area's first gourmet restaurant, a conference center, a cooking school and an inn. The various ventures became collectively known as the Eagle's Nest.

The Eagle's Nest Winery currently offers six of its own wine varieties, with each wine named for some part of the town's cultural history. For example, early pioneers that set off from Pike County and navigated the Mississippi River were known as "Pikers." These men had a reputation for being somewhat haggard-looking by the end of their travels. Once they found a place to settle, they would send for their families. According to Karen, when the women arrived, they "had a reason to blush" at the scruffy appearances of the men. This piece of regional history yields us Pikers Blush, a light, fruity and slightly sweet varietal. Be sure and inquire about the names of the other Eagle's Nest wines when you are visiting.

Cory Bomgaars of Les Bourgeois Winery takes the lead in hand-crafting the unique wines offered by the Eagle's Nest. The Stoeckleys are very pleased with their working relationship with the staff at Les Bourgeois. Karen notes that within the state there is a trend of larger wineries with ample production capabilities helping to supply the smaller wineries, and the vintners seem to really enjoy it.

"Cory and the others at Les Bourgeois have been tremendously helpful and very good to work with," Karen adds.

The Stoeckleys are impressed with the way that the people within the wine industry are eager to help each other. The Eagle's Nest offers a selection of wines from many other Missouri wineries, as well as a limited number of wines from Napa Valley, California. The Stoeckleys regularly feature wines from newly opened wineries around the state. Each year, the Eagle's Nest hosts a Winter River Fest and invites seven wineries from around the state to have their wines featured. Each October, the winery also holds a Winemaker's Dinner, with six courses, each accompanied by a different wine. Karen makes French chocolate truffles to enjoy with her favorite wine, the Port.

The restaurant menu at the Eagle's Nest Bistro consists of a variety of gourmet dishes and desserts, and the dining area offers a majestic view of the Mississippi River. Karen studied culinary arts in Italy, France, Japan and America. She is also food editor for *Missouri Life Magazine*. When it comes to fine food, she's got plenty of experience. Her unique menu is made up of specialty breakfasts, lunches, dinners and desserts, plus specials of the day (such as the delectable Cajun Chicken Pasta). Karen is proud to offer "the only place in town without a deep fryer."

The oldest of the four buildings that make up the Eagle's Nest dates back to 1859. In the center of the buildings is a wine garden and patio. A 10-foot, 100-year-old stone wall provides protection from the wind in cooler weather and helps maintain a cooler climate during the hot summer months. It's the perfect place to dine if you are looking for a fantastic, secluded outdoor area.

After a day of relaxing at the winery or exploring Louisiana, the inn at the Eagle's Nest is the perfect place to rest your weary head. It offers seven rooms, each with televisions, phones, luxurious bathrobes and private baths. You can relax in the jacuzzi tub in the solarium room or at the bistro or coffee bar. There is a private guest lounge overlooking the garden, and even more features yet to come, including an elevator and additional rooms.

On your wine country adventure, the Eagle's Nest is one stop that should not be missed. It offers a step back in time with all of the comforts of today.

THE EAGLE'S NEST WINE LIST

Current Offerings:

BUFFALO FORT NORTON: Missouri's own Norton grape blended with a Colorado Cabernet and aged in oak barrels creates a wine with a bouquet of violet and earth tones and a rich fruit flavor.

MISSISSIPPI RIVER ROUGE: This light style red wine is made with Chambourcin, Cabernet and other red grapes for a delicious semi-dry finish.

PIKERS BLUSH: Made with the Native American Catawba grape that reflects the seasons, sun and rain in a light, fruity and slightly sweet finish.

RED BUD: A blend of Catawba and French-American hybrid red and white grapes, this semi-sweet wine leaves the taste of raspberry or cherry tones on the palate. Served chilled.

RIVIERA DE SEL: A blended, crisp semi-dry wine in the French tradition leaves tones of citrus and spice on the palate.

SWEET LOUISIANA BASYE: A semi-sweet to dry blend of Vidal and Muscat grapes is full of floral aromas and a taste of tropical fruit with a crisp subtle finish.

The Italian heritage of the Polesel family gives a home-style feel to Villa Antonio Winery.

VILLA ANTONIO WINERY

3662 Linhorst Road, Hillsboro, MO 63050

(636) 475-5008

www.villaantoniowinery.com

Hours of Operation:

May to October: Wednesday through Sunday 11 a.m. to 6 p.m.

Extended Patio Hours on Friday and Saturday Evenings

HOW TO GET THERE: Travel I-55 South to Exit 180 (Pevely). Turn right onto Route Z and travel 1.1 miles. Turn right onto Sandy Creek Road and travel 2.7 miles. Turn left onto Johnston Road and continue to Linhorst Road. Turn right onto Linhorst Road and the winery entrance will be on your left.

Italian wine country is closer than you think. In fact, it's less than 45 minutes from downtown St. Louis. On a rustic and relaxing farm owned by retired electronics store owner Antonio Polesel and his wife, Fernanda, is a small family-run winery that exquisitely preserves the distinctive influence of Antonio's birth and upbringing in northern Italy.

Villa Antonio means "Tony's house" in Italian, and that's exactly what the winery started out as. The Polesels refer to the establishment of the winery as "retirement gone haywire." Nevertheless, it is a fulfillment of a life-long dream of

Antonio "Tony" Polesel relaxes on the porch. Villa Antonio means "Tony's house" in Italian.

Antonio's. He's been making wine since he learned the art from his father and crafted his first varietal while still living in Italy.

Antonio (Tony) and Fernanda moved to the 40-acre farm after retiring in the 1990s. The land had plenty of picturesque, gently sloping hills covered with fields and pastures. Antonio began to visualize rows of grapevines covering them and planted the first vines. The winery now boasts seven acres of vineyard with more than 4,000 vines. Villa Antonio produces about 3,000 gallons of nine wine varieties, with plans to add at least three more varieties in the near future.

The winery's tasting room is located in an historic 1800s cabin that the family remodeled themselves. Tony is not only a skilled winemaker but also a talented craftsman. He made the tasting room's bar and wine rack from trees on the property. His son and general manager, Thomas, is an engineer by trade and oversaw the addition of a detailed outdoor pavilion and patio.

Villa Antonio offers seven-course, Old World gourmet dinners made from scratch by Fernanda herself. Dinner is served in one of the two fireside dining rooms in the cabin or on the cabin deck and new pavilion. Fernanda's specialty is traditional Italian cookies called biscotti, but by reservation she will prepare a mouthwatering Italian-style dinner that may include one of several recipes that utilize fruits and vegetables grown right on the premises. The dinners are intended to be opportunities for guests of Villa Antonio to interact with the staff and other guests. The claim is that people seldom leave Fernanda's dinners without having made new friends.

The Polesels' "do-it-yourself" attitude is reflected in virtually every aspect of their establishment. Sometimes called the "best kept secret in Jefferson County," Villa Antonio had times when they first opened when almost no one showed up. However, as the "secret" gets out, business has doubled in volume every year.

The grounds of Villa Antonio Winery are the perfect place to "seal the deal."

Despite this growth, the Polesels insist that they don't want to become a massive operation but will strive to keep it small and offer visitors a personal touch. The Polesel family is working together, making sure that a visit to Villa Antonio will rank among the best in terms of product and service.

VILLA ANTONIO WINE LIST

Current Offerings:
CAYUGA WHITE: A light dry white with a fruity character and a hint of oak.
CHAMBOURCIN: A full-bodied, dry, oak-aged red with a fruity aroma.
CHARDONEL: A full-bodied dry white with intense flavor and aroma.
GOCCIA d'ORO: A special blend of premium white grapes.
NORTON: A rich, full-bodied dry red with spicy overtones and berry flavors.
ROSETTO: A semi-sweet blush with a fruity character.
ROSSO VALENTINO: A light sweet red with a wonderful aroma and a lingering, fruity flavor.
SEYVAL BLANC: A crisp, dry white with a fruity character and a hint of oak.
VINA ROSA: A light, oak-aged, dry red varietal.

Recent Arrivals
in the Eastern Region

CLAVERACH FARM & VINEYARDS

570 Lewis Road, Eureka, MO 63025
(636) 938-4996
www.claverach.com

Claverach specializes in the production of wines bottled with minimal filtration or other intervention. There are about seven acres of vines planted with Norton, Petite Verdot, Chambourcin, Seyval, and Vignier grapes. The name Claverach is Welsh for "Clover Fields," and in fact, clover is grown in the vineyards to naturally enrich the soil. This is central to their sustainable farming philosophy. Currently, Claverach wines are available at many of the fine wine shops and restaurants in the St. Louis area. Check website for hours and availability.

COPIA URBAN
WINERY & MARKET

112 Washington Avenue, St. Louis, MO 63101
(314) 621-7698
www.copiawine.com
Hours of Operation:
Open Daily 9 a.m. to 11 p.m.

As a new addition to the eastern wine region, Copia Urban combines traditional American cuisine with a progressive twist. The wine market offers an array of products from gift baskets to wine accessories to gourmet food items, as well as a vast selection of wines from around the world.

The winery exhibits high ceilings, warm hues and exposed brick walls. The open display kitchen equipped with a brick oven is situated at the back of the restaurant, while a glass-enclosed wine cellar, reaching from floor to ceiling, separates the main dining room from the bar. Enjoy a bottle of wine and an assorted cheese plate in the courtyard, in the upper and lower wine cellars, or by the fireplace in the lounge area. Copia Urban Winery has accommodations for any occasion.

Copia Urban is the third urban winery in the United States. It is located in the downtown loft district of St. Louis. All of their current house wines are through a partnership with Les Bourgeois. See website for their complete wine list.

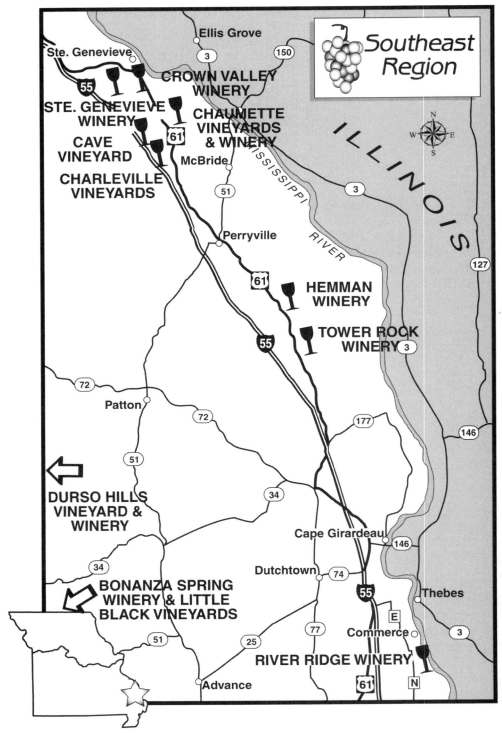

Ellis Grove

Ste. Genevieve

CROWN VALLEY WINERY

STE. GENEVIEVE WINERY

CHAUMETTE VINEYARDS & WINERY

CAVE VINEYARD

McBride

CHARLEVILLE VINEYARDS

Perryville

HEMMAN WINERY

TOWER ROCK WINERY

ILLINOIS

MISSISSIPPI RIVER

Patton

DURSO HILLS VINEYARD & WINERY

Cape Girardeau

Dutchtown

BONANZA SPRING WINERY & LITTLE BLACK VINEYARDS

Thebes

Commerce

RIVER RIDGE WINERY

Advance

SOUTHEAST REGION

The southeastern wine region includes a visit to Missouri's oldest permanent settlement and some great drives through gorgeous rolling Ozark terrain. This corner of the state was a particular highlight for me, given its rich, early French history. In fact, Ste. Genevieve holds a full quarter of all surviving French Colonial architecture in the Western Hemisphere.

This region stands out for offering the whole array of winery experiences—from one of the smallest to one of the largest. This area has seen extensive development in recent years that firmly anchors it as a long-term quality tourism destination. Come and explore—to appreciate yesterday's pioneers, and to embrace new traditions now taking root.

The Bolduc House, built in 1770, is regarded as the most authentically restored French-American house in the nation. It is open for tours April through November.

EXPLORING SAINTE GENEVIEVE

Cave Vineyard, Charleville Vineyards, Chaumette Vineyards & Winery, Crown Valley Winery, Sainte Genevieve Winery

B&Bs • Eats • Historic Homes • Lodging • Museums
Parking • Post Office • Restrooms
Sainte Genevieve Tourist Information Center: (573) 883-7097 or (800) 373-7007
www.ste-genevieve.com

Sainte Genevieve, regarded as the oldest permanent settlement in the state, was established by French Canadians in the 1730s who followed Pere Marquette, Joliet and LaSalle down the Mississippi to settle the Illinois Country. "Ste. Gen" was named in honor of a female saint—the patron saint of Paris. Founded on the western bank of the Mississippi River, Ste. Gen marked the French foothold on the western frontier. The population of the town grew quickly because of its convenient river location, access to Ozark lead mines, abundant salt springs and rich gumbo soil.

In 1762, the territory was transferred to Spain and the young town became an outpost for the Spanish government. The French-American town continued to grow rapidly and absorbed a wide mix of cultural influences. Life was more communal among the French-Americans than among their English counterparts, and French and Native Americans lived in relative harmony.

Though it was the fertile river bottoms that allowed pioneers to thrive, the Mississippi River also devastated the community several times. One of the most severe floods came in 1785, when the city was covered by more than fifteen feet of water. The town was then moved to its current location, a bit farther from the river. It now sits beyond the reaches of all but the highest of floods. In later years, as river traffic and mining interest decreased, agriculture and German settlement helped the town survive.

Ste. Genevieve contains the largest number of surviving French Colonial houses in the United States. Numerous sites are open to visitors, some of which are early vertical log cabins—the preferred construction method of settlers here. The mix of commerce and cultures, both then and now, makes Ste. Genevieve truly unique. Today many bed & breakfasts, restaurants, antique and specialty shops add to the experience of visiting the largest collection of 18th Century Creole, or French-American, structures in the Western Hemisphere.

A good place to begin exploring is the Great River Road Interpretive Center located at 66 South Main Street (corner of Main & Market). They provide a complete listing of historic homes and museums. Their phone number is (800) 373-7007. Be sure to watch their Ste. Genevieve video. A walking tour tape is available at several B&Bs and at the information office. The tour of museum houses begins with the elegant Maison Guibourd Valle house at Fourth and Merchant. The next stop is the museum and then the Felix Valle House State Historic Site. The home tour also visits the Bolduc and Bolduc-LeMeilleur houses operated by the Missouri Chapter of Colonial Dames. Visit the Amoureaux House to view a wonderful scale model of the community, circa 1830. Across the road are the bottoms that were cultivated by the early farmers, who plowed in long, narrow strips from river to bluff.

Be sure and visit the Bolduc House, constructed around 1770. The nearby Felix Valle House State Historic Site is also a must see. This vertical log house dates to 1790. Many other 19th Century churches and homes also add to the charm and appeal of the town's central square and its rich history.

The Steiger Haus Bed & Breakfast here is also worth noting. Instead of a typical night's stay, guests are treated to an evening of murder mystery theater as guests try to figure out "who dunnit." Invite a house-full of your friends and spend a night unlike any other. Call (573) 883-5881 for more information.

While exploring Missouri Wine Country in Ste. Genevieve County, check out the Little Hills Express for winery tours. The company offers round-trip scenic rides in a 10-passenger limo along the local wine route, or Route du Vin, from downtown Ste. Genevieve to tour the area's unique wineries–Cave, Crown Valley, Chaumette and Charleville. There are morning, afternoon and evening tours. Reservations are necessary. Call (800) 788-4948 or (573) 883-TAXI or visit www.littlehillsexpress.com.

For forty years, Ste. Genevieve has hosted Jour de Fete, an August festival honoring its French heritage. The name of the event translates roughly to mean "Day of Feast." The festival embodies crafts and crafters, arts and artisans, exhibits and tours, beer gardens and wine tasting, art shows and antiques, and historical tours and reenactments. Browse several hundred booths and local shops, or enjoy food, games, music, contests, and sporting events. The event also includes one of Missouri's finest car displays, the Classic Cruisers Car Show.

Nearby: Be sure to visit Kaskaskia Island, Illinois—reachable only through Missouri—to see the church and the Kaskaskia Bell, gifted in 1740 by King Louis XV. Be sure to hear their Lewis & Clark story. The kids will enjoy taking the nearby ferry across the Mississippi. Tour nearby Fort de Chartres, enjoy the underground boat ride at Bonne Terre Mine, hike in beautiful Hawn State Park on Route 32, (573) 883-3603, and learn about Missouri's lead belt at Missouri Mines State Historic Site. There are also great hiking trails in the Whispering Pines and Pickle Creek Natural Areas located nearby.

Bed & Breakfasts

Chateau Sainte Genevieve
(573) 883-2800

Inn St. Gemme Beauvais
(573) 883-5744 or (800) 818-5744

Somewhere Inn Time
(573) 883-9397

Jon Hael Gasthaus
(573) 883-5881

Falk House
(573) 883-5881

Southern Hotel
(573) 883-3493

Main St. Inn
(573) 883-9199 or (800) 918-9199

Steiger Haus
(573) 814-5881

Annual Events

February: King's Ball—a 200-year-old tradition
May: Annual Spring House Tour, Garden Walk, La Fete Française
June: Missouri Antique Show & Sale, Fort de Chartres
Rendezvous, French Heritage Festival
August: Jour de Fete—the area's largest craft fair, Family Festival
September: Fort Kaskaskia Traditional Music Festival
October: Fall Harvest Festival, Autumn Daze
November: Winter Rendezvous
December: Annual Country Christmas Walk, Historic French Christmas

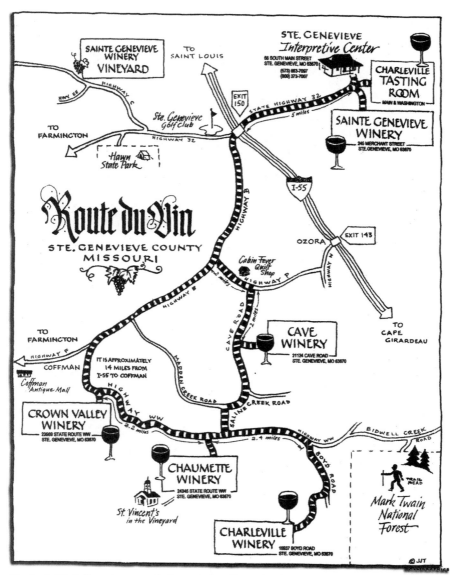

Route du Vin is the primary route through Ste. Genevieve's wine country. Be sure to request a copy of the "Discover the Mississippi River Hills" map at the Ste. Genevieve Tourism Information Center, or at one of the area wineries.

NATIONAL TIGER SANCTUARY
Preservation through Education
(573) 483-3100 or (877) 317-3100
www.nationaltigersanctuary.org

HOW TO GET THERE: Located 12 miles west of Sainte Genevieve in Bloomsdale. Take US 61 West to I-55. Take Exit 157 toward Bloomsdale. Travel west on Route Y about a quarter-mile and you will reach the sanctuary.

A Close Encounter with Wildlife Made Possible by the National Tiger Sanctuary

We had already forded a rockbed creek that drowned the entire Jeep, as we charted a quick course between towering sycamores. After ratcheting the Jeep into 4-Lo, we pointed 'er up an impossibly steep, rock-strewn mountain trail. After several tight maneuvers, we enter flat land again.

To my side, I sense movement in the overgrowth. Despite the blur of orange speed, my eyes lock with the piercing predatory eyes of a 700-pound tiger, slung low, moving stealthily toward the open-topped Jeep, which had become momentarily bogged down by the thick overgrowth around us. Just then, my peripheral vision makes out four more male tigers sprinting toward the kill, honing in on their hapless prey (me). Just as my mental projector reels up the final showing of "this was your life," I exhale, feeling my final breath leave my body.

Keith's voice tugs on my moment, and my eyes refocus on the 20-foot fence just a foot away, all that separates 3,500 pounds of hungry tigers from me, their prospective dinner. I live to see another day...

Be sure to visit the sanctuary, especially if you have kids. This visit is like nothing you'll ever see again. The sanctuary has five tigers, one of which is an albino: Vincent, Dee, Paul, TJ, and Max. "They are all from the same litter and love public attention. They are animal ambassadors to help us become more aware of our environment," said Keith Kincaid, who operates the sanctuary with Judy McGee and Georgia Wohlert. Give their cats Siegfried and Roy a good ear rub too.

BONNE TERRE MINE:
Deep Earth Diving & Underground Boat Tours

"One of America's Top Ten Adventures" by *National Geographic*

Those of us that prefer to remain on *terra firma* have a host of descriptive terms for deep water: the drink, the inky depths, the abyss. A fear of the deep—and of the unknown—is practically universal. Now imagine coupling that fear of deep bottomless water with another healthy fear—a fear of going underground. Now add a billion gallons of water, remove your natural air supply, and stir.

It is in just such a place below Southeast Missouri's green fertile fields where thousands annually trek, choosing to leave the clear blue skies behind and walk down an old mule path underground to a flooded, abandoned lead mine to embrace an abyss on an unfathomable scale.

The town of Bonne Terre, French for "good earth," perhaps should have been named "good water." The community of Bonne Terre offers no clues to what lies beneath. The Bonne Terre Mine, once the world's leading lead producing mine, is now an internationally renowned scuba diving location. The diving here, dubbed deep earth diving, allows adventurous scuba divers to plunge right into the heart of Missouri's past—to glimpse a world reclaimed by nature.

The only telltale sign of the old mine's existence is the pyramid-sized chat pile that dominates the skyline, looming large over the town. Of the mine's five levels, the top level is dry, making it accessible to hikers and sightseers. The damp 62-degree air feels comfortable year round. Levels 2 and 3 are used for divers. As I enter the beginning of the mine's catacomb of enormous rooms, I crane my neck to scan its rock ceiling almost 100 feet above. I catch sight of some old scaffolding, ladders, an old dynamite case and a drill. Exactly as the workers left them on their last day of work almost 40 years ago. Tours of this top level are given to visitors who are not looking for an underwater experience. The electric-motor-driven pontoon boat allows everyone the chance to peer into the crystal clear water and to contemplate the inky depths that lurk in the shadows. It's an adventure your kids will not forget!

But the real magic is underwater, on the bottom three levels of the mine, which are completely flooded. Divers that have sampled the mercurial blue hues of the world's oceans come here in throngs to do just that. Thanks to 500,000 watts of light pumped throughout partially flooded mining chambers, visitors dive into a 58-degree water world—a world where time stands still.

After the mining facility closed in 1962, the workers left their tools of the trade where they lay. The hum of the pumps that had kept the mines dry ceased forever. Over the ensuing years, natural seepage of groundwater and springs slowly flooded the cavernous space, creating one of the world's largest subterranean lakes. The limestone rock, considered solid by most people, actually acts as one gigantic filter—straining out impurities, leaving the mine filled with clean, clear water.

One man's flooded mine is another man's treasure. Cathy and Doug Goergens, owners of West End Diving in St. Louis, opened it in 1981.

"The first time I walked in here," Doug said, "I couldn't believe the vastness of the mine. How huge it was. Pillars rising from 50 to 200 feet from floor to the ceiling. And the water was so clear. Since there's no salt water, no sea life, tide or current to stir the sediment, the water is just crystal clear. And it doesn't matter what the weather is doing outside. Inside it's constant temperatures year-round."

"Absolutely crystal clear—that's really the claim to fame of the Bonne Terre mine," Doug said. "It's like a time machine. You enter the mine, you enter the water, and you are literally going back in time. Time stopped down here in 1960. Diving the mine is very peaceful and tranquil. It's you and the element and that's it. It's a purist joy. Because its purist diving."

In such a foreign environment, safety always comes first. Every diving party has a guide. And every dive has a dive plan, which is discussed in detail before anyone dons his or her gear. Our group of divers said goodbye to the sun, entered the mine through the old mule entrance, and headed down into a series of stairs and circuitous pathways. Football field sized rooms wove between Herculean-sized pillars 50 feet in diameter. The roof of some rooms hovered a hundred feet above our heads in places. Bright lights illuminated our steps, but the shadows of this monstrously huge complex easily enveloped the majority of the mine system. It seemed to go on forever in every direction...

:::Splash::: As I drift to a depth of 40 feet, the lights from above illuminate the sky blue water with 100-foot visibility. I float along, weightless in the eerie silence of this ghostly place. I slowly ease myself forward with a few kicks of my fins, drifting only three feet above the contours of the mine's floor. Mammoth pillars loom large, and a distant overhead light, twinkling like a bright moon, helps me to keep my bearings. Fist-sized rocks are strewn across the mine floor—each and every one pried from this solid piece of limestone pursuing the mine's rich veins of lead—some of the purest that can be found in the entire world.

Beyond my 100-foot envelope of visibility a wall of impenetrable blackness awaits. For me, it seemed hungry, ready to consume a greenhorn diver like myself. The blackness seemed to draw me toward it like a black hole. It was a place devoid of all light and life. A place where fears take hold. A place that doesn't easily let go.

Remnants of Bonne Terre's bygone mining days haunt the dive: pick axes and shovels are still strewn about the mine. An ore car waits for a one-ton load of lead ore that will never come. Around another bend, a rock drill still juts from a hole drilled decades ago. A set of stairs once used by the miners to get to work leads into darkness to a timekeeper's shack below. A ladder still rests against a wall—now a useless climb to oblivion. A locomotive, once used to haul lead and laborers, rests upon its side like a shipwreck in an underground ocean. And upon the walls are telltale signs of the lode: thin, silvery, veil-like veins of lead ore, now a half-forgotten footnote to the building of a nation.

"Magnifique!" said Jacques Cousteau, when he dove at this underwater labyrinth in 1983. He and his crew came expecting to dive for a day, and ended up staying a week, my dive instructor tells me. Cousteau's visit literally put Bonne Terre on the diving map for good.

Doug summed it up well. "It's like a ghost town. It's like you're a cowboy cruising through town and nobody's home. It is a dive through history."

It is difficult to envision the hard life of a miner in these silent chambers. Working sometimes 500 feet underground, with only the light from a dim carbide headlamp, hundreds of men—generations of miners—toiled lifetimes away here assisted by railcars, mules, dynamite and good old Missouri can-do. These miners created a subterranean city complete with its own rail system, machine shops, buildings, and even a movie theater.

Bonne Terre mine operated from 1864 until the price and grade of lead ore dropped and in 1961 the mine closed forever. It was the largest lead mine in the world. Up to 5,000 men were employed here by the St. Joseph Lead Company at the peak of production. From solid rock they removed some 30 million tons of ore. *Thirty million tons.* In their path they have left gothic pillars and sweeping stone arches and a series of cavernous rooms, some measuring 200 feet tall and several hundred feet across, and a labyrinth of tunnels and shafts. The mine extends roughly one mile north and south, and two miles east to west, its five levels extending more than 300 feet below the surface.

Whether you are on a family vacation looking for a place to explore on a hot summer day, or a scuba diver who thinks you have seen it all, the Bonne Terre Mine offers more than a fascinating look into Missouri's past. More importantly, it offers a safe platform from which to explore, push your personal limits and contemplate the stories that must still lie guarded by its shadowy depths.

West End Diving offers scuba diving certification courses throughout the year. Or if you are a certified diver already, contact St. Louis-based West End Diving for more information on how to dive the mine. Call (888) 843-3483 or visit www.2dive.com. The high season for scuba diving is October through April. The high season for the boat and walking tours is May through September.

NOTES

SAINTE GENEVIEVE WINERY
245 Merchant Street, Ste. Genevieve, MO 63670
(573) 883-2800
www.saintegenevievewinery.com
Hours of Operation:
Open daily 11 a.m. to 5 p.m.

HOW TO GET THERE: The winery is located in Ste. Genevieve's French Colonial Historic District on Merchant Street, between Second and Third Streets.

Established in 1984, the Sainte Genevieve Winery is located in a 5,000-square-foot turn-of-the-century home. The winery features a complete line of premium and traditional wines from fresh grapes and fruit that is either grown in their 13-acre vineyard or purchased from area vineyards and orchards.

The winery and vineyard were started by Chris and Hope Hoffmeister on their 400-acre farm. One short year later, the winery outgrew the small farm building in which it was originally housed and the Hoffmeisters relocated to the current location. The winery's growth has not slowed since its inception and its owners are always planning for expansion. To ensure their capability to accommodate guests as they grow, their daughter, Elaine Mooney, recently returned from California State University with a degree in enology.

The second floor of this beautiful home has been transformed into a bed & breakfast called Chateau Ste. Genevieve. The elegant rooms are decorated in Queen Ann décor. A delicious gourmet breakfast is served in the morning.

When you visit the Sainte Genevieve Winery you will have a chance to share in the Hoffmeisters' love of wine. Stop in for a free tasting.

SAINTE GENEVIEVE WINE LIST

Current Offerings:

AMOUREAUX: A semi-sweet white blend of Vidal and Muscat Canelli grapes.

APPLE: Made from apples from Diebold's orchard in Southeast Missouri, this wine has wonderful authentic apple aromas.

APRICOT: Just a tinge of acid on the palate makes this wine taste refreshing.

BEAUVAIS: A dry red, hearty, very drinkable wine.

BLACKBERRY: One of the sweetest wines made at Sainte Genevieve Winery. Winner of numerous awards, including bronze at the 2006 Missouri competition.

BOLDUC: A semi-dry red blend of Chambourcin and Norton grapes. Blackberry and black pepper aromas and a full mouth feel.

CHERRY: Tastes just like cherry pie. A nice level of sweetness, combined with a spicy, cinnamon, clove on the palate. This wine wins the most awards.

CHRISTMAS PLUM: Made from fresh plums. Ideal for holiday gatherings.

CONCORD: Fermented dry, and sweetened to taste.

ELDERBERRY: Made from local wild elderberries. Very sweet, but very fresh.

LAROSE ROSE: Easy to drink, not too sweet, not too dry.

RED CURRANT: Crimson in color, and a marvelous taste.

RED RASPBERRY: Sweet, but has a little acid to balance it out.

SEYVAL BLANC: A dry white wine, barrel fermented, and aged in Missouri oak.

STE. GEMME: A semi-dry blend of barrel-aged Seyval and Vidal with a wonderful full mouth feel, just a tinge of oak aromas, and a lot of fruit on the palate.

STRAWBERRY: Pink colored and very smooth and semi-sweet.

VALLE RHINE: A semi-sweet white wine made in the traditional German Rhine style. A lot of red and green apple flavors and aromas.

VIDAL BLANC: Dry wine aged in stainless steel.

Saltpeter Cave was named by early French settlers
who used the saltpeter they mined to make gunpowder.

The tasting room at Cave Vineyard was constructed over the top of Saltpeter Cave.

CAVE VINEYARD

21124 Cave Road, Ste. Genevieve, MO 63670

(573) 543-5284

www.cavevineyard.com

Hours of Operation:

April through November: Wednesday through Monday 11 a.m. to 6 p.m.

November through March: 11 a.m. to 5 p.m. Closed major holidays.

HOW TO GET THERE: Take I-55 Exit 150. Go west on Hwy 32 and take an immediate left onto Hwy B. Continue six miles, turn left onto Hwy P, continue two miles, turn right onto Cave Road and continue two miles to the winery.

In 1995, Marty and Mary Jo Strussion found 155 acres of land nestled in the rollings hills of eastern Ste. Genevieve County. With its large cave and picturesque topography, they decided it would be a perfect place to retire. They bought the land and built a house. Soon after, they began planting grapes and Marty's vision of building a winery began to take shape. By 2002, they had 14 acres of grapevines planted and had constructed a winery on top of the cave. The vineyard includes four varieties of grapes: Chardonel, Traminette, Chambourcin and Cynthiana/Norton. Their first harvest of these vines was in August 2003. Marty and Mary Jo are now producing close to a dozen wine varieties.

The cave was named Saltpeter Cave by early French settlers who mined it for saltpeter in the 1700s. They then used the saltpeter to make gunpowder.

As I sat at a cafe table in the cave, I savored a glass of wine and enjoyed the relaxed mood of this great spot. Today, the cave is mostly inhabited by wine enthusiasts kicking back and enjoying live music performances. Musician Josh Driskill performs every Saturday from mid-April through mid-November.

The cave is 35 feet high and 100 feet across and goes back 900 feet. It is lighted and has picnic tables. A stream travels under a bridge and collects in a pool near the mouth of the cave. A blend of comfortable seating and several rows of oak barrels complete the rustic ambience. A wooden walkway serves double duty as a dance floor if the mood strikes.

The coolness of the cave can be a nice break from the summer heat. In the wintertime, icicles that form around the mouth of the cave are a captivating sight. During cold weather, propane heaters are set up near the entrance to keep visitors comfortable. The cave is easily accessible by a paved path (only 200 yards from the winery to the mouth of the cave).

The tasting room, located on top of the cave, offers samples of fine wines. Visitors can sample the wines here, in the covered shelter out in front or in the cave. According to the Strussions, their most important accomplishment is bringing family and friends together to enjoy fine wine in a unique and relaxing atmosphere.

The coolness of the cave is a nice break from summer heat
and provides a perfect spot to enjoy a glass of wine.

CAVE VINEYARD'S
STRUSSIONE WINE LIST

Current Offerings:

CAVE ROCK RED: Full-bodied and fruity, this sweet red wine has a bouquet of berry fruits coupled with floral and spicy notes.

CHAMBOURCIN: A medium-bodied dry red wine. It produces a fruity aroma with hints of cocoa.

CHARDONEL DRY: A full-bodied dry wine that has been oak barrel-aged, producing a fresh and fruity taste on the palate. A pear aroma on the nose.

CHARDONEL LATE HARVEST: A full-bodied sweet dessert wine with a complex nose. It has flavors of dried apricot, figs and raisin with a hint of spice.

CHARDONEL OFF DRY: An off-dry fresh white wine with exotic fruit flavors of pineapple, dried apricot and coconut.

CHARDONEL SWEET: An elegant and fruity sweet wine. Aromas of apricot and raisin with a hint of spice.

NORTON: This full-bodied dry red wine has been barrel aged. It offers hints of black cherry and cinnamon.

TRAMINETTE: A full-bodied sweet wine with hints of rose petals and licorice.

WHITE CHAMBOURCIN: A semi-sweet rosé wine produced from Chambourcin grapes. It is fresh and fruity with hints of raspberry.

Joal Russell, co-owner of Charleville Vineyards.

Charleville Vineyards was named for François Chauvin
dit Charleville, who settled on the land in the 1700s.

CHARLEVILLE VINEYARDS

16937 Boyd Road, Ste. Genevieve, MO 63670
(573) 756-4537
www.charlevillevineyard.com
Hours of Operation:
Wednesdays and Thursdays Noon to 6 p.m.
Friday through Sunday 11 a.m. to 7 p.m.

HOW TO GET THERE: From St. Louis, take I-55 south to Exit 150. Turn right, then immediately left on Hwy B. Travel 14 miles and turn left on Route WW. Travel four miles, turn right onto Boyd Road and then right again onto the Charleville Drive.

In the mid-1700s, Joseph Chauvin dit Charleville was captain of the French Militia in Illinois. His youngest son, François, also served. François assisted George Rogers Clark, brother of William Clark, in the capture of Vincennes during the Revolutionary War. For his service, he was granted 200 acres of land near Ste. Genevieve. It was there that he died in 1793.

The descendants of the Charlevilles, Jack and Joal Russell, are pleased to introduce one of Sainte Genevieve County's newest wineries. Charleville Vineyard offers a charming, rustic country setting high above the Saline Creek Valley.

The winery was named in honor of François, Joseph, and Joseph's wife, Genevieve. Not far from the winery, in historic Ste. Genevieve, is where François Chauvin dit Charleville received his original land grants in *Le Grand Champ,*

An 1860s log cabin has been re-constructed at Charleville Vineyards
and now serves as a bed and breakfast and offers indoor seating.

loosely translated as the great field. Le Grand Champ offered early pioneers a unique system of farmland allotments. Each farmer worked one long strip of land reaching all the way to the river—ensuring that each farmer had easy access to river commerce. This great field, an integral part of early Ste. Genevieve life, can be seen from Amoureux House, a state historic site.

Back at the winery, a panoramic view of the vineyards awaits you from some of the highest points in Ste. Genevieve County. The Russells currently have 11 acres in production: seven of Chardonel, and four acres of Norton. The *St. Louis Post-Dispatch* wrote that Charleville has a "million dollar view." The view can only be rivaled by the great mix of people that make this their favorite hangout. As you relax on the patio enjoying the view, you can sip on one of Charleville's delightful hand-crafted wines. The Russells are proud to offer small lots of very distinctive wines for your tasting pleasure. They also offer hiking, bonfires, horseback trails and hay rides by arrangement. The Russells have also reconstructed an 1860s log cabin, which serves as a bed & breakfast and offers indoor seating.

Charleville Vineyard is also one of the only wineries in the state that has their own on-site microbrewery. With four to five beers on tap, you're sure to find a favorite. Their wheat and their amber are both very popular.

Charleville Vineyard is one of few wineries in the state that offers two wine tasting locations. The other is located in the historic district of French Colonial Ste. Genevieve, at the corner of Main and Washington. This location offers a tasting room and a gift shop that features Charleville wines, handmade quilts, willow baskets and gourmet coffees and candies, (573) 883-2308.

CHARLEVILLE WINE LIST

Current Offerings:

BARREL FERMENTED CHARDONEL: A fine dry white wine aged in Missouri oak. Fruity with oak overtones.

BARREL FERMENTED NORTON: A spicy yet smooth Norton with rich berry tones.

CHAUVIN: A dry white wine that is light and crisp.

FRANCOIS: Aged in Missouri oak, this is a light-bodied dry wine.

GENEVIEVE RIVARD: This sweet white wine is light and fruity.

LATE HARVEST CHARDONEL: Made when harvests are plentiful enough to leave several rows of grapes hanging until mid-November. Exquisitely sweet.

OFF DRY CHARDONEL: This Chardonel is light and slightly sweet.

Chaumette staff member Russ Carmichael describes Chaumette's wine selections to guests.

CHAUMETTE VINEYARDS & WINERY

24345 State Route WW, Ste. Genevieve, MO 63670

(573) 747-1000

www.chaumette.com

Hours of Operation:

March through October: Monday, Wednesday and Thursday 10 a.m. to 5 p.m.
Friday and Saturday 10 a.m. to 8 p.m.; Sunday Noon to 5 p.m.
November through February: Call for hours.

HOW TO GET THERE: From I-55, exit at Hwy 32 (Exit 15). Go west 100 feet to Hwy B. Go south 14 miles to Coffman, then take Hwy WW approximately 2.5 miles and look for the Chaumette sign.

Just a few miles from the historic riverport, in the heart of Ste. Genevieve County, are 310 acres of lush meadows and quiet splendor that are now home to Chaumette Vineyards & Winery. Amid gracefully rolling hills, carefully tended vines and captivating views is this new addition to Missouri's wine industry. The winery has received rave reviews. *Sauce Magazine,* a St. Louis publication, ranked the winery in the top five area wineries and restaurants.

The French name, "de la Chaumette," goes back as far as the 13th Century. It persisted through the Reformation and the French Revolution. In the 17th Century,

Jean de la Chaumette left France and came to the New World. Loosely translated as "little roofs" the Chaumette name now belongs to the winery and its products.

Hank Johnson is a retired executive president of a St. Louis insurance company. He discovered his appreciation for wine in the 1960s while traveling in Napa Valley, California. Since then, he has developed great knowledge of and appreciation for the wine business. In 1992, he planted his first vines. Today, Hank is a leading pioneer of new techniques to improve the health of the grapes. Most notably, his trellising methods have been shown to improve vine nutrition. The result is a variety of incredible wines. Johnson now has 30 acres of vines and bottles some 6,000 cases of wine a year.

Chaumette holds true to the region's French heritage. The tasting room is patterned after the vertical-log houses of early French Colonial Ste. Genevieve. An art gallery and gift shop are packed with genuine French merchandise. French delicacies are offered for weekend lunches. The wines are vinified in a French style. French entertainers are occasionally present. There is a garden of French herbs and a boules court. Boules is a French game similar to bocce. True to the French rules, you must play with a glass in your hand.

During one-hour tours, visitors can examine different trellising methods that are used for growing Chaumette's grapes. The tours teach the difference between the Smart-Dyson Ballerina, Vertical Shoot Positioned and B-Lateral Kniffen methods. The different styles of trellis were set up after consulting with Richard Smart, a leading authority on grapevine trellising. Reservations are required.

Hank Johnson also conducts informative and fun weekend classes that will enable all visitors to verbally describe their appreciation for a wine's unique tastes, aromas and mouth feel. Call the winery for more information.

St. Vincent's in the Vineyard Chapel is situated on a wooded hillside above
a small lake with a magnificent view of the valley and the vineyards of Chaumette.

What vision of France would be complete without an historic chapel? Visit Chaumette's own St. Vincent's in the Vineyard Chapel, which is available for weddings, receptions, banquets and other events.

Johnson's vision of a French-style vineyard and winery has taken shape nicely in the pastoral setting of central Ste. Genevieve County. Take a journey to Provence without ever leaving Missouri.

CHAUMETTE WINE LIST

Current Offerings:
ASSEMBLAGE: A full-bodied blend crafted in a northern Rhone style. Aromas of cherry, strawberry and citrus peel, with hints of black pepper and spice.

BOUVET BLANC: A semi-sweet white wine that is light and fruity with aromas of pear, peach, honey and a hint of spicy ginger.

DRY CHARDONEL: Crisp, clean and light-bodied with citrus aromas.

ESTATE CHARDONEL: Burgundian in style. Full-bodied with apple and pear, then tropical fruit and mango, finishing with hints of vanilla and toast.

HUGUENOT RED: A sweet red wine with an enticing blend of raspberry and cherry.

LATE HARVEST CHARDONEL: A sweet white wine. Full-bodied with rich flavors of apple, honey and apricot.

MISSOURI BLUSH: A light-bodied, fruity, semi-sweet red wine. Aromas of cherry, raspberry and citrus peel.

NORTON: A dark, dry red wine. Tastes of cherry, leather, smoke and cigar box. Aged in American oak. Characteristics reminiscent of a fine Syrah.

THEBEAU CHARDONEL: Aromas of pineapple, lemon zest and vanilla.

SEMI-DRY CHARDONEL: Light-bodied with aromas of apricot and tropical fruit.

"SPONTANEOUS" CHARDONEL: Produced by spontaneous fermentation from wild yeasts present on the grapes. Citrus aromas of grapefruit and Meyor lemon, with a supple, round mouth feel.

Regal gates welcome guests to the sprawling Crown Valley estate.

CROWN VALLEY WINERY

23589 State Route WW, Ste. Genevieve, MO 63670

(866) 207-9463

www.crownvalleywinery.com

Hours of Operation:

April to October: Monday through Friday 11 a.m. to 5 p.m.

Saturday & Sunday 11 a.m. to 7 p.m.

November to March: Monday through Sunday 11 a.m. to 5 p.m.

HOW TO GET THERE: From I-55, take Hwy 32 west. Make a quick left onto Hwy B. Travel 14 miles on Hwy B. Turn left on Route WW at Coffman. Crown Valley Winery is one-quarter mile on the right. From US Hwy 67, take Hwy 32 east, through four stoplights. Continue straight on Hwy OO for one mile then turn left onto Hwy F. Travel 12 miles on Hwy F, turning right onto Route WW at Coffman. Crown Valley Winery is one-quarter mile on the right.

Joe Scott, owner and proprietor of Crown Valley Winery, spent a large portion of his youth in the Coffman area. Various business interests and a love for the countryside led him to acquire some 8,000 acres of land here, including an Angus beef ranch and a pig farm. In 1998, Joe introduced grapevines that he acquired from neighbor and owner of Chaumette Vineyards, Hank Johnson. He originally planned to simply sell the grapes but soon realized that he had an ideal spot on which to build a winery of his own.

Upon his decision to build, Joe flew to California to tour the vineyards of the famed Napa Valley and the West Coast. Inspired by the Fess Parker Winery in

Santa Ynez, he began plans for what would become a 44,000-square-foot building constructed of stone, copper, carved oak, wrought iron and stained glass. The structure houses the complete winery production process, from crush pad to automated bottling equipment. Forty-minute wine tours are offered and are a perfect crash course in winemaking. One feature of the tour is the tank room, which contains 39 stainless steel tanks that hold up to 110,000 gallons of wine, equal to 500,000 bottles. Two man-made caves were formed to allow Crown Valley's wines to age in oak barrels. With nearly 850 barrels, each holding almost 60 gallons of wine, it's an impressive site indeed.

The vineyard consists of almost 200 acres of vines. Crown Valley boasts more Norton grapes than any other vineyard in the country. Buffalo, elk, donkeys goats and even llama call the Crown Valley estate home. There was even an island built to accommodate two swans. Visitors 21 and over can hop on the Crown Valley Trolley and take in all of the sights of the carefully tended vineyards and manicured landscapes, followed by a mini safari to see the animal life.

Visitors to Crown Valley Winery are quick to liken it to something straight out of Napa Valley. For a small fee, visitors can sample seven wines from a list of Crown Valley's 36 offerings and receive a souvenir wine glass.

Crown Valley also has several other outlets, located in Farmington, St. Louis and Clarksville. Crown Valley's Farmington wine store is located at 930 East Woodlawn, right off of Highway 67. Call (573) 431-9992.

Crown Valley's store in St. Louis is called The Wine Experience. It is located near Highway 270 at 12478 St. Charles Rock Road, in the same plaza as Best Buy and Office Depot. Call (314) 739-4722 for directions and information.

Or visit the Port House, situated inside the private resort Tievoli Hills, located just off of Highway N in Clarksville, Missouri.

Two man-made caves house nearly 850 barrels of Crown Valley wines.

CROWN VALLEY WINE LIST

Current Offerings:
BLACKBERRY WINE: Juicy and sweet, ripe and fresh with a rich texture.
CHAMBOURCIN: Deep burgundy in color, aged in American and French oak barrels for 20 months. Fruity aromas with hints of cocoa and complex spices.
CHARDONEL DRY: A dry white wine aged nine months in stainless steel. Fresh and fruity with pear and lemon flavors and has a long finish.
CHARDONEL LATE HARVEST: A white wine with intense flavors of ripe fruits, dried apricots, figs and raisins. The rich texture and well-balanced structure on the palate ends with a hint of vanilla and honey.
CONCORD: A sweet and fruity Concord.
CROWN HERITAGE: An exclusive white Missouri blend with bright scents of ripe fruit, fresh lemon and a hint of honey and oak aromas. In the mouth you feel ginger, honey and tart pear that unfold into a long fresh finish.
CROWN PRESTIGE RED: A blend of Syrah and Grenache aged in French and American oak for nine months. Features red fruit aromas from the Grenache and intense spices from the Syrah.
FRONTENAC: A pleasant cherry aroma with berry and plum notes.
GEWÜRZTRAMINER: A flowery and spicy white with notes of licorice and rose. Full-bodied with a long and pleasant finish.
LEGACY: A full-bodied red wine with soft tannins with flavors of black currant that persist to the finish, plus scents of violet, dill, fresh figs, black pepper, cinnamon and blackberries.

Viognier

CROWN VALLEY WINERY
AMERICAN WHITE WINE

13% ALCOHOL BY VOLUME

MALVASIA BIANCA: A white wine aged with oak chips. A high intensity of fresh grapefruit, peach and pineapple with a touch of vanilla. A very full-bodied wine.

MERLOT VINTNER'S SELECT: A classic example of Merlot. Highly complex aromas with spices and fresh red fruits. Elegant and full-bodied with silky tannins.

MUSCAT OF ALEXANDRIA: A sweet white wine with fresh and subtle aromas of exotic fruits, hints of vanilla and spice and a rich and pleasant fruit finish.

NORTON: Made from Missouri's premier red grape, the Norton. Very soft tannins, complex berries and an intense, full-body finish. Aged for 10 months in French and American oak barrels.

PETITE SIRAH: A red wine made with grapes from Lodi, California. Aged 18 months in French and American oak barrels. It is unique compared to most Petite Sirahs thanks to its fruitier flavor.

PINOT GRIS: A classic Pinot Gris with honey, pear, peach and grapefruit flavors on the nose. The palate gives you a mouthful of apricot, pear, baked apple and vanilla, with an aftertaste of honey and grilled almonds.

PINOT NOIR: Made using the style of the Alsace wine region. Fresh notes of red berries with a light body throughout the palate, finishing with a note of refreshing raspberry. This red wine is best served fresh at 50 degrees.

PINOT NOIR VINTNER'S SELECT: A classic example of a Burgundy-style Pinot Noir. Aged exclusively in new oak, this red wine presents a typical aroma of red fruits, blended with violets and vanilla notes.

PORT: A Norton and Chambourcin Port aged in French oak barrels for 22 months. Aromas and flavors of black cherries in the forefront. Light raisin and prune notes are prominent. A hint of peppery spice and a toasty caramel note from the oak barrels. Richly fruited but complex. Mouth-filling, yet not too sweet or rich.

RASPBERRY WINE: Sweet and crispy with fresh raspberry flavor, the palate is sweet and refreshing.

ROSÉ: A blend of Chardonel, Grenache and Chambourcin. A fresh and fruity wine.

SAUVIGON BLANC/COLOMBARD: A white blend of half Sauvignon Blanc and half Colombard that boasts intense, complex aromas of grapefruit and exotic fruit, with a touch of mocha and vanilla. Fresh and fruity with a long and pleasant finish.

SEYVAL BLANC: Aged 16 months in oak barrels, this white wine presents highly complex aromas of fruit and hints of vanilla. Dry and crisp with a fresh, clean taste. Oak aging adds hints of butter and honey.

STRAWBERRY WINE: Elegant and sweet, ripe and fresh.

TRAMINETTE: A new and upcoming variety in Missouri, the nose of this white wine presents aromas of litchi, rose petals and licorice, with a subtle hint of vanilla. Full-bodied with a long and fresh finish and a note of honey.

VIGNOLES: A bouquet of flowers and exotic fruits on the nose with a hint of coconut and vanilla. The fresh finish is long and intense with a spicy aftertaste.

VIGNOLES LATE HARVEST: A late harvest white wine with a very complex nose with aromas of raisins, dried apricot and spices.

WHITE ZINFANDEL: Sweet with bright berry notes, a harmonious balance and a slight acidity.

HEMMAN WINERY

13022 Highway C, Brazeau, MO 63737

(573) 824-6040

www.hemmanwinery.com

Hours of Operation

Friday through Sunday: Noon to 6 p.m.

HOW TO GET THERE: From I-55, take Hwy 61 north to Hwy C. Follow Hwy C to Altenburg. Turn left on Hwy A. Once in Frohna, turn right on Hwy C to Brazeau. From Perryville: Take I-55 Exit 129 and turn east. At the second stoplight past McDonald's, turn right on Hwy 61 South. Follow Hwy 61 to Uniontown, then turn left on Hwy A to Frohna. Turn left on Hwy C to Brazeau.

I reckon there will be a few people reading this, who might choose to skip Hemman Winery after seeing that there's no triple-gold-medal-winning Norton on their wine list. What a shame. For me, Hemman epitomizes what Missouri wine country is all about. Turn off the beaten path, open your mind, be ready to enjoy a newfound destination with real charm and great wines. Hemman delivers on every level. After sampling umpteen Chambourcins elsewhere, here's your chance to dive into some new wine tasting territory.

Where else will you ever be able to sample a rhubarb, plum or dewberry wine? I don't even know what a dewberry is.

"We make country wines—primarily sweet and semi-sweet and a couple of dry wines," said Corey Hemman, one of a handful of family members that have made this dream become a reality. Corey and his family produced 23 different wines this year—5,000 gallons of stored sunlight and sugar—highlighting fruits as myriad as apricot, apple, mulberry and plum.

The Hemman family has been making fine wines and setting them aside for special occasions since the 1830s. For more than five generations, the Hemman family has passed down the art of making home-style wine. "We learned it from Al, Al learned from his mom, she learned from her dad, who brought it over from Germany in 1839. Everyone had been trying to get us to sell it and it was a demand-type thing," Corey said.

The Hemman Winery opened their doors to the public in 2003. Now they've set some aside for visitors, to help make everyone else's occasions a little more special. Whether for an hour or an afternoon, Hemman Winery is a relaxing little spot to visit, sit on the porch and enjoy some sausages, cheeses and wines.

"When you're here, there's always a Hemman here—Dad, Mom, Lisa or I. It's a family operation. We take turns on weekends... Thursday night we were pressing until 1 a.m... the next day we're out picking... This is in addition to us all having 'regular' jobs."

The Hemmans of Hemman Winery include Doug (left) and his wife
Bonnie (not shown), Dorothy & Al (center), and Corey & Lisa (at right).

Despite the hard work and long hours, Corey is quick to quote a sign tacked up on the blacksmith shop: "A Day in the Country Is Worth a Week in the City."

As I peer into a vat of fermenting Chelois, a locally harvested grape, Corey tells me: "This year we picked 300 gallons of blackberries... Everything is local but our cranberry. It's really been booming. It's taking off. A lot of local farmers are looking for ways to diversify. All this hill ground is perfect for growing grapes."

Visiting Hemman and the Brazeau community (pronounced BRAZAWW) is the closest thing to jumping into a dusty old postcard of country life from 100 years ago. Brazeau is a neat cluster of well-preserved buildings at the proverbial bend in the road. A restored blacksmith shop, bank, school, general store and a few other structures sew up this neat quilt of life from 100 years ago. The thread, of course, is the can-do spirit of the local residents.

How big is Brazeau? "I usually say 35 and a bunch of dogs," said Dorothy Hemman, matriarch and wine sample pourer.

Their most popular item is the "Front Porch Special," a bottle of chilled wine, crackers and cheese. The winery's tasting room and gift shop are located in the old country store in Brazeau. The building was built 150 years ago. It was a general store until it was shuttered in the early 1970s. Now the hardwood floors are enjoying a new life in a new century as a steady stream of customers walk through those old general store doors.

Hemman is a well-kept secret enjoyed almost completely by locals. Other than a few groups of motorcyclists touring the gorgeous curves of Highway 61, this place hasn't even been discovered yet by St. Louis daytrippers.

A community highlight is the Christmas Walk, the first weekend in December, when all of the historic buildings are open for tours, and the town is aglow with candles and holiday spirit.

The museum is open by appointment only. You can also book a stay at Aunt Carrie's Tea House, which has three bedrooms and is very inexpensive. For more information, call (573) 824-5394. Or call the winery.

Nearby: The Seventy-Six Conservation Area is right around the corner from the winery. Also nearby is the Bollinger Mill State Historic Site in Burfordville. The 19th Century mill and its neighboring covered bridge offer a glimpse of an earlier time. The mill dates to the Civil War period. It is a massive four-story stone and brick building where visitors can observe corn being ground into meal by water power—just as it was done long ago. The Burfordville Covered Bridge standing alongside stretches its 140-foot span across the Whitewater River, which powers the mill. Begun in 1858, it is the oldest of only four remaining covered bridges in Missouri. Bring a picnic to enjoy this pleasant reminder of a bygone era.

Wine maker Corey Hemman continues the family tradition of making fruit and grape wines.

HEMMAN WINE LIST

Current Offerings:

APPLE: Made with 100 percent sweet Steffens apples. Like taking a bite out of the real fruit.

BLACKBERRY: Made with 100 percent local blackberries, this semi-sweet wine has a rich color and fruity flavor.

BLUEBERRY: Delicate flavors make this a fresh and fruity wine. Made with local fruit.

BRAZEAU BLEND: A semi-sweet blend of Catawba and Concord wines, this local favorite has the perfect balance of fruit flavor.

CATAWBA: A sweet white wine with full Catawba flavor. Hemman's most requested wine.

CHAMBOURCIN: A dry red wine, medium-bodied, with a fruity aroma and cherry and earthy/spicy complexity.

CHARDONEL: A semi-sweet smooth white wine, delightfully rich in flavor.

CHARDONEL DRY: A smooth white wine. Fruity, rich in flavor with an oak finish.

COUNTRY DAYS: A sweet wine with rich red color, Concord grape and blackberries, loaded with fruit flavor.

EARLY BIRD: Early harvest on the Concord grape. A semi-sweet, light red wine with a hint of tartness. Loaded with fruit flavor with a crisp finish.

NIAGRA: An elegant, rich and sweet white wine.

PEACH: Made with 100 percent locally grown peaches. Full of fruit flavor.

PIESTENGAL–RHUBARB: That's right, a wine made out of rhubarb! Just like the old-fashioned pie you remember.

RASPBERRY: Made with 100 percent raspberries. Often mixed with tea.

RED SUNSET: A deep, rich, semi-sweet red with an earthy taste.

STRAWBERRY: A sweet, succulent, fresh-out-of-the-patch flavor.

VIDAL BLANC: A dry, well-balanced, white wine with a smooth, round flavor and nice fruit aroma.

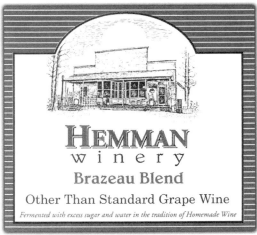

NOTES

Guests at Tower Rock Winery are encouraged to feed the fish.

TOWER ROCK WINERY

10769 Highway A, Altenburg, MO 63732
(573) 824-5479
www.tower-rock-winery.com
Hours of Operation:
Tuesday through Sunday Noon to 6 p.m.

HOW TO GET THERE: From the North: Take I-55 Exit 117. Go east to Hwy 61, then north through Old Appleton. Continue to Uniontown, and turn east on Route A. You'll come to Frohna first, then Altenburg. From the South, take I-55 Exit 105 at Fruitland. Go northeast on Hwy 61 and over the auction barn hill just north of town. Turn right on Route C to Altenburg. Turn right on Route A. The winery is two miles east of Altenburg, half a mile past the lumber processing plant. Look for the lake and signs. Turn just before the lake. The winery is just down the road.

Tower Rock Winery, located a few miles from a massive rock formation known as Tower Rock, is another new addition to the expanding wine community in southeastern Missouri. Tower Rock Winery was founded by Bob and Cheryl Breuer. Their winery offers a variety of red and white French hybrid wines as well as seasonal fruit wines.

Each year, the Tower Rock Winery crew creates 5,000 bottles of wine from the grapes grown right in their own vineyard, which is part of the Ozark Mountain viticulture area. Whether tasting on the screened-in patio near the lake or at an inside table, visitors to Tower Rock Winery are sure to find a wine they enjoy.

On any given afternoon, visitors may witness Bob feeding the fish in the lake with the help of his trusty assistant, Casper the Friendly Wonder Dog. For those who prefer more of a "hands-on" experience, a fish food dispenser is located nearby. Guests are encouraged to feed the fish and will likely witness an impressive wake of circling fish as a result.

TOWER ROCK WINE LIST

Current Offerings:

ALTENBERGER: A blend of Traminette and Chardonel. A semi-sweet wine with spicy flavors. As it ages the spicy flavors are enhanced, plus flavors of apricots, apple and honey seem to develop.

CHAMBOURCIN: A smoky, fruit aroma, medium-bodied, dry red wine with hints of cherry and spicy complexities.

CHARDONEL: A dry white wine made from a hybrid of Chardonnay and Seyval grapes, aged in oak barrels.

CYNTHIANA: A dry red wine with berry flavors aged with American oak that give hints of vanilla to the taste.

CYNTHIANA RESERVE: A young, full-bodied, rich berry-flavored, dry red wine. Aged on French oak to give a well-balanced mouth feel.

MISSOURI APPLE WINE: A fruit wine made in the style of a premium dry white wine. A great fruity aroma, well-balanced and perfect full-mouth feel.

MISSOURI PEACH WINE: A fruit wine made in the style of an off-dry white wine. A medium-bodied wine that's well-balanced.

MISSOURI SPICED APPLE WINE: A fruit wine made dry, but aged on Apple Pie Spice to give this wine a holiday feel and taste.

TOWER ROCK RESERVE (NY 73): A semi-dry red wine, full-bodied with pepper characteristics and aged with American oak.

VIDAL BLANC: A dry wine with fruity flavors of grapefruit and lemon.

VIGNOLES: A dry wine with floral aromas and fruity flavors. Acidity is higher than most wines, giving the full-mouth feel and an enjoyable aftertaste.

To early explorers, Tower Rock marked an eerie transition into the unknown. Upon first crossing past it, new deckhands would either have to furnish spirits or be dunked.

TOWER ROCK:
Witness to History

Tower Rock juts out of the slow muddy waters of the Mississippi River about a hundred miles south of St. Louis. On November 26, 1803, Meriwether Lewis climbed this limestone formation and dropped a cord from the top to determine that it was 92 feet high.

One report called it a "colossal tree stump." To me, it looks more like a mini-me version of Wyoming's Devil's Tower, featured in the movie *Close Encounters of the Third Kind.* It juts out like a limestone mesa out of the Mississippi River about 300 feet off the riverbank in Perry County, Missouri. This unique eminence has been known over the years as Tower Rock, Grand Tower, Grand Tower Roc, and La Roche de la Croix.

A knob of rock this size (the roughly flat summit measures approximately three-quarters of an acre) would probably not be afforded a second glance in someplace like the Badlands, but along the Mississippi River, it's an anomaly that has attracted awe, fear and even ownership disputes. As one author wrote: "Tower Rock has the paradoxical distinction of being both unique and unremarkable. There is nothing else like it along the Mississippi, yet from the point of view of geologists, it is merely an erosional remnant, not appreciably different from many others across the face of the globe, that (for reasons they do not attempt to explain) was overlooked by the river as it ground away the surrounding rock."

Tower Rock has played a prominent role in rivermen's psyches for centuries. It played a role much like crossing the Equator. Upon first crossing past the Tower Rock, new deckhands would either have to furnish spirits or be dunked.

Pere Jacques Marquette paddled by Tower Rock in 1673. In his journal, he wrote that it is "a place that is dreaded by the savages because they believe the Manitou is there, that is to say, a demon that devours travelers."

Perhaps the superstition had its roots in truth, since a dangerous eddy forms between the rock and the shore during high water. That dangerous eddy at one time in the 1800s even drowned an entire wedding party, after capsizing their boat after the bride and groom exchanged vows on the rock.

During the summer of 2003, the river fell so low that for only the second time in the memory of local residents the stone shelf between the rock and the mainland was left dry and visitors could walk out to it. The rock became an instant attraction.

Some believe Tower Rock is the nation's smallest national park. The theory was spread by Robert Ripley in his book *Believe It or Not* in 1933. The myth has been perpetuated in a notation on the Corps of Engineers' river navigation chart.

EXPLORING COMMERCE

River Ridge Winery

Parking • Post Office • Restrooms
Commerce Museum: (573) 264-3960

Commerce is possibly the oldest community west of the Mississippi still in its original location. While you won't find much about this place in the history books, there are a lot of stories here waiting to be told. The Commerce Historical Society publishes regular newsletters—about 24 pages in length—and is even conducting an archaeological dig of a pre–Civil War site. The society's newsletters and recovered artifacts can be found at the Commerce Museum.

On the next page is a brief history written by Dixie High. Mrs. High and her husband, Jack, are transplants to Commerce from Las Vegas, Nevada. She serves as caretaker to the museum, editor of the *Commerce Newsletter*, secretary of the Commerce Historical Society, member of the Scott County Tourism Committee and secretary of the Commerce Better Community Club. In her spare time she's a freelance photographer.

Special Essay:
COMMERCE
by Dixie High

The sign states it was founded in 1790—though there's a question about when it was first settled, since a map printed in London shows one of the Pittman's settlements was here prior to 1770. Commerce sits on its original site. Even with all the floods, no levee or floodwall has ever been built to protect the town, or to obscure the beautiful view of the showboats and the barges going up and down the Mississippi. Once the site of major industry and one of the main ports for boats, barges and showboats, now Commerce is struggling to stay afloat and can only wave to the river traffic since the docks are gone.

Visitors to Commerce have included the Czar of Russia, and Bill Cody's family and sister-in-law were from here. A lot of citizens prior to 1900 came to Commerce and left for other parts once they got their start here. Once the site of many hotels, restaurants, bowling alleys, movie houses, doctors, lawyers, judges— and Scott County's first newspaper—now it has an auto repair shop, two churches, a community hall and a museum in a 100-year-old church and a winery.

Commerce is on the south end of the bluffs known as Crowley's Ridge. The King's Highway originally went along the river through Commerce, but the floods made upkeep too expensive so it was changed to Benton. But one can still see some of the old roadbed if you walk along the river just north of Commerce. The railroad came here and many residents can remember the old depot, though all that remains are a few iron spikes in the dirt.

Commerce was the site of a "retaliation" during the Civil War. On August 10, 1861, Captain Price of the Missouri State Guard received a letter from Colonel Marsh. It said that if the people in Commerce, or their property were attacked that night, the hostages would be killed and bitter revenge would be taken upon certain persons... In 1863 an average of only $1.59 worth of food and supplies could be made per person per month, due to the war.

Some of the homes destroyed in the FEMA flood buyout in 1996 were built with cypress wood more than 100 years ago. But it was wrecking machines, not the mighty Mississippi that finally pushed them over. Only 13 people left because of the FEMA buyout and more lots are being cleared for new homes.

While some old homes were destroyed, many others continue to stand as monuments to the people that worked so hard more than 100 years ago to help build this river town.

River Ridge Winery's outdoor pavilion is a perfect place to enjoy live music or to give Lucky the dog a good belly rub.

RIVER RIDGE WINERY

County Road 321, Commerce, MO 63742

(573) 264-3712

Hours of Operation:

Open daily 11 a.m. to 6 p.m.

Closed Christmas.

HOW TO GET THERE: If going northbound, take I-55 south from Cape Girardeau to Exit 80 (Benton). Turn west and go two miles. Then turn right on Hwy E, and go 10 miles to Commerce. Then turn north on County Road 321 and go three miles. The winery will be on your right. If going southbound on I-55, take Exit 89 (the Scott City Exit).

L ocated on the Mississippi River at the scenic Crowley's Ridge, River Ridge Winery is located in a farmhouse that dates back to 1894. The winery was established in 1993.

Winemaker Jerry Smith and his wife, Joannie, produce up to 5,000 gallons annually and tend a six-acre vineyard on the hill behind the winery. Smith says the people in and around Commerce have welcomed and supported his vineyard.

Hand-tended grapes are used to make River Ridge's high-quality dry and semi-dry table wines. As many as five years may be needed from harvest until they are served. Smith ages his wines in Missouri white oak barrels. "We just can't quit

Keller Ford, the assistant winemaker at River Ridge, is an excellent host in the tasting room. He shares his extensive knowledge of the wine's finer points, in a language easily understood by even wine country newbies.

experimenting. This year we have nearly 20 different wines for sale," Jerry said. "We're the only ones in the state I know of growing voignier and sauvignon blanc."

Jerry offers a mix of about 80 percent dry wines, with the rest being a mix of semi-dry and after dinner wines.

Smith says he wanted to start a vineyard and make wine for most of his

While touring River Ridge's well-managed vineyard, winemaker Jerry Smith
was quick to add, "This is really where the wine is made. My job is to not screw it up."

adult life. Smith, a retired Navy fighter pilot, and his wife have lived in New Orleans, California and Greece. Smith is happy to be realizing his dream, and also taking part in the rejuvenation of Missouri wines.

Drop by the winery for a complimentary tasting or a full service meal at the Fermentation Room Cafe, where the motto is "always innovative and delicious." Food can be enjoyed indoors, or outdoors on the patio or in the pavilion. The winery also has a selection of cheese, sausage and bread for an afternoon picnic by the river or in the vineyard. While visiting River Ridge, be sure to browse their showroom full of unique wine-related items. They are open for weddings, private wine tastings and special dinners.

As Jerry likes to say, "Come as a customer, leave as a friend."

Nearby: Be sure to visit the Yule Log Cabin Christmas Store, located nearby. Be sure and ask for directions. River Ridge Winery also has an overnight cabin available for guests.

RIVER RIDGE WINE LIST
Current Offerings:

CABERNET SAUVIGNON	JOIE DE RIVIERE
CHAMBOURCIN	NEW YORK MUSCAT
CHARDONEL	NOONER
CHARDONNAY	ROSE
CYNTHIANA	SERENDIPITY
DESSERT VIGNOLES	TRAMMINETTE

Recent Arrivals
in the Southeast Region

BONANZA SPRING WINERY

1004 S. Westwood
Poplar Bluff, MO 63901
(573) 778-9966 or (573) 686-1413

This family-owned and operated winery is located in the bootheel area of the state. Bonanza Spring Winery and Little Black Vineyards derives its names from the natural spring that flows through the 600-acre farm into the Little Black River in Ripley County. The Kingery family invites you to visit their tasting room at the winery on Business 67 South in Poplar Bluff, adjacent to the Bottle Shop. The family grows Vignoles grapes that produce a fruity, flavorful wine. Also produced in the winery are Cayuga, Chardonel, Chambourcin, and Norton wines. Open weekends–call for tasting room hours.

DURSO HILLS
VINEYARD & WINERY

110 N. Harding Street
Marquand, MO 63655
(573) 783-8324
www.dursohills.com

Durso Hills Vineyard and Winery is nestled in the hills of Madison County in the rural town of Marquand. The vineyard overlooks town and Castor River Valley, which always provides entertaining smallmouth bass fishing. The small tasting room and gift shop are housed in a one-hundred-year-old house. In its earlier years it was a drug store and part of the practice of a local doctor, Doctor Gale. The winery is in the historic heart of the town and shares a quiet tree-lined street with the park and historic Sitze log cabin. The front porch boasts a serene view of Marquand's city park. Durso's wine list includes a dry red, a sweet red, a white, a dry white, and a Giovanna. More wines will be released in upcoming years.

THE BEST & THE BIGGEST

THE BEST

Medalists at the 2006 Missouri Wine Competition

Governor's Cup ~ Best of Show

Augusta Winery • 2004 Vignoles

Best Dry Red Wine: Tower Rock Winery • 2004 Cynthiana

Best Semi-Dry Red Wine: Augusta Winery • Reserve Red

Best Dry White Wine: Montelle Winery • 2005 Seyval Blanc

Best Semi-Dry White Wine: Augusta Winery • 2004 Vignoles

Best Sweet White Wine: Stone Hill Winery • 2005 Vignoles

Best Sweet Red Wine: Augusta Winery • River Valley Red

Best Late Harvest / Ice Wine: St. James Winery • 2004 Late Harvest Vignoles

Best Dessert / Fortified Wine: Mount Pleasant Winery • 2002 Vintage Port

Best Sparkling Wine: Stone Hill Winery • 2002 Blanc de Blancs

THE BIGGEST

By gallons of Missouri wine sold, retail and wholesale

St. James Winery—242,070
Stone Hill Winery—167,171
Les Bourgeois Winery & Vineyards—57,239
Mount Pleasant Wine Co.—37,449
Montelle Winery—28,964
Hermannhof Winery—28,328
Crown Valley—21,165
Adam Puchta Winery—19,649
Augusta Winery—17,879
Blumenhof Winery—8,561

From Missouri Grape and Wine Program, Missouri Department of Agriculture

BUDDING WINERIES RIPE FOR EXPLORATION

Here's a list of new wineries to be featured in future editions. For a complete listing of new wineries, call the Grape and Wine Program in Jefferson City at (800) 392-WINE.

Le Cave Vineyards
6696 Jasmine Road
Billings, MO 65610
(417) 744-1925

Williams Creek Winery
310 South Hickory Street
Mount Vernon, MO 65712
(417) 466-4076

THE BASICS OF WINE TASTING

The FIVE STEP Wine-Tasting Method

The basics of wine tasting can be condensed into five simple steps. Keep in mind that the conclusions to be drawn using this method are all relative. What you see, smell and taste in a wine can only have meaning when it is compared to the wines you've tasted before. If you are a beginner, it's time to start building your wine taste index and training your palate by drinking different wines.

SEE

Hold a glass of wine in front of you, against a white background to help you see the finer shade of the wine. You're looking at the clarity and the color of the wine. Look to see how light or dark the wine is; color can be a gauge to its age. Red wines lose color with age whereas whites gain color. When you describe what you see, compare it to something you've seen before (if it's not too obscure).

SPIN

Swirl the wine gently in the glass to release the bouquet. Swirling releases chemicals that combine with air to produce a better smell. The spin also reveals the wine's legs. These are the little streams of wine that run down the glass slowly after the spinning stops. Thicker legs generally mean a higher alcohol content.

SNIFF

Your sense of smell is more sensitive than your sense of taste, so take your time. To train your nose you should try and memorize the smells of some standard wines and let these sensory memories be a guide to experiencing more wines.

SIP

And now for the moment we've all been waiting for, the drink, the sip. Let the wine coat every area of your mouth so that all of your taste buds will have a chance to work. Try and recognize the different flavors and qualities possible in a wine.

SET

Kick back and ponder what you've just tasted. Does it linger pleasantly? Decide whether you like it or not. In the end, drink what you like!

Three More Simple Rules

Although many wine experts suggest enjoying wine through a complicated code of etiquette, only three rules really matter:
1. Hard liquor impairs the taste buds for appreciating the subtleties of wine.
2. Choose the wines you enjoy.
3. Enjoy the wines you choose.

Selecting a Wine

Tradition plays a big part in shaping the rules regarding the pairing of certain wines with different types of foods. Often, cultural biases have further confused the issue. Also, some wine purists suggest that wine should stand alone and not be considered with food—that food only gets in the way of the wine.

A simplistic view of some of the basic tenants of wine and food pairing could be summed up "red wine with meat and white wine with fish." As useful as this may sound, this generalization is limiting and perhaps borders on meaningless.

So, how does one match the perfect wine with the food on the table? Today, it has become popular to "drink what you like" and many people now choose wine and food pairings according to their tastes and not a series of rigid rules. But, as good a solution as this might sound, there are pairings that can affect (positively or negatively) the wine or the food.

Some Recommendations:

(The following are not rules—In the end, drink what you like!):

Pair white wines with simple dishes, particularly those that highlight fish and shellfish. The more acidic whites tend to complement these dishes nicely. Try a Riesling with some smoked fish.

Pair red wines, especially those high in tannins, with more complex and deeply textured foods. A natural pairing is a young Norton with a steak.

Pair sweet wines with cheese. A sweet wine will support the rich and salty flavors of many cheeses.

Dry wines and sweet dishes do not make a particularly good match. Sweet dishes should be enjoyed with sweet, full-bodied wines.

Is there a guide for the ordering of wine? Yes, and again, no. The order in which you select different types of wine (with food or alone) can affect the flavors and sensations that you experience. A standard convention is dry before sweet, young before old and ordinary before fine. Again, drink what you like.

Cooking with Wine

In addition to its utility as a savory beverage, wine can also be a particularly useful ingredient. Wine imparts favorable flavors to many foods. When wine is added to hot foods, the alcohol evaporates (along with the calories) while the flavors remain. Wine also acts as a tenderizer and can be added to marinades to improve the texture and taste of many meats.

As a rule—dry white wines tend to complement light and delicate foods like chicken and fish, while red wines are used with beef and heartier fare. Sweet rosé and white wines can be used to supplement the tastes of a wide array of fruit and vegetable dishes. A better rule—DON'T BE AFRAID TO EXPERIMENT. A little wine is unlikely to spoil the flavor of any dish; more likely, you will be pleasantly surprised by its addition.

HOW TO STORE
AND CARE FOR WINE

Store wines in a dark, cool place, either upside down or laying the bottles on their sides. This prevents the cork from drying out, which serves to protect the wine from exposure to oxygen. After opening, store the unused portion in its original bottle, corked, laying on its side, in the refrigerator. Most oak-aged wines will be more flavorful and complex if enjoyed at cool cellar temperature (50° F or warmer), not ice-cold. Wine is very oxygen-sensitive, so use it up as quickly as possible.

If It Tastes Good... Drink It!

The case for immediate gratification
by Glenn Bardgett

In the wine world, there seems to be some confusion as to when a wine should be enjoyed. Many people seem to think the older a wine the better it is. Few things in this business, or any other, could be more wrong.

It's been said that the French drink their wines too early because they're afraid the socialist government will confiscate them; that the British drink their wines too late because they admire anything old; and that Americans drink their wines at just the right time because they don't know any better.

The truth is that the proper time to drink a wine is when it tastes best. There is very little in the way of a general rule that can be made. If you judge or predict Missouri wines by looking at other regions of the world, you may be making a big mistake. Certainly some, if not most, of our Nortons can age and compare with the great reds from anywhere in the world. But most other Missouri grape varieties are meant to be purchased, opened and enjoyed in a relatively short time after release.

If the Seyval, Vidal or Vignoles that tasted so great at the winery sits in your hot apartment, or near a sunny window, you may be in for an unpleasant surprise when you finally open it. Yes, storage is important to long-term wine-aging potential, but nearly all our wines taste good when we buy them. Why hang on to them and risk the chance of the wine deteriorating?

People have told me about wines they enjoyed at the winery but were disappointed with when they opened a bottle a year later. I reply, "So, why did you keep it so long? If it tastes good, drink it."

As a lover of Missouri wines, it distresses me to hear complaints from an ill-informed consumer who believes the older the wine is the better it is. My advice: Don't get carried away when you find a wine you like. Buy a six-month supply, drink and enjoy, then go back for more. While you sip your whites, let your Nortons age. Ask the winery about the wine's aging potential, then store the wine in the coolest, darkest, dampest place in your home. My suggestion is always, "Find the place in your home that most resembles Meramec Caverns."

NEW WORLD GRAPES
An Introduction to Early Grape Cultivation
Compiled from *Vintage Missouri*
by Robert Scheef

Before their discovery of North America, Europeans knew of only one species of wine grapes, the classic varieties of *Vitis vinifera* ("wine bearing"). Along with such exotic botanical specimens as corn, tomatoes and tobacco, the grapevines found in North America presented a challenge in taxonomy to 17th Century botanists, since there were more grape varieties growing naturally between the Atlantic and the Pacific than in any other place in the world.

A Foxy Flavor

The first colonists to settle Jamestown tried to make wine from the strange new grapes, that easily slipped free of their tough skins. They made wine—at least a drink enough like wine—to accompany their first Thanksgiving dinner. When crushed, these native grapes gave off a pungent aroma described as "foxy." For some writers of the time the term simply meant "wild." For others, the word conveyed the odor of the animal's wet fur. Over time, "foxy" came to mean any strongly foreign taste or smell of wine, including an overpowering flavor of the grape.

Early attempts to cultivate imported varieties failed to an even greater degree than the trials with native grapes. Occasionally, the European vines lived into their third year and began yielding fruit, but they rarely matured to full-bearing age.

Vinifera vines in the colonies seemed as tenuous as orchids in Antarctica. Mysterious pests and unknown plant diseases also decimated the fragile vines. Even Europe's most seasoned vintners were unable to grow *Vitis vinifera* in North America at this time.

Let the Grafting Begin...

In the 19th Century viticulturists realized the country's tremendous potential for producing wine. They needed a vine resistant to weather and disease like the native varieties, but which yielded grapes with the qualities of the European varieties. To tap this potential, decades of experiments ensued, grafting and cross-pollinating between native and European vines. Simply by planting *vinifera* vines beside native *labrusca*, the process of toning down the foxy quality of the native species had begun.

In the early days of plant hybridization it took years, even decades, to develop a new plant strain. Standard procedure was to surgically cross-pollinate two plants, then work with the seeds that resulted. Results could not be determined until viable plant hybrids survived. And then, only after several years of cultivation would the plants reveal whether their fruit made acceptable wine.

The onset of Prohibition curtailed further research and nearly erased the life's work of early scientists. A few varieties, such as Munson's Muench grape, Jacob Rommel's Elvira and Nicholas Grein's Missouri Riesling, escaped the purge and survived to produce wine in Missouri after Prohibition.

Among early pioneering viticulturists was Texan T.V. Munson, who developed more than 300 hybrids, two of which he named for his Missouri colleagues Friedrich Muench and Hermann Jaeger. Hermann Jaeger was a grape-breeder from Neosho, Missouri, who in 1867 advised French viticulturists to graft their *phylloxera*-devastated vineyards onto wild Ozark vine roots. He shipped them 17 carloads of rootings and was later awarded the Cross of the French Legion of Honor.

George Husmann of Hermann also spent part of his life looking for the perfect grape for Missouri soils. In 1866, the year after the Civil War ended, Husmann penned his first book, *The Native Grape and the Manufacture of American Wines*. Husmann, like Jaeger, also shipped millions of *phylloxera*-resistant vines from Missouri to reestablish European vineyards. In St. Louis, he founded the *Grape Culturist*, one of the earliest American periodicals on viticulture, and wrote several more books. Husmann was the first professor of horticulture at the University of Missouri. He headed west in 1881 to become a winemaker in California's Napa Valley. Once there, he helped to stamp out the *phylloxera* plague. He then produced prize-winning wines for the Talcoa Vineyard of Napa and the Oak Glen Vineyard of Chiles Valley until his death in 1902. Even today, some of his experimental vines, named Dry Hill Beauty, still bloom in a vineyard near Hermann.

Today, at the Fruit Experiment Station in Mountain Grove, enologists continue to seek out hybrids suited to Missouri growing conditions. Two premises guide their work: to find the grape that will become what Chardonnay was to Burgundy; and to support viticulture as a profitable form of agriculture.

NATIVE GRAPE VARIETIES

A merican species have played a major role in the world of wine, as disease-resistant rootstock and breeding stock. Only one species, *Vitis rotundifolia*, makes drinkable wine without *vinifera* influence. This is called scuppernong or muscadine, a wine associated with the southern Atlantic states. All other so-called "native grapes" evolved as varieties either through chance pollination with *vinifera* or through experimentation

The following list treats varieties found in the wild separately from varieties bred with a purpose in mind. Many experts consider members of the latter group such as Elvira, Missouri Riesling, Niagara and Delaware to be native varieties— offspring of American parents. The recorded history of these grapes, however, suggests that they are actually engineered "American hybrids" and, thus, suitable for inclusion in the following section.

Catawba (*V. labrusca*) In the 1820s, Revolutionary War hero Major John Adlum of Maryland cultivated Catawba cuttings from a neighbor's garden. He named these vines after the Catawba River in North Carolina. In 1823 Adlum sent one of his early Catawba vintages to his friend, former president Thomas Jefferson. Catawba is durable and productive, though it is prone to fungal diseases. It is a good grape for juices or for adding a fruity character to blended wines.

Isabella (*V. labrusca*) William R. Prince (1795–1869), a horticulturist from New York, believed this vine originated in South Carolina. Named for the wife of an amateur grape grower, the Isabella became almost as widely planted as Catawba prior to the Civil War. In Hermann, Jacob Fugger vinted this grape to contribute to the city's first vintage in 1848. Regarded as one of the more promising *phylloxera*-resistant rootstocks, cuttings of Isabella traveled worldwide.

Concord (*V. labrusca*) In 1849 Ephraim Wales Bull of Concord, Massachusetts, propagated a prolific and hardy vine from wild *labrusca* seeds he had gathered near his home. Three years later he exhibited the Concord to the Massachusetts Horticultural Society. More than the Alexander, Isabella and Catawba, the Concord heralded the dawn of commercial winemaking in America. Horticulturists spread Concord cuttings like children trade sports cards and marbles.

Hermann's George Husmann received "a few eyes" of Concord from an Illinois grower in 1855. In his 1885 book, *American Grape Growing and Wine Making*, Husmann wrote:

> . . . *Will with skillful handling and a little artificial heat, make*
> *a wine of fair quality, of very enlivening and invigorating*
> *character, which is emphatically the "poor man's" drink, as*
> *it can be produced cheap and is just the beverage he needs,*
> *instead of the poisonous compounds called whiskey and brandy.*

Norton (*V. aestavalis*) The Norton, once regarded as the best grape for red wine, was cultivated by Dr. Daniel Norton of Virginia, who believed the vine was a chance cross between the *vinifera* Miller's Burgundy and the Bland grape, a *labrusca* variety. Critics of this genealogy, however, point out that these parents don't flower at the same time, making cross-pollination unlikely. The controversy of the plant's origins, like that of California's Zinfandel, cloaks this grape in mystery.

Hermann's early vintners sought an evaluation of one of their first Norton vintages from Nicholas Longworth, recognized in his time as "the father of American grape culture." Repeating his earlier dim assessment of the Norton grape, Longworth judged the wine to be unpleasant. Husmann took the opposite stance on the Norton's future:

> *There is perhaps no other grape which has given such uniform satisfaction as this and although I have warmly praised and recommended it from the first, I have seen no reason to retract a single word which I have said in its favor...*

Cynthiana (*V. aestivalis*) Like the Norton, the source of the Cynthiana grape lurks in mystery. Many experts consider them to be one and the same grape. Many Missouri winemakers believed Cynthiana would become America's grape for red wine. In 1883, the Bushberg Catalogue proudly announced that the Isidor Bush & Son and Meissner Cynthiana had won the First Medal of Merit at the world exposition in Vienna. The next year French experts at the Congrès de Montpellier voiced unequivocal praise. They described the Cynthiana of Mr. Bush as "a red wine of fine color, rich in body and alcohol, reminding us of old Roussillon wine," an accolade they bestowed also on the wine of "Poschel & Sherer," the founders of Hermann's Stone Hill Wine Company.

GRAPE FACT

Laid to rest by science

There's a controversy in Missouri's tasting rooms that is as old as the vines. Some vintners believe that Norton and Cynthiana are two distinct varieties of grapevines, that one came from Virginia, the other from Arkansas... But, of course, there are other connoisseurs who will attest, with equal certainty, that these grapes are the same. The people who say we have two names for one grape are now supported with results of recent protein analysis, which show virtually identical compositions. So perhaps this perennial bone of relatively amicable contention will finally be buried—along with so many other myths, old wives' tales and other "flat earth" notions.

HYBRID GRAPE VARIETIES

The following list begins with 19th Century American hybrids that many viticulturists classify as native grapes. The French hybrids, often called French American hybrids in recognition of a genealogy traced back to Hermann Jaeger and his colleagues, were developed in France. Other hybrids, such as Cayuga and Steuben, have been developed in the United States.

American Hybrids

Elvira Most histories of winemaking in America credit Jacob Rommel of Hermann with developing this cross between *Vitis riparia* and *Vitis labrusca*. According to the local history of Gasconade County, however, Jacob Rommel, Jr., produced this grape in his father's nursery around 1880. In his 1895 work, *American Grape Growing and Wine Making*, George Husmann states that Jacob Rommel's Elvira first bore fruit in 1869.

Husmann lauded the vine for its hardiness to withstand the worst of Missouri winter temperatures, its resistance to disease, its high productivity and its ability to yield fine wine. Husmann described Elvira as "a beautiful greenish-yellow wine, without foxiness and a delicate and full aroma, resembling Riesling."

Missouri Riesling Another pioneering viticulturist in Hermann, Nicholas "Papa" Grein, also crossed a *riparia* seedling, this one known as Taylor, with a *labrusca* variety. The resulting hybrid, Missouri Riesling, resembled its German namesake only in color. About Missouri Riesling, Husmann wrote that it was "said to make an exquisite white wine."

Delaware Some plant historians claim that the Delaware, a chance cross between *labrusca* and *vinifera* parents, was the last native variety found in the wild. Winemakers have used the Delaware in their wines for more than 100 years. Husmann described it as "a nice little grape, sweet and luscious for the table and makes a fine wine." Friedrich Muench, meanwhile, said Delaware "makes our best and most fiery white wine, very like the finest Rhinewine."

George Husmann was a pioneer viticulturist in Hermann. Some of his experimental vines, named Dry Hill Beauty, still bloom in a vineyard near Hermann.

Niagara The Niagara was developed in 1868. Husmann described it as a cross between Concord and Cassady, another American hybrid. In his notes he describes its berry as "large, slightly oblong, semi-transparent, greenish-white, bronzed in sun, adheres well to the bunch, flesh tender, sweet and melting, good flavor, skin tough and bears handling well."

Muench One of T.V. Munson's creations, the Muench grape produces a crisp, dry red wine. This species was used extensively as breeding stock by Munson and by Hermann Jaeger.

Friedrich Muench once said, "With the growth of grapes, every nation elevates itself to a higher degree of civilization."

French–American Hybrids

Seyval Blanc Produced from grapes developed by Seyve-Villard (1895–1959), Seyval Blanc wine is one of the most popular varieties east of the Rocky Mountains. Many people regard the Seyval Blanc as the finest French-American hybrid.

Vidal Wine made from Vidal grapes often has the luscious buttery fullness of a Chardonnay more than the crispness of a Seyval. While its first impression often only tickles the olfactory fancy, a lingering finish embeds a well-made Vidal in the memory taste buds. Its use in blends makes Vidal perhaps the most widely planted wine grape in France.

Vignoles This hybrid shows a particular fondness for Missouri's soil and climate. Vignoles vines are winter hardy, and the buds are more frost resistant than other varieties since they open later. The small, compact bunches of mature fruit produce an excellent dessert wine.

Rayon d'Or This white-wine grape was one of Albert Seibel's (1844–1936) early hybrids. Through an intermediary, Seibel received seeds of Hermann Jaeger's American hybrids in 1886. With these seeds Seibel did further grape hybrid research in the St. Julien vineyards of Bordeaux.

Villard Noir and **Villard Blanc** This red-wine grape creation of Seyve-Villard was described by Philip Wagner in *Grapes into Wine* as capable of making a "firm, well-balanced wine."

Chelois Chelois once piqued the hopes of Missouri winemakers to produce a notable red wine. From Kansas City to St. Louis, wine lovers enjoy debating how to pronounce this exotic name. In general, Missourians around St. Louis prefer the pronunciation that rhymes with Illinois.

Chancellor Chancellor is a widely planted grape in Missouri, finding its way into many proprietary blends. Vinted in a nouveau style, the grape yields an appealing red table wine that does not require years of age to soften its inherent acids.

Chambourcin Developed by Joannes Seyve (1900–1966), this red-wine grape ripens late and produces a highly regarded red wine. Though it has been susceptible to infection, it remains a promising variety in Missouri vineyards.

Baco Noir Originally known as Baco 1, this hybrid was one of the first grapes planted after 1933 on commercial scale in vineyards east of the Rockies. In Missouri planting of Baco 1 declined as winemakers turned to Chambourcin and Chancellor, varieties that typically require less aging to soften tannic acids than Baco Noir.

American French-American Hybrids

Cayuga White This variety was created at the New York Agricultural Experiment Station in 1972 and is used to produce off-dry wines.

Steuben Developed in New York. The Steuben's lavender grape is most frequently used to blend white wines.

EUROPEAN GRAPE VARIETIES

The following European species, referred to as *Vitis vinifera*, were brought to North America in the 1700s. Until the 1950s they were considered too fragile to be grown successfully in this climate. Today, however, due to improvements in viticulture, many are thriving in Missouri vineyards.

Chardonnay The white-wine grape of Burgundy, France, Chardonnay contributes its characteristic buttery sensation to the wines of Chablis and Champagne. As much a feeling as a taste, Chardonnay's full butteriness is balanced by an apple-like hardness and crisp acidity. The wine is commonly aged in small oak barrels, a practice that leaves a spicy trace of charred wood in the bouquet and flavor.

Riesling Also known as Johannisberg Riesling, this grape produces the fruity wine of the Rhine Valley. Using the *Spatlese* and *Auslese* technique, Riesling grapes reach intense honey sweetness due to *Botrytis cinerea*, the "noble rot," a skin fungus that removes water and intensifies sugar and flavor. In Alsace, Rieslings are also vinted, though in a drier style than the typical Rhinewine of Germany.

Cabernet Sauvignon The red-wine grape of Bordeaux, Cabernet Sauvignon makes a full-bodied wine that requires long cellar-aging to soften brash tannin. In a balanced wine, the taste of raspberry or blackberry fruit often shines through, offset by herbal overtones. Oak-aging can lend a cigar-box quality to its bouquet.

Pinot Noir The red-wine grape of northern Burgundy, Pinot Noir also plays a significant role in making champagne. With legions of fans who cheer this grape as the number one red-wine variety in the world, the best vintages are smooth and lightly perfumed. Scents of leather or cherries may rise from its bouquet. With less tannin than Cabernet Sauvignon, Pinot Noir is often called an elegant wine.

GRAPE FACT

Is the cork sinking?

Someday you may not need a corkscrew to open Missouri's finest wines. The 2,000-year-old symbol of quality wine—the cork—could be replaced by the ubiquitous screw cap. (Perhaps even more jarring to our aesthetics, a plastic cork, Cellucork, has enjoyed success out in California.) Why the possible shift? It comes down to money, of course. The world supply of quality cork is dwindling, so prices are rising. A winery may spend 25 cents on a cork, whereas an aluminum cap is half a penny.

Cork trees in Spain, Portugal, Tunisia and Morocco are 20 years old before they offer much quality material—and 50 when they really produce the highest grades of cork used in Missouri.

Vineyard crews across the state use both hand- and machine-picking methods.

GRAPES INTO WINE
An Introduction to the Winemaking Process

Winemaking is a process that involves science, timing and a bit of good luck. Although the basic steps involved are easy to outline, one of the best ways to understand the many steps in winemaking is to visit a local winery. From grape harvest to bottling, many smaller Missouri wineries offer interested individuals a chance to participate in the art of winemaking.

Since the time when the first palatable fermented-grape beverage—the first true wine—was enjoyed, many have strived to perfect the process of making pleasing alcoholic beverages from grapes. Today, high-tech processes and advances in agriculture have increased the complexity of a relatively simple fermentation process that has remained virtually unchanged for centuries.

Step 1: The Grape Harvest

Grapes are harvested at the peak of ripeness. One might assume that gauging the ripeness of grapes involves a bit of luck. Although there are many unknowns, vintners obtain an accurate measure of ripeness through the use of a refractometer. A refractometer (read in "degrees Brix") indicates the grape's sugar content, which, as you might of guessed, corresponds to ripeness. Once picked, the harvested grapes are destined to become wine.

Step 2: Crushing

From human feet to high-tech mechanical presses, the result is the same. Grapes are crushed and juice is freed from the skins. It is here that the juices begin to flow.

Step 3: Pressing

Red and white wines take a slightly different course at this stage: Grapes used to produce red wines remain in contact with their skins for several days while those used to create whites are pressed immediately. It is the contact with their skins that yields the robust colors and distinctive tastes of reds. For the pale whites, the juice is immediately gently pressed free of the seeds, skins and stems.

Step 4: Fermentation

Primary Fermentation

The juice or "must" is transferred to containers typically made of stainless steel, oak or concrete. While the majority of wines are produced in large open containers, premium reds and whites are frequently fermented in small oak barrels to impart an oak taste to the wine. Yeasts are then added. Feeding on the sugar contained in the skins, these microbes (either natural or synthetic varieties) produce alcohol and carbon dioxide as metabolic by-products. Temperature greatly influences the activity of yeasts, so vintners must pay close attention to this step. Modern refrigeration—like a cool, old wine cellar—allows for uniform and accurate regulation of vat temperature throughout fermentation.

Secondary Fermentation

Production of some white wines involves "malolactic fermentation." This additional step invokes the transformation of malic acid into lactic acid. The second fermentation produces a wine with soft tones.

Fermentation ends when most of the natural sugars have been converted to alcohol. At this point most wines typically have an alcohol content of 7-14 percent. Common labels assigned to wine, such as "dry" or "sweet" are directly linked to the amount of sugar remaining after fermentation has stopped. Dry wines have very little sugar remaining whereas sweet wines have higher sugar contents. Dessert and ice wines are typically the sweetest wines. The term "residual sugar," frequently abbreviated RS, provides a measure of the sugar content that remains in the wine. Typically, the RS value ranges from 1 to 2.5 grams per liter. Dry wines have lower RS values than sweet wines.

Step 5: Aging

At this stage, the wine (both red and white varieties) often appears cloudy and has a rough smell. White wine is commonly aged only a few months and in stainless steel tanks. Premium whites, especially those crafted from Chardonnay and Seyval, may be aged in small oak barrels. When in the confines of oak, whites are often aged "sur lie"—they remain on the yeast sediment.

As for red wines, most endure a much longer aging period. Oak barrels, known as "barriques," are used to store the wine as it matures. Aging in oak barrels is more critical for reds than whites, as the oak serves to combat the tannins that are found in red varieties. These barrels are usually made of either oak from France or white oak from Missouri.

Step 6: Clarification

Sediments are the by-products of fermentation and aging processes. Removal of this unwanted matter is also known as "fining" and can be accomplished by any of a wide variety of methods. Vintners often add beaten egg whites, gelatin or bentonite (a type of clay) to remove the suspended particles from the wine.

Step 7: Filtration

This step adds clarity to the wine and is done just prior to bottling. Many vintners object to clarification and filtering. They argue that vigorous removal of lingering particles robs the wine of important aspects of its character and identity.

Step 8: Addition of Sulfites

Sulfites are added to preserve the wine. A sulfur-based compound, such as sulfur dioxide (SO_2), is a natural by-product of the fermentation process, and is commonly used to sterilize and protect wine from spoilage.

Step 9: Aging in the Bottle

Wine is a living product that matures even after the cork is in place. In the bottle, the alcohol, pigments and tannins combine and interact to produce changes in the body of the wine. The growth of a wine in the bottle is continuous (unless the wine has been pasteurized) and time can impart positive or negative effects.

Stone Hill Winery's Apostle Cellars are where old and new meet: historic cellars, age-old barrel design, and state-of-the-art winemaking.

MAKING WINE AT HOME

The nation is affected with grape fever. I firmly believe that this continent is destined to be the greatest wine-producing country in the world. America will, from the Atlantic to the Pacific be one smiling and happy Wineland, where each laborer shall sit under his own vine and none will be too poor to enjoy the purest and most wholesome of all stimulants, good, cheap, native wine.

— George Husmann, 1866

THE GENERAL PROCEDURE

These instructions serve as a basic outline to home winemaking. Some recipes available from your local supplier may call for changes.

1. Get everything ready ahead of time. Double check to make sure all tools and ingredients are at hand. Keep everything that will touch the wine sterilized. Sterilize something twice if you think it may be contaminated. Use glass instead of plastic, since air can seep through plastic over time; and use no metals other than stainless steel, since the chemicals in wine can dissolve many other metals.

2. Always dissolve solid additives in a little water or juice before adding to must.

3. Add all the ingredients, with the exception of yeast, to the primary fermenter and stir until completely dissolved. Don't add all the water if working with a large (5 gallon plus) batch. It is much easier to stir a small amount.

4. Adjust specific gravity (S.G.) to about 1.09.

5. Dissolve crushed Campden tablets and add to must. Let must stand for about a day and then add yeast.

6. Ferment until most of the foaming subsides. The rule of thumb says that this should take about a week. At this point the S.G. should be about 1.03.

7. Transfer to a secondary fermentation container, preferably glass. Be sure to carry over a bit of the sediment from the first container. Strain out any fruit solids (if needed). Allow room for foaming. When the foam has run its course (3–24 hr.) top off with cool water or cool wine. Attach the air lock.

8. Ferment until the wine clears. You may want to add a clarifying agent at the beginning of this stage if the recipe didn't call for it to be added at the beginning. You can also usually wait to add a clarifier even if the recipe called for it at the beginning. Clearing can take three weeks or a few months.

9. Add dissolved Campden tablets (one per gallon) to aging container (glass) then move wine into this container. Top off with cool water and attach air lock.

10. Let set for 2 weeks. If it hasn't produced any more sediment it may be bottled. If you decide to age it, rack it (move the wine off the sediment) every 3 months.

HOMEMADE WINE RECIPES

For the beginner, it's simpler to make homemade wine using juice concentrate than grapes. These recipes make one gallon, but most home winemakers say they come out with better wine when they make a larger batch (just multiply by five). Good luck and happy winemaking!

Blackberry Wine

This is an excellent fruity wine with good body.
Make sure the blackberries are fully ripe and well cleaned before use.

Ingredients

3 lbs. blackberries • 2 ¼ lbs. sugar • 1 gal. water • 1 Campden tablet
yeast • yeast nutrient • pectic enzyme • 1 tsp. acid blend

Wash blackberries and place in fermenting vessel. Crush then add a gallon of boiling water. Cool then add pectic enzyme and acid blend and leave for 24 hours. Add the yeast, nutrient and sugar and stir well. Cover and leave for 4–5 days, stirring daily. Pour into a dark fermenting jar and fit a bung and airlock. Wait another 10 days, rack off for the first time. Allow to ferment out and then add the crushed Campden tablet. Clear and bottle.

Strawberry Wine

It is always nice to relax with a light fruity wine on a hot day.
Strawberry wine is the perfect wine for such an occasion.

Ingredients

3 lbs. strawberries • 2 ¼ lbs. sugar • ¼ tsp. grape tannin • ½ tsp. citric acid •
1 gal. water • wine yeast • yeast nutrient • pectic enzyme

Use ripe fruit with all bruised flesh removed. Cut up and add to fermenting bin. Add the sugar, citric acid and tannin, then add boiling water. Stir until sugar completely dissolves. Cool, then add the pectic enzyme and stir. Let stand for 24 hours, then add yeast. Put in a warm place to ferment. Stir daily for first five days then rack into a carboy. Fit airlock and bung and return to a warm place. Rack off after fermentation and again after 2 or 3 months. Strawberry wine is best when relatively young, though time maturing smooths the flavor. Be careful to ensure that the wine has fully finished fermenting before bottling, as it is not that uncommon for strawberry wine to begin fermenting in the bottles if corked too early. Makes 6 servings.

Make Your Own Fresh Blueberry Wine

by E. Crystal Cornell

There are several resources that you'll need. Time and patience are the most important ones, since winemaking is a slow process. In addition, you'll need to buy certain equipment and supplies. It also helps to set aside a cool wine storage area. This space would also be handy for keeping the large fermenter bucket, which can take up space in your house.

Blueberry Wine, Recipe and Procedures

(makes five gallons)

Suggested equipment and supplies:

Sugar scale hydrometer
Fermentation bag
Lever-type corking machine
Bottles and corks
Two 6-gallon polyfermenters
Yeast energizer
Pectic enzyme
Acid blend
Campden tablets
Potassium sorbate
Montrachet wine yeast

1. Dissolve 10 pounds of sugar in one gallon of water.
2. Mix with 4 gallons of water in fermenter; dissolve sugar. Add 5 Campden tablets. Draw one gallon of the solution to be saved and added in step 7.
3. Crush 12 pounds of blueberries and strain through fermenter bag into fermenter. Keep pulp in fermenter bag, tie and place in fermenter.
4. Add: 7 teaspoons acid blend
        2 teaspoons pectic enzyme
        2 teaspoons energizer
        Stir and cover, but do not seal.
5. After 24 hours, add one package of Montrachet wine yeast.
6. Stir daily, squeeze fermenter bag and check specific gravity.
7. When specific gravity lowers to 1.03 (in about one week), squeeze fermenter bag and remove bag from fermenter. Transfer the wine to a clean fermenter; add the 1 gallon of sugar solution saved in step 2; dissolve and add 5 Campden tablets; seal and add the air lock.
8. When fermentation is complete (in about four weeks, very little carbon dioxide bubbling through air lock), transfer to clean fermenter, measure specific gravity (should be approximately 1.000), taste for desired sweetness and adjust specific gravity (2 ounces sugar per gallon will raise specific gravity about .005 units).

A final specific gravity of 1.000 to 1.002 will result in a dry wine. After adjustment, add 5 Campden tablets, seal the fermenter and reattach the air lock.
9. After two or three months, transfer the wine to a clean container, make a final adjustment of specific gravity, add potassium sorbate to prevent any further fermentation and bottle.

THE HOME WINEMAKER'S DIARY

by Mark Flakne

*All you need to be assured of success in this life
is ignorance and confidence.* —Mark Twain

Day 1: I've taken a big step today, Diary. I visited the local wine and beer supply store to pick out my ingredients and picked the brain of a helpful and knowledgeable clerk. I decided to go with bulk ingredients instead of a kit for two reasons: First, it was cheaper and gave me enough chemicals for another batch; second, I thought I could learn more about making wine if I did it from scratch. When I got home I couldn't wait to get started. I read the recipe on the back of the can of grape concentrate a couple of times and checked my ingredients. When I had my stuff together I chucked it all in the primary fermenter and let the yeast go to work. Then came the hardest part, the waiting.

Here are a few things to remember next time: (1) Everything that comes in contact with the wine should be sterilized, using a method recommended by the supplier or someone else who knows what they're doing. (2) Keep in contact with the supplier. They can be, in any moments of vino-confusion, magically transformed into wine gurus ready to bestow their wisdom—as long as you call between 9 a.m. to 5 p.m. Tuesday through Saturday. (3) Read, read, read... you can never know too much—$45 or more is a lot to waste on a botched batch.

Day 7: I buzz home at lunch hour and pop the top off the fermentation bucket, hoping to be overwhelmed with the foam of fermentation. No such luck. The sugary grape sludge is just setting there staring at me with a blank gaze, free of any sign of CO_2.

Day 8: I awake with thoughts of hungry little yeasties grinning from ear to ear as they chow down on the syrupy must of their 5 gallon world. I hop out of bed and run to check my wine. I pull back the top to see what I have been waiting for all this time, small patches of tiny bubbles on the once barren surface. A small but important step in the right direction. Once again I put the lid in place and give the bucket a triumphant swirl (to keep the yeast working).

Day 9: I give the bucket a swirl and hear the happy gurgle of gasses escaping through the clear plastic airlock that sits atop my bucket like some weird hood ornament from the 1960s. After work I hurry home, open the door to the spare bedroom and my eyelids slowly peel back. The walls that were once white are splattered with purple polka dots. The area around the airlock is caked with the remnants of wine foam. I can't resist a peek so I pull back the lid to see my dreams realized—a healthy growth of wispy foam six inches thick. "It's alive! It's alive!" I scream with a wild-eyed grin. My celebration comes to an abrupt halt as my wife plops a wet rag in my hand and stares at the wine-splattered walls not saying a word. "It's alive, it's alive... "

Day 10: I construct a makeshift tent from a towel and a coat hanger and fit it over the airlock. The gurgles are steady but I decide to sterilize my mixing spoon (a half-inch dowl rod) and give my concoction a stir. The foam rises, nearing the bucket rim. I put the lid back in place and leave the yeasties to do their thing.

Day 11: The foaming has subsided a bit, but with a brisk stir it comes back to life. It is now time to start thinking about the first racking. I'll wait a few days.

Day 12: I stop by the supply store to pick up some Campden tablets and ask a few questions. The owner says that using wood to stir is not recommended. He tells me that as a rule of thumb I should wait to rack the wine until it has fermented for one week. Needless to say, I purchase a long plastic spoon.

Day 13: Well, Diary... I just finished racking my wine. When the first taste of my concoction passed my lips I was elated. It was actually palatable, carbonated and yeasty, but it tasted good to me. The racking went smoothly. I couldn't figure out how to use the valve on the siphon tube so I popped it off and racked it the old-fashioned way, I pinched it off. The foaming took off immediately and this pleased me. Perhaps it will subside tomorrow.

Day 14: After work I return to the supply store to pick up some Sparkolloid clarifying agent so that I will be ready to top off the carboy. When I arrive home I check my wine to see that the foaming has stopped. I add the Sparkolloid according to the directions on the package, top the wine off with cool water and apply the airlock. Now, once again, all there is to do is wait.

Days 15–43: I watch and wait. Slowly my wine begins to clear. I can't wait for my next chance for a taste.

Day 44: Today I racked the wine. I was tempted to try and bottle a bit, but after tasting it I decided that some bulk aging would be in order. It tasted horridly bitter. I think I'll put the carboy in a safe place and forget about it for a while.

Day 74: (A month later) I must bottle now or forget the whole thing. I pop the top on the carboy and siphon the contents into the bottling bucket. I try a sip. Not bad! Not the best wine that has passed my lips but certainly not the worst.

Day 75: Hallelujah! Twenty-five bottles of wine and no place to go. I've died and gone to heaven!

HISTORY OF THE BOTTLE

*If you decide to make your own wine you will undoubtedly need
to bottle it. The following information, while educational, will
also provide you with a load of conversational cannon fodder
perfect for any occasion where a bottle is present.*

The history of the wine bottle starts with the discovery of silica, or glass as a chemical compound. Today, of course, we know glass exists in nature, as obsidian and rock crystal (quartz) minerals, and is beautiful both in its untouched shape and after craftsmen have used it to create jewelry.

The Roman scholar, Pliny the Elder, tells the tale of Phoenician merchants traveling from Syria to Egypt with a cargo of *natron* (sodium carbonate, then used for ceramic pastes and as a cleaning agent). After stopping at the mouth of a river with sandy banks, the merchants unloaded the blocks of natron and cooked dinner. One of them happened to place a hot pot on top of a block. They were later surprised to find that the heat of the fire had melded the sand and *natron* together. *Voilà!* Glass!

Bladder, c.1725

Now it's true that glass is made from a mixture of sand, soda and limestone—but this melting and fusion occurs only at temperatures of 1500°C (2700°F), or greater—far above the boiling temperature achieved by a Phoenician cooking pot. That is to say, you need a furnace designed to obtain and maintain those tremendous temperatures.

The oldest glass furnace was discovered in Egypt in 1891 and dates back to 1370 B.C., during the reign of Amenhotep IV. In this excavation were found numerous glass beads and bottles. The bottles were made using a painstaking method that was substantially unchanged until the first blown glass was produced, more than 1300 years later.

Blown glass began in Syria, around 50 B.C. Perhaps some enterprising glassmaker decided that the iron rod used to catch and spin glass threads was unnecessarily heavy and awkward to wield. When the solid rod was replaced with a hollow rod, perhaps the glassmaker blew down the length of the rod to help keep it cooler near his hands. That must have been a keen moment of delight when the molten ball of glass at the other end of the rod suddenly expanded into a bright translucent bubble, glowing and shimmering in the light of the fire. It would be self-evident that when cooled, it would serve admirably as a container for liquids.

Shaft & Globe, c. 1680

Possibilities for new sizes, shapes and forms stretched into the infinity of the imagination. Artisans have focused their creativity on glassware ever since, throughout the world. Colored glass, cut glass, engraved glass, glass with jewels—from the simplest shapes to the most ornate—all have enriched our appreciation for glassmaking.

The Glass Bottle Comes Into Its Own

It wasn't until the 17th Century that glassmaking technology advanced to the point that more or less uniform-sized bottles could be consistently produced. At this point, a marriage was possible between the bottle and the cork stopper. The modern international wine trade is a child of this union. When vintners started bottling and corking their wines, they no longer had to ship their product in bulky, awkward clay vessels or wooden barrels. The quality of the wine was not spoiled or changed by its container; in fact, the cork and the glass bottle both benefited the wine in its maturing process.

During the 18th Century, wine bottles evolved into the sizes and shapes we recognize today. Made from black glass they became taller and more cylindrical and most assumed the form of today's Burgundy bottle. The first machine to make wine bottles was used in Cognac in 1894, and the age of truly uniform bottle shape and size had begun.

Why So Many Different Shapes?

During the 19th Century, wine bottles developed into particular shapes according to the regions from which their contents came. Today, most of the world's great viticulture regions have their own distinctive bottle shapes.

The high-shouldered Bordeaux bottle may have developed its particular shape because older red Bordeaux varietals often have sediment settled at the bottom. When the wine is poured into decanters or glasses, the shoulder helps prevent sediment from escaping with the wine. All red Bordeaux wines, such as Cabernet Sauvignon, Merlot or Cabernet Franc, are aged in green glass—while all white Bordeaux varietals, such as Sauvignon Blanc or Semillion, are aged in clear glass (with a few exceptions in green).

The elegant, sloping-shouldered Burgundy bottle can also contain either red or white wine. In both France and California, Pinot Noir and Chardonnay are the classic varietals bottled in this shape. Pinot Noir is usually found in green glass whereas Chardonnay may be found in either green or clear glass. In California, Chenin Blanc and Rhone varietals are also usually bottled in this shape.

Onion, c. 1700

Modern Manufacture

Wine bottles are made differently today than they were in Cognac in 1894. Visitors to a major bottle manufacturing plant are struck by the automation of the entire process. One huge facility in California uses eight different machines that can mold over 200 different shapes and produce 1 million bottles a day. Each bottle undergoes extensive testing for clarity, symmetry, uniform neck diameter and strength as it rattles and rolls down the line. Time from the furnace to the shipping carton? A mere one hour and fifteen minutes!

Modern
Bordeaux

The furnaces and molds are awesome. A batch of raw materials is tipped into a furnace and fired and mixed for 24 hours before the glass is completely molten and mixed. A combination of gas and electricity is used to maintain a temperature of 2700°C, much higher than the minimal melting point for glass ingredients, but necessary because of the large volume to be melted. The molten glass is dispensed in pre-measured billets and shot into molds directly beneath the furnace. This mold first forms the bottle neck; after 5,000 years this hasn't changed. The rudimentary bottle shape is then lifted into a second mold where it is blown into its final shape. Glowing brilliant orange, it is deposited on a moving belt to begin a process of cooling and testing on its hour-long trip to its shipping container. Perhaps the first Egyptian glassmaker would feel at home in this roaring, flame-lit modern environment and admire a process that remains unchanged in its transforming essence, but revolutionized in its precision and speed.

Modern
Burgundy

Compiled from an article in the Simi News

The Punt of the Bottle

GRAPE FACT

Sparkling wine bottles have an indentation at the bottom. For carbonated wines stored under great pressure, it's essential. The depression, or punt, relieves the pressure on the base. Without the punt (or kick, as it is also called) the pressure could blow out the bottom. For non-carbonated wines, the punt's been there since glass was first blown by hand. A pontil, or wooden stick, was used to secure the bottom of the bottle while the glass blower spun and blew the neck end. Naturally, the stick indented the bottom of the still molten glass. Today, higher quality molded glass bottles do not require the punt, but almost all fine wine bottles retain the punt, more out of tradition than necessity.

WINE COUNTRY MEMENTOS

Preserving Labels

Preserving a favorite wine label is a great keepsake of a memorable event with friends. To preserve the label, fill the empty bottle with hot water and place it in a bucket of hot water. It usually takes about 3 to 8 hours for the label to peel off.

Take the label out and lay it between two paper towels, followed by a layer of newspaper. Then leave on a counter-top and cover with several heavy books, until it dries.

Creating Corkboards

To make a useful bulletin board, or corkboard, from your explorations, drink a lot of wine, or pester friends and family enough so that they save all their corks for you. Decide how large a board you want for your den, office or kitchen wall... and when you think you have enough, use a hot glue gun to glue corks lengthwise to a smooth base surface.

STARTING A VINEYARD

*Farmer and artist, drudge and dreamer, hedonist and masochist,
alchemist and accountant—the winegrower is all these things.*
— **Hugh Johnson** *Vintage: The Story of Wine*

Starting a vineyard is one of the most challenging agricultural endeavors one could ever undertake. As one vintner attests: "Starting a vineyard is a lot like eating an elephant. You have to do it one bite at a time." Many vintners will readily tell you that planning, patience and persistence are all essential, along with the much-needed dollar.

Just suppose you read the following steps and begin on the first step tomorrow... It could easily take five years before you would be ready to press grapes for wine (assuming the crown gall didn't get you). So what follows is probably just some interesting reading. But if you do have several acres of land and about $6,000 for each acre and a lot of free time, here's your basic outline to an exciting new way of life.

If you lack the land, labor or loan, remember that even a few grapevines can benefit a home's landscape. A few vines not only produce grapes but provide shade on arbors, trellises and other structures.

Choosing the Land

Missouri grapevines prefer elevated, "frost-free" sites, like bluffs, ridge tops and gently sloped hillsides. Vines on these sorts of sites with good air drainage are less prone to early frosts—which kill emerging flower clusters and reduce potential harvests. The worst places to start a vineyard are small hollows, wooded sites and river bottoms, where frost is more likely to occur. To be profitable in today's market, 30–60 acres are recommended, unless a winery is planned also.

As far as the soil goes, grapevines need a lot of oxygen. Therefore, drainage is important. Healthy vines also need about two feet of unobstructed soil each for healthy root systems.

If a site has all these qualities, its soil should then be tested for its alkalinity or acidity. If tests show a pH outside the range of 5.5. and 6.5, fertilizer or lime should be applied to bring the pH to the recommended level.

Preparing the Site

Preparation is of paramount importance in starting a vineyard. Success comes down to the health of the root systems, which support the vine throughout the life of your vineyard. A diligently tended vineyard can "live" for at least 25 years.

Applying organic matter a year before planting will give young vines a healthy start for several reasons. It will recharge the soil with nutrients necessary to establish a healthy root system. It will also help to offset the cost and labor of introducing fertilizer (which you will have to do eventually).

It will also make the soil easier to work. To reduce the presence of weeds and other plants in a young vineyard, it is important to work the ground over with a plow and disc the fall before cuttings are planted. After the ground has been worked up, a cover crop like cereal rye or hairy vetch will further reduce weeds.

Ideally, vine rows run north to south to get the most sun. But, if a steep slope precludes this orientation, then east to west will do. Erosion can damage a vineyard much more than less-than-perfect sun exposure. Rows should be planted perpendicular to steep slopes, or along the terraces of rolling hillsides.

Choosing Varieties of Vines

Many Missouri growers are adding French-American hybrids and seedless table grapes to their traditional grape varieties. There are many people with good advice on this issue. Whatever you decide, it's best to order vines one or two years before you plant. Also, culls and two-year-old plants don't seem to fare as well as one-year-old dormant-rooted cuttings. It's also best to diversify your rootstock, since the popularity of specific wines, and therefore demand for a particular grape, continue to change. Consider a grape like Norton, that can be used alone or blended with other varieties, to strengthen your ability to evolve with the industry.

Planting the Vines

When you begin to plant, you will either be planting clippings or one-year-old vines. Clippings arrive with three or four buds, are about 12 inches long and have no root system. They are dipped in root hormone or "root grow" and then planted directly into rows. When the stems arrive from the nursery, refrigerate them or plant them immediately if weather permits. Another option is to purchase bare rootstock. Care should be taken to spread the root system as wide as possible.

Use a tractor to cut a furrow to ease planting. Many growers cut a furrow down the row and then plant by hand. Holes should be dug about ten inches deep. Make sure the sides of the hole are not smooth and glazed if using a mechanical auger, since this creates a "pot" effect, which prevents the roots from spreading out. Two vines are usually planted in the same hole, to ensure a keeper. To allow for the best sun exposure, plant the vines six feet apart. Prune the stems down to their two best buds to focus their growing energies, and water each stem well.

GRAPE FACT

A Grape is a Grape...

Even though there is great demand for our grapes, Missouri is not the most profitable place to operate a vineyard. The grapes grown in California's Napa and Sonoma Valleys command as much as $2,500 a ton, whereas Missouri's premium red Norton grapes sell for half of that amount, depending mostly on the weather.

To try and fill the demand for Missouri-grown grapes, the state offers financial incentives to grow more. To qualify, growers must agree to produce at least three years, with at least a 1.5-ton yield per acre. They must also contract with a processor to buy their fruit. This program is expected to net 39 acres capable of producing on average about five tons of grapes each, enough to make about 250,000 bottles of wine.

Training the Vines

Accounts vary on whether trellises should be installed at planting time, or a year or two down the road. Growers do usually agree about one thing: the trellis should be built to last at least as long as the vineyard. Replacing rotted posts and sagging lines can quickly equal the cost of the initial trellis system.

The point of a trellis is to give the leaves the most sunlight possible, so they can produce hardy plants and high-quality fruit. A standard stretch of trellis has two posts set between 17 and 24 feet apart along a row, with two wires running between them, two and six feet off the ground.

Sometimes growers use old telephone wire to cut down on costs. If you know someone with a long hedgerow of Osage Orange, you can cut expenses even more by using these native hardwoods rather than buying treated posts.

The importance of a strong trellis system will not become obvious until it's too late to fix it. Many hours of hard work resupporting existing trellises can be saved each year by starting out with the strongest trellis system you can devise.

Irrigation

Since the quality and depth of soils around Missouri differ greatly, so does the need for irrigation systems. Studies have shown that vineyards in Missouri that use trickle irrigation systems tend to produce a higher quality and quantity of grapes than those relying on rainfall. Like so many other elements of a vineyard, an irrigation system should be planned out long before the first plant goes in the ground. Most systems are costly. If it's out of your price range, you're not alone— healthy grapes also come from non-irrigated vineyards.

Advice on the Vine

So you haven't been scared off yet? Well then, fold down the corner of this page for easy reference. First, I would contact the Department of Agriculture's Grape and Wine Program, P.O. Box 630, Jefferson City, MO 65102: (800) 392-WINE. Or write the Department of Fruit Science at Missouri State University's Research Campus, Mountain Grove, MO 65711. Or call (417) 926-4105. Also, it's worth noting that the University of Missouri–Columbia's Institute for Continental Climate Viticulture and Enology, within the Food Science Department, has developed advisory and research programs that focus on enhancing Missouri's wine industry, and will eventually be offering courses: (573) 882-2121. Other Missouri universities, such as Mineral Area College, also offer courses in viticulture and enology. For more information, call (573) 431-4593.

Annual Viticulture Field Day

This annual event is held at the State Fruit Experiment Station in Mountain Grove, Missouri. Speakers give presentations on all aspects of commercial grape growing and provide updates on current viticulture research. Tours of the various research plots and facilities are also offered. Anyone interested in grape growing is welcome to attend. Call (417) 926-4105 for more information.

The Missouri Winemaking Society

The Missouri Winemaking Society is a group of amateur winemakers who meet monthly to share experiences and to promote wine production. Since the society began in 1977, several members have opened their own commercial wineries. Visit www.mowinemakers.org for more information.

GRAPE FACT

Persian Connoisseurs

While digging in the Zagros Mountains of northern Iran, archeologists from the University of Pennsylvania recently found a yellowish residue in a 7,000-year-old pottery jar. The chemical makeup of that residue suggests that humans were fermenting grapes by at least 5000 B.C.

Omar Khayyam, a 12th Century Persian poet, told a story to bring these experiences to life: In the Persian royal court, servants stored grapes in urns for snacking. One day the grapes in one urn started to bubble and smell strange. A young woman seeking an end to her life to escape her constant headaches found this urn and thought the juice was poison. But the wine put her to sleep, a sleep from which she woke feeling unusually refreshed. Thus, according to Khayyam's tale, humans discovered fermented grape juice to be a relaxing libation and a medicinal tonic.

EDIBLE LANDSCAPING

Grapevines around a home can offer a precious bit of romantic shade on a hot August afternoon or simply provide fresh fruit for desserts (or wine). Since vines can live 75 years, training them to trellises, arbors and pergolas creates a long-term landscape attraction. If a structure is near the house or where people pass by frequently, most birds will leave the grapes to you.

Trellises

A trellis is a single wire running between two sturdy posts, about six feet above the ground. The grapevine's trunk grows straight up to the wire, then two shoots are trained along the wire in opposite directions to make cordons. Fruiting canes arise every eight inches along the cordons, and shoots drape down on either side forming the curtain. This system is great for the home landscape if you want to make a dense-looking hedge about six feet tall or grow the greatest number of varieties in the least amount of space. Yields and sugar levels will be high, and pruning, spraying and picking are easier.

Pergola

A pergola is a series of sturdy poles with exposed rafters. Pergolas have open sides so you can see through them, with the grape foliage overhead, and are usually built to shade patios and walkways. The structure's openness allows breezes to pass through and creates an island of comfort in a hot summer landscape. Each vine should have at least an eight-by-eight-foot-square area to cover.

Arbors

When using an arbor, most people plant vines on both sides of an arch-like structure and train them to grow over the arch. The tendency is to prune too lightly, since the idea is to cover the structure with foliage as soon as possible. But light pruning leads to a tangled mass of trunks and canes that then produce poor grapes. Be patient. Prune and train the vines to one trunk and try to leave short fruiting canes, as with a trellis system. To do this, start early on by tying a healthy cane in a vertical direction. Also prune the fruiting canes at intervals of two or three feet. If these canes are limited to a few buds, the main trunk will become stronger.

A Note on Pruning

Perennial pruning keeps the vines from running wild, which maximizes the potential harvest and improves the fruit quality. Grapes produce fruit only on one-year-old branches, or canes. Without pruning, the fruit-bearing canes spread farther and farther from the trunk. By leaving only the healthiest canes the plant can focus its energy into new growth, and increase the fruit's sugar content.

BIBLIOGRAPHY

Adams, Leon D. *The Wines of America.* 4th edition. St. Louis: McGraw-Hill, 1990.

Bardgett, Glenn. "If It Tastes Good... Drink It!" *Missouri Wine Country Journal.* Vol. 7. No. 1. Hermann: Wein Press, spring 1996.

Barnickol, Lynn. "What's In a Barrel?" *Missouri Conservationist,* August 1993.

Borwick, Jim, et al. *Forgotten Missourians Who Made History.* Columbia: Pebble Publishing, 1996.

Burnett, Robyn, and Ken Luebbering. *German Settlement in Missouri.* Columbia: University of Missouri Press, 1996.

Church, Ruth Ellen. *Wines of the Midwest.* Athens: Ohio University Press, 1982.

Denny, James M. "History and Cultural Resources along the Katy Railroad Corridor: Sedalia to Clinton Section." Missouri Department of Natural Resources, Division of Parks, Recreation and Historic Preservation November 1991 (unpublished).

Denny, James M., Gerald Lee Gilleard and Joetta K. Davis. "Cultural Resources along the Missouri, Kansas and Texas (Katy Trail) Railroad Route, Sedalia to Machens, Missouri." Missouri Department of Natural Resources, Division of Parks, Recreation and Historic Preservation. September 1986 (unpublished).

Denny, James M. "Manitou Bluffs Section of the Missouri River." Jamestown: Manitou Publications, 1996.

Dicarlo, Henry, and Chad Finn. "Home Fruit Production: Grape Training Systems." Agricultural Publication G06090. Columbia: University of Missouri–Columbia. October 1993.

Dufur, Brett. *Exploring Lewis & Clark's Missouri.* Rocheport: Pebble Publishing, 2004.

Dufur, Brett. *The Complete Katy Trail Guidebook,* 8th Edition. Rocheport: Pebble Publishing, 2005.

Earngey, Bill. *Missouri Roadsides: The Traveler's Companion.* Columbia: University of Missouri Press, 1995.

Frishman, Robert, and Eileen Frishman. *Enjoy Home Winemaking: A Guide for the Beginner.* 3rd edition. Westport: Crosby and Baker, 1995.

Gabler, James M. *Wine into Words: A History and Bibliography of Wine Books in the English Language.* Baltimore: Bacchus, 1985.

Godley, Lee N., and Patricia O'Rourke. *Daytrip Missouri.* Fulton: Aphelion Publications, 1996.

Hesse, Anna Kemper, ed. *Little Germany on the Missouri.* Columbia: University of Missouri Press, 1998.

Joseph, Robert. *The Wines of the Americas.* Los Angeles: HP Books, 1990.

Lockshin, Larry. *Establishing a Vineyard in Missouri.* MU Extension Division. Science and Technology Guide.

Meagher, Phyllis. "The Stark Star Shines Again." *Missouri Wine Country Journal.* Vol. 2. No. 1. Hermann: Wein Press, spring 1991.

McMillen, Margot Ford. *A to Z Missouri: The Dictionary of Missouri Place Names.* Columbia: Pebble Publishing, 1996.

Parenteau, Jan. "A-Frame on Bluff Touches Many Lives." *Rocheport Chronicles.* Vol. 2. No. 4. fall 1994.

Pinney, Thomas. *A History of Wine in America: From the Beginnings to Prohibition.* Berkeley and Los Angeles: University of California, 1989.

Robinson, Jancis, ed. *The Oxford Companion to Wine.* Oxford: Oxford University Press, 1994.

Scheef, Robert F. *Vintage Missouri: A Guide to Missouri Wineries.* St. Louis: Patrice Press, 1991.

Sichel and Ley. *Which Wine: A Wine Drinker's Buying Guide.* London: Harper and Row, 1975.

Thomas, Marguerite. *Wineries of the Eastern States.* Lee, Mass.: Berkshire House Publishers, 1996.

Wagner, Philip. *American Wines and Winemaking.* New York: Alfred Knopf, 1961.

Zraly, Kevin. *Windows on the World: Complete Wine Course.* New York: Sterling, 1997.

WINE COUNTRY ON THE WEB

Missouri Wine County: www.missouriwinecountry.com
This site is dedicated exclusively to Missouri wine country. Features include regional winery information and a detailed calender of events.

Interactive Katy Trail: www.bikekatytrail.com
For a biking adventure in Missouri wine country, this online guide is a perfect starting point. It lists lodging, services, tips, maps, you name it!

The Wines of Missouri: www.missouriwine.org
This site is sponsored by the Missouri Wine & Grape Board. This great resource contains historical information, awards and wine country events.

WINE GLOSSARY

Acetic: A sharp vinegary odor; volatile acidity. Too much makes the wine undesirable.

Acid: One of the four descriptive tastes of wine. This taste may sometimes be described as tart or sour and is linked to the areas on the sides of the mouth and tongue.

Air Lock: A loop of hard plastic or glass tubing. When filled 1/3 full of water or sterilizing solution, prevents air from going in while allowing fermentation gasses out. Used to keep bacteria laden air away from the wine while allowing CO_2 to escape.

Arms: Temporary side extensions of the main vine stem—the basal portions of former canes that were left after pruning.

Aroma: The scent of grapes that comes from a wine. Professional tasters make a distinction between aroma and bouquet: young wines have aromas and the more complex qualities of aged wines have bouquets.

Astringent: A rough, puckery taste caused by excess tannin, especially in young wines; diminishes with age in the bottle.

ATF: Federal Bureau of Alcohol, Tobacco and Firearms. This agency oversees the production of wine in the United States.

Aurore: A white French-American hybrid grape producing lighter styled soft, fruity wines often finished off-dry. Generally produced in the eastern United States.

AVA: American Viticultural Area.

Bacchus: Greek god of wine also commonly known as Dionysus.

Baco Noir: A red French-American hybrid grape producing a hearty red wine with some similarities to Cabernet Sauvignon. Generally grown in vineyards in the Eastern United States and widely used in Missouri.

Balanced: Having all natural elements in harmony.

Beaujolais (bo-zho-LAY): Fruity and light red Burgundy wine from the region of Beaujolais, France.

Big: Describes a wine full of body and flavor, high degree of alcohol, color and acidity.

Bitter: This is self-descriptive; sign of ill health caused by inferior treatment, i.e., excessive stems during crush or metal contamination.

Bloom: The dusty, whitish covering on a healthy grape on the vine. Helps the grape retain moisture and protects it from spores.

Body: The weight and substance of wine in the mouth; actually a degree of viscosity dependent on percentage of alcohol and sugar content.

Botrytis Cinerea (bow-TRIED-iss sin-eh-RAY-ah): Known as the "noble rot," this mold forms on the grape, making the grape suitable for the production of special types of wine.

Bouquet: How a wine smells to the taster. This term has been used since the 1800s to describe the complex blend of mature wines. Professional tasters often disagree as to when a wine's smell changes from an aroma to a bouquet.

Brilliant: Bright and sparkling; opposite of dull and cloudy.

Brix (bricks): A scale that measures the sugar content in grape juice before fermentation.

Brut (brute): The driest champagne style.

Cabernet Sauvignon (cah-burr-NAY Sow-vee-NYOH): A popular red California varietal. Usually aged for a long time to soften, this wine can produce very complex tastes.

Canes: The mature shoots, those which have become woody after growth has ceased. Fruiting cane merely refers to a one-year-old cane that has the potential to bear fruit.

Carboy: A five-gallon glass container used in the home winemaking process.

Catawba (ka-ta-ba): A *labrusca* grape that is native to America. It is often used in Missouri wines and in wine produced in the eastern United States. It produces sweet white and blush wines and may also produce dry and sparkling wines.

Cayuga (ki-u-ga): A white American hybrid varietal, producing a light-bodied, fruity, semi-dry wine.

Chablis (shah-BLEE): The northern region of Burgundy, France; any wine made from Chardonnay grapes grown in the Chablis district.

Chambourcin (sham-BOR-sin): This French-American hybrid red grape is grown both in the eastern United States and France. It produces fruity red and rosé wines with a distinct aroma. It is an important grape for the Missouri wine industry.

Champagne: This French region produces the only sparkling wine that can truly be called champagne.

Chancellor: A red French-American hybrid known to produce high quality red and rosé wines.

Chaptalization: The process of adding sugar to the juice before fermentation.

Character: The positive and distinctive taste giving definition to a wine.

Chardonnay (shahr-dun-NAY): This wine is the preeminent dry white of California. It is often barrel-aged to produce oak flavors that complement its fruit character.

Chateau (shah-TOH): A house with a vineyard, winemaking facilities and wine-storage facilities on the premises.

Clarity: Wine should have a clear color, should not have cloudiness or visible particles.

Clean: A well-balanced wine with no offensive smell or taste.

Cloying: Too much sweetness and too little acidity.

Color: Wine reflecting proper color of variety; i.e., Vidal Blanc should not be brown.

Common: Adequate, but ordinary.

Concord: A red grape grown widely in Missouri. This grape was partially responsible for the survival of the early Missouri wine industry.

Corky: A disagreeable odor and flat taste of rotten cork.

Crown Gall: A bacterial disease that affects vines. Typically the disease forms fleshy growths on the lower portion of the trunk. Often causes vine death.

Cynthiana (SIN-thee-ana): Thought by some to be the same as Norton, a red American hybrid variety widely used in Missouri. Descriptors of the wine include spice- and coffee-like.

Decanting: A process for separating the wine from its sediments that involves pouring the wine from its bottle into a carafe.

Degorgement (day-gorzh-MOWN): Removal of sediment from the bottle during the making of champagne.

Delaware: A pink-colored American variety used to make sweet, dry and sparkling white wines of high quality when handled correctly. Eastern United States.

Depth: A rich, lasting flavor.

Dosage (doh-SAHZH): A mixture of cane sugar and wine used in the making of champagne.

Dry: Completely lacking sugar or sweetness; not to be confused with bitter or sour.

Earthy: A peculiar taste that the soil of certain vineyards gives to their wines.

Elegant: Well-balanced with finesse and breed.

Enology: The study of wine and the winemaking process.

Estate-bottled: Wine that is produced and bottled by the vineyard owner. Most Missouri wines are estate-bottled.

Fat: Full-bodied but flabby, which in white wines is often due to too much residual sugar—when applied to red wines, means softness and maturity.

Fermentation: The process by which yeast combined with sugar and must produces alcohol; the process of juice becoming wine.

Finesse: Breed and class that distinguish a great wine.

Finish: The taste that wines leave in the end, whether pleasant or unpleasant.

Flabby: Overly soft, almost limp, without structure.

Flat: Dull, unattractive, low in acidity—in sparkling wines; wine that has lost its sparkle.

Flinty: Steely, dry wine, with an odor, and flavor recalling gunflint.

Flor: A kind of yeast produced during some sherry production.

Glossary

Flowery: A flowerlike bouquet.

Foch: A red French American hybrid producing deeply colored wines thought by some to be "Burgundian" in character. This variety is used in Missouri.

Fortified Wine: Wine combined with grape brandy to increase the alcohol content.

Foxy: A pronounced flavor in wines from native American grapes usually in young wines.

Fruity: An aroma and flavor from fresh grapes found usually in young wines.

Full: Full body and color—applied to wines high in alcohol, sugar and extracts.

Gamay (gah-MAY): Red grape used to produce Beaujolais wine.

Green: Harsh and unripe with unbalanced acidity. Causes disagreeable odor and raw taste.

Hard: Tannic without softness or charm; may mellow with age.

Harsh: Excessively hard and astringent; can become softer with age.

Ice wine: A wine made from grapes that have been left on the vine until frozen. The grapes are then harvested and immediately pressed—this porcess yields wine with a higher sugar content.

Insipid: Lacking in character and acidity; dull.

Labrusca: A species of grape native to North America, it belongs to the *Vitis* genus. Concord, Isabella and Catawba grapes are all members of this class. Wine made from this species often has a pronounced flavor described as foxy.

Legs: When a glass of relatively strong wine is tipped just a bit and then set down, the thin streams of wine running slowly back down the inside of the glass to the wine's surface are the legs, or tears.

Light: Usually young, fruity, acidy and with little carbon dioxide.

Long-vatted: Process by which a wine takes on a rich, dark red color by fermenting with the grape skins for a long period of time.

Mellow: Softened with proper age.

Merlot (mehr-LOW): A popular Bordeaux-style red wine similar to Cabernet Sauvignon.

Metallic: An unpleasant bitter taste from improper treatment.

Must: The pre-fermented grape juice and sugar mixture.

Musty: A disagreeable odor and stale flavor; moldy.

Norton (NOR-ton): A native of Virginia, this grape produces a rich, full-bodied red wine, dry in character which has a unique spiciness.

Nose: Bouquet.

Oxidized: Having lost freshness from air contact, often leaving a sherry-like aroma.

Petite Sirah: A very dark-skinned red grape that produces wines with an inky color. The wine tends to be robust, rustic and simple, often with black pepper in the aroma and taste. This grape is grown successfully in California and Missouri.

Phylloxera (fill-LOCK-she-rah): An aphid, or louse, that destroys vineyards by eating vine roots.

Pinot Noir (PEE-noh NWAHR): This red grape from the Burgundy region of France produces a red wine that is lighter in color than a Cabernet or Merlot. This grape has met limited success in Missouri.

Punt: The concave indentation on the bottom of wine bottles, essential for champagnes, just cosmetic on regular table wines.

Rack: The removal of clear wine from the sediment.

Residual Sugar: Measure of the sweetness of a wine.

Rhineland: English name for the region of Germany known as the Rheinhessen and includes theRheinterrasse. This famous region is dominated by Riesling vines and is admired for its ability to produce some of the finest German wines. (Sometimes used in reference to Missouri's Hermann viticultural area.)

Riesling: A white grape grown in Germany and Missouri.

Ripe: The full-tasting of ripe fruit without a trace of greenness.

Rosé Wines: Wines colored any shade of pink, from barely noticeable to pale red.

Rounded: Well-balanced and complete.

Sauvignon Blanc (SOH-veen-yown BLAHNK): This white French grape has declined in use because of the popularity of Chardonnay. This grape produces different flavors when grown in different temperatures.

Seyval Blanc (say-VAL blahnk): This French American hybrid is used all over the eastern United States in many different wines. The dry wines coming from this grape are sometimes similar to a French Chablis. This grape grows well in Missouri.

Sharp: Excessive acidity—defect usually found in white wines.

Short: Leaving no flavor in the mouth after initial impact.

Smoky: Descriptive of a bouquet.

Smooth: Of silky texture that leaves no gritty rough sensation on the palate.

Soft: Suggests a mellow wine—usually low in acid and tannin.

Sound: Healthy, well-balanced, clean tasting.

Sour: Like vinegar—wines that are spoiled and unfit to drink.

Spice: The definite aroma and flavor of spice from certain grape varieties.

Spurs: These are one-year-old canes (preferably originating near the trunk) shortened to two buds. Shoots (and later canes) develop from the spur buds. One of these is selected as a fruiting cane for the following season, thus "renewing" the fruiting wood.

Sulphury: A disagreeable odor reminiscent of rotten eggs—if smell does not disappear after pouring wine, this is an indication of a faulty product.

Sweet: High content of residual sugar either from the grapes themselves or from added sugar or arrested fermentation.

Tannic: Sharp, with excessive acidity and tannin; may be necessary in long-lived wines.

Thin: Lacking body and alcohol. Will not improve with age.

Velvety: A mellow red wine with smooth, silky texture leaving no acidity aftertaste.

Vidal Blanc (ve-DAL blahnk): This grape produces a variety of wines including a German-style Riesling—a popular Missouri wine.

Vigorous: Healthy, lively, firm, youthful; opposite of flabby and insipid.

Vignoles (vin-YOLE): A white French-American varietal. This grape possesses complex flavors and aromas, and produces wine ranging from dry to dessert-style wines.

Vinifera: A European species brought to North America in the 1700s. Until the 1950s it was considered too fragile to be grown successfully in this climate. Today many of the most popular grapes grown in Missouri belong to this species.

Vintage: The year or growing season that produced a particular wine; can also refer to the physical process of picking grapes and making wine.

Viticulture: The art and science of growing grapes.

Watery: Thin without body and character.

Weinstrasse: German for wine road (Sometimes used in reference to Missouri's Augusta viticultural area.)

Woody: Odor and flavor of oak due to long storage in barrels.

Yeasty: Smelling of yeast as in fresh bread, often signs of secondary fermentation.

Photo & Artwork Credits

Hundreds of photographs spanning more than one hundred years of Missouri winemaking history were used to create this book. Many thanks to Jim Anderson at the Missouri Grape and Wine Program, who allowed extensive reprint permission from their archives. Additional credits go to the owners of Missouri wineries who also generously submitted photographs. Several photographs do appear without credits since many archived images did not include the photographers' names.

Many thanks to the following people for providing images or artwork: R.C. Adams, Terry Barner, Archie Beatte, Curtis Bourgeois, Lisa Finger, Mark Flakne, Lucinda Huskey, Randall Hyman, Miriam Krone, Mary Mueller, Kimberly Small, Jane Toben, Rick Truax, Sue Vanderbilt, Michael Vosburg, Sandy Watts, John Wilding. Pen & ink sketches by Martin Bellmann. Cover photograph by Miriam Krone. All other photographs by Brett Dufur.

INDEX

INDEX

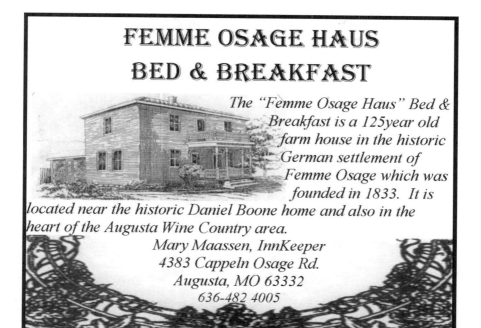

FEMME OSAGE HAUS
BED & BREAKFAST

The *"Femme Osage Haus" Bed & Breakfast is a 125year old farm house in the historic German settlement of Femme Osage which was founded in 1833. It is located near the historic Daniel Boone home and also in the heart of the Augusta Wine Country area.*

Mary Maassen, InnKeeper
4383 Cappeln Osage Rd.
Augusta, MO 63332
636-482 4005

STONE HILL WINERY
Hermann, Missouri

HISTORIC
CELLAR TOURS

PICTURESQUE VIEWS

CHARMING
RESTAURANT

AWARD-WINNING
WINES

FREE TOUR
with purchase of second tour at regular price. Coupon not redeemable for cash.

Located just 3 miles south of the McKittrick Trailhead
1110 Stone Hill Hwy. • Hermann, MO 65041
573-486-2221 • www.stonehillwinery.com